A Walk in the

PARK

For Beginners
Tropical or Western Astrology

A Walk in the Park
For Beginners -Tropical or Western Astrology

K2

INDIA • UK • USA

Copyright © K2, 2022

All rights reserved. No part of this publication may be reproduced, stored in a retrieval system, or transmitted in any form or by any means, electronic, mechanical, recording or otherwise, without the prior written permission of the author.

This book has been published with all reasonable efforts taken to make the material error-free after the consent of the author. The author of chapters is solely responsible and liable for its content including but not limited to the views, representations, descriptions, statements, information, opinions and references ["Content"]. The publisher does not endorse or approve the Content of this book or guarantee the reliability, accuracy or completeness of the Content published herein. The publisher and the author make no representations or warranties of any kind with respect to this book or its contents. The author and the publisher disclaim all such representations and warranties, including for example warranties of merchantability and educational or medical advice for a particular purpose. In addition, the author and the publisher do not represent or warrant that the information accessible via this book is accurate, complete or current.

Paperback ISBN: 978-93-5574-247-6
eBook ISBN: 978-93-5574-249-0
First Published in October 2022

Published by Walnut Publication (an imprint of Vyusta Ventures LLP)
www.walnutpublication.com

USA
6834 Cantrell Road #2096, Little Rock, AR 72207, USA

India
#625, Esplanade One, Rasulgarh, Bhubaneswar – 751010, India
#55 S/F, Panchkuian Marg, Connaught Place, New Delhi - 110001, India

UK
International House, 12 Constance Street, London E16 2DQ, United Kingdom

Dedication

This book is dedicated to all the Scorpio friends and clients of mine who opened their doors to personal secrets. I had considerable learning experience within my family too. Although I must have erred a hundred times, very few lost hopes in my reading of horoscopes. So, I dedicate this book to many and include my siblings, cousins, friends and their families.

I will not forget my father who gave the impetus and my only teacher Late Mr. Ramrao Kurdur, Asst. Comm. of Police, Maharashtra. They both could point their fingers that showed what to see. I still wonder…. their finger had no point…. it was showing a lot more than something single. I still feel that I could not see everything it pointed at. Perhaps that was the reason I constantly searched. What I found I have bared before you all.

Foreword

It was the month of October, 1980. My mother was suffering with cancer and my mind was under stress with my final year examinations on one end and a constant worry if my mother would survive. My father used to give consultation in astrology to friends and an occasional new face would drop by too. I was quite good at palmistry then. But my optimism was failing in front of me as what I had told my mother that she would survive no matter what was slowly bringing in guilt. She had become frail and the chemotherapy treatment was not bringing relief. Under these circumstances I felt I should learn astrology from my father just to find if my mother would survive. To discuss at home and learn was difficult because my mother would get irritated with our discussion of astrology. So, I would accompany my father to the local railway station both ways and the fifteen minutes I would get from him were valuable. Those days there were very few books on astrology that were available to read and self-understand. One needed a teacher. Besides, there were several schools of astrology in the Vedic system (Sidereal system); but were too far from home to attend regularly. One just could not pick up any book and start understanding a subject like astrology. After a few weeks of my toiling under tutelage one evening my father had returned from work early. He had decided to spend more time today to teach a few new topics. He said to me, "Let's take a walk in the park today". Those words keep ringing in my ear. I was delighted that I would get more time with him that day. I was twenty-two and sometime thereafter I became very serious about this subject. I lost my mother in mid-December and I was more determined than before to see the end if it existed for the subject of astrology. I have not seen that till this day.

Then I decided that I must make sure that the end doesn't arrive at all. You readers have the capacity to take this subject further. Just carry some passion in your heart and give it everything you can.

This book has been written with all beginners in mind. Of course, there are easier books written for beginners too and the net is waiting to be used. Still when you finish all easy books you will crave for more. This is where I come in; be determined to survive the space trip. You will need to look around and understand everything. You must know your way well enough. Do not make it a one-way trip but do get back and tell me your story. If not anyone else, I am always waiting to know more. I will be waiting at the point of splash down of your space ship; look around.

Contents

Introduction 1

Chapter I
The Symbols for the Planets 5

Chapter II
Aspects 7

Chapter III
The Nodes - Part One 20

Chapter IV
The Sun - Part One 36

Chapter V
The Sun - Part Two 80

Chapter VI
The Moon 116

Chapter VII
Planet Mercury - The Identity 142

Chapter VIII
Planets Jupiter and Mars 173

Chapter IX
The Two Systems 189

Chapter X
The Nodes - Part Two 195

Chapter XI
The Nodes - Part Three 214

Chapter XII
Planet Venus 226

Chapter XIII
The Outer Planets 248

Chapter XIV
The Disorders 260

Chapter XV
An Exercise 278

Chapter XVI
Epilogue 288

Introduction

Miles: Sometimes you gotta say "What the fuck", make your move. Joel, every now and then, saying, "What the fuck", brings freedom. Freedom brings opportunity, opportunity makes your future. So, your parents are going out of town. You got the place all to yourself.
Joel Goodson: Yeah.
Miles: What the fuck.
Tom Cruise is Miles in Risky Business.

♏ It was the year 2015 and the month was April. I was at the Shamwari Game Reserve at Paterson, not too far from the city of Port Elizabeth, Eastern Cape, South Africa. This is a privately owned animal reserve where the animals live in their natural habitat. This habitat is 12 square kilometers. It is quite vast; has both open lands and thick forests. Kruger National Park in Limpopo and Mpumalanga, South Africa is much bigger and one can experience adventure amidst wild animals. These game parks have serendipitous mysteries attached to them. One actually has to fall into a haystack in search of a needle. Some do find the farmer's daughter there!!!

I planned to see these wild animals from close quarters in the company of Game Marshalls in their safari van. My interest was just that much. I had not studied the flora and fauna of this land before going. I just decided and left after seeking some advice at the University in Durban, where I taught Marine Engineering. It just happened that some unexpected wishes came true on their own. There were wonderful animals no doubt but wonderful birds and flowers got my attention. The flowers here were huge with large petals and a gamut of colours on them. The roses were called grandiflora and floribunda, seeing their sizes and colour. I did not venture to sniff them for the fear of some wild insect getting into my nose but just their sight was enough to think, "These too are there to see and they exist".

Besides, there were butterflies, honeybees, and caterpillars crawling over the stems of flowers or stuck underneath the leaves was a delight to watch, if we had curiosity. The Marshalls at the game would deliberately make us walk in the bushes to make sure we saw everything the Park had to offer. I came home with wonderful thoughts and cherished these more than the pictures I had taken with my camera. Perhaps all youngsters who happen to read this book have a small lesson here? To have a desire to predict something much before a certain event happens is both thrilling and satisfying. But to identify certain dormant issues that are around in an unassuming manner is more reassuring to self than to the client who has come to consult.

Imagine someone who has no idea of what a tiger is capable of and is on an elephant's back sitting and going through a forest. I am sure that person will enjoy the ride until a tiger is noticed and gets to see it in its habitat. Assuming that the tiger is not interested and does not bother who is watching it or who isn't. What if someone like me is going through such a forest? I have seen a video in which the tiger leaps over the head of the elephant and takes a bite off the mahout's arm. Imagine my state of mind while going through the thick forest at Corbett Park, India, on an elephant's back with my family! My thoughts were getting churned into an imagination that was scarier than a horror movie. "What if the elephant slipped over the slippery undergrowth?", "What if the tiger attacked from the side instead of the front?" "What if the elephant began to run in panic?" So many of such thoughts raced through my head until the ride was finally over and the attempt at spotting the tiger was also a disappointment.

The picture created by the earlier video on 'YouTube' described the possibilities vividly in my head. This knowledge was over and above what I had learned in school about the nature of a tiger and the havoc; these animals create year after year in the Sundarbans of West Bengal. Honestly, someone would stand up to me and say, "If you are so scared why you went on an elephant ride into the forest?" But does fear ever stops us? Has anyone refused a ride on a roller coaster? I still don't know what can ever stop us unless we lose curiosity. Coming to the point, that I had identified what a tiger is all about, I was able to and had let myself go wild just thinking of possibilities.

So, friends let us start identifying who is who. The game hasn't begun yet. Once you get to know what is a tiger-like, what is an elephant, giraffe, rhinoceros, ape, and zebra are like then predicting them or what is likely to happen could be easier. I forgot there are jackals and foxes to see if you are lucky. Do you know the difference? Then there are mountain zebras and zebras of the plains. There are two types of rhinoceros too; a black one and a grey one, a browser and a grazer. But you should know who is who. Then if you see ostriches do remember the sign Libra suits these the most; for these are inseparable mates. An ostrich gets completely depressed if it loses its mate. It just does not want to live. It cannot take another ostrich for a matter. That is why whenever an ostrich is put down for meat its mate is not spared. Now that you know so many animals and a few birds, this book will be interesting to read. You have a lot to identify and remember. Your memory will come in handy when you sit to predict. I have discussed plenty of charts to show the analysis. First, feel confident in using the steps of analysis. Then write it down in a sequence. Then read and re-read. If you feel satisfied and you feel a burning desire to say whatever you feel or think then write that too. Think for the last time, "Is it relevant and necessary?" Then go ahead, say it. It is 'deliverance', that is the name of the game.

The interesting thing about the book is that most issues that a beginner wants to know have been discussed or shown. What is necessary to begin with is also shown. What one may need to develop in the future is very personal. For a layman to say with confidence that I know what astrology can do is given in the book. Everyone can be an astrologer provided that someone special is ready to go through the fundamentals. That my readers, is shown here.

Chapter-I
The Symbols for the Planets

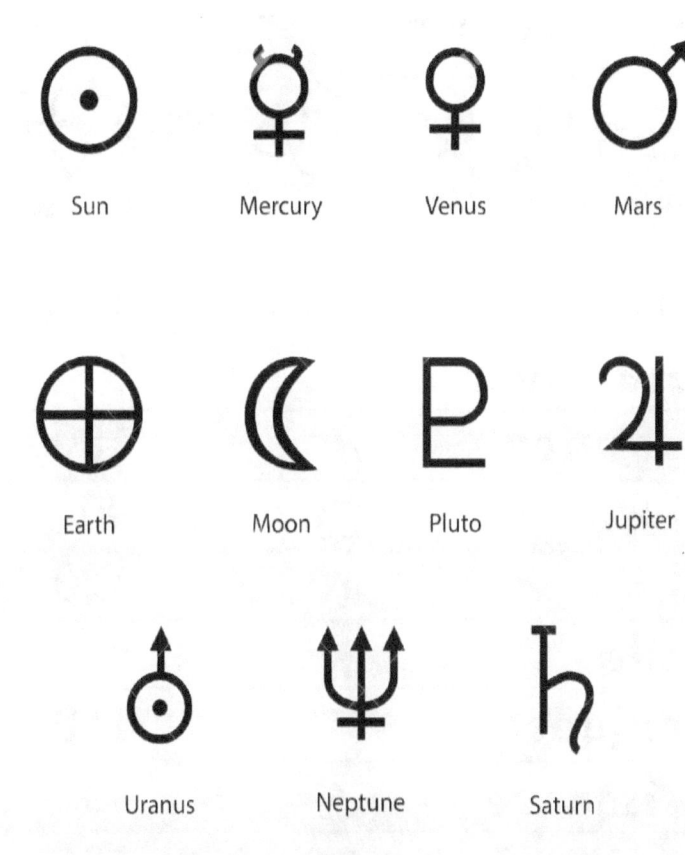

MC	Midheaven's Cusp, 10th house cusp.
ASC	Ascendant, 1st house cusp.
DES	Descendant, 7th house cusp.
IC	Imum Coeli, 4th house cusp.

The Zodiacal Signs

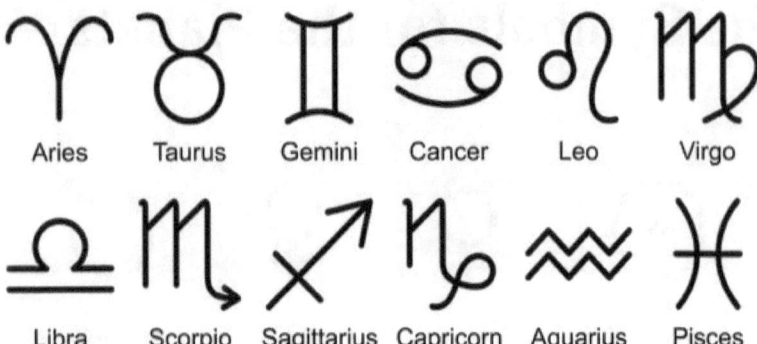

ASPECTS	SYMBOLS	ANGLES
Conjunction	☌	0
Opposition	☍	180
Square	□	90
Trine	△	120
Sextile	✶	60
Inconjunct	⊼	150
Semisquare	∠	45
Sesquiquadrate	⚼	135
Semisextile	⋎	30

Chapter-II
Aspects

Eddie Felson: You gotta have two things to win. You gotta have brains and you gotta have balls. Now you have got too much of one and not enough of the other.
"Fast Eddie" was played by Paul Newman in the Colour of Money.

Conjunction	☌	0
Opposition	☍	180
Square	□	90
Trine	△	120
Sextile	✶	60
Inconjunct	⊼	150
Semisquare	∠	45
Sesquiquadrate	⚼	135
Semisextile	⋎	30

The Aspects

The aspects are a way of laying down a road for a connection to happen. The planets do not get connected otherwise. With each type of connection, the planets cause an influence to build. The influence is usually from a more powerful planet to the lesser one. Sometimes an aspect can be between two minor or less powerful planets too. Their effect is usually for a lesser period. Who are these powerful planets? All the outer planets are powerful. Who are the less powerful planets? All the personal planets are the less powerful planets. Aren't there any forces to influence the outer planets? The eclipses, both lunar and solar can influence the outer planets through aspects when they are within an orb of 5^0 with them. Only planet Saturn among the outer planets can be influenced by other outer planets. Planet Jupiter is one co-operative planet that agrees to help increase the effect of any planet's aspects. For example, say, if Uranus aspects planet Mars in one of the ways, and simultaneously there is another aspect from planet Jupiter taking place with Mars then, whatever effect Uranus produces over planet Mars gets magnified. The Uranus aspect could be either stressful or comforting to planet Mars but that is not distinguishable to planet Jupiter. It will simply increase the effect by threefold.

Let us understand these aspects one by one.

The Conjunction

When two planets come close to each other, within an orb of 5^0, it is called a conjunction. The effect of this aspect stays as long as the separating orb remains less than 3^0. Separation happens due to a difference in the speeds of the two planets while transiting. In a natal chart, there are no transiting planets. In that just check if any two planets are close to each other within an orb of 5^0 from each other. Sometimes the planets can be in different houses or signs too.

There is a special phenomenon called 'a planet combust' sometimes. This happens when the personal planets come close to the Sun while transiting and remain within an orb of 8^0 with the Sun. Under such circumstances, the planet loses its power to the Sun. The Sun assumes the characteristics of the planet that is combust and brings about a change in its own characteristics. We could call it a 'double role' as if! In a natal chart to a planet combust may be noticed and we must apply the rule as explained above.

When a transiting personal planet like planet Mercury, Venus, or Mars transits over the natal Sun in a chart, then the planets do not become combust and their power is not lost to the Sun. The transiting planets are simply motivators to all other planets in the chart including the Sun. The motivation sometimes might not happen if the speed of the transiting planet is very high. If the personal planets transit over the outer planets, the personal planets are overpowered, and these have to act according to the wishes of the outer planets.

For example, the fastest transiting body is the Moon. While transiting over any planet, say conjunction is about to happen with planet Saturn, the full transiting period could take about six to eight hours. The Moon, which always wants to keep a cheerful outlook, turns serious, morose, and worrisome for those six hours. This is after considering an orb of just 2^0 for the fast transit. That is one reason why our moods fluctuate each day. If a planet say, Venus is stressed due to some other aspect from any other planet, then too instead of cheer we could turn pensive during the six hours of a Moon transit over planet Venus.

There is an underlying theme to the conjunction aspect. One must use this before applying the aspect to make it easier to understand. A conjunction always sends out a message, ***"I must fulfil this responsibility. I cannot avoid. I shall put best possible effort to be successful"***. Sometimes it could be a conjunction of three planets. This does not mean the conjunction is very strong. Sometimes any two planets may have characteristics that are conflicting each other. That reduces the strength of one of the planets. In the chart shown below, planet Saturn is stressing planet Mercury. This reduction is exaggerated by planet Jupiter's presence in the conjunction. The net effect is that planet Mercury is highly stressed that it begins to produce a negative effect. The bearer of this aspect will be an individual who will show the actual suffering. Probably would be looking for relief through intoxication during that conjunction.

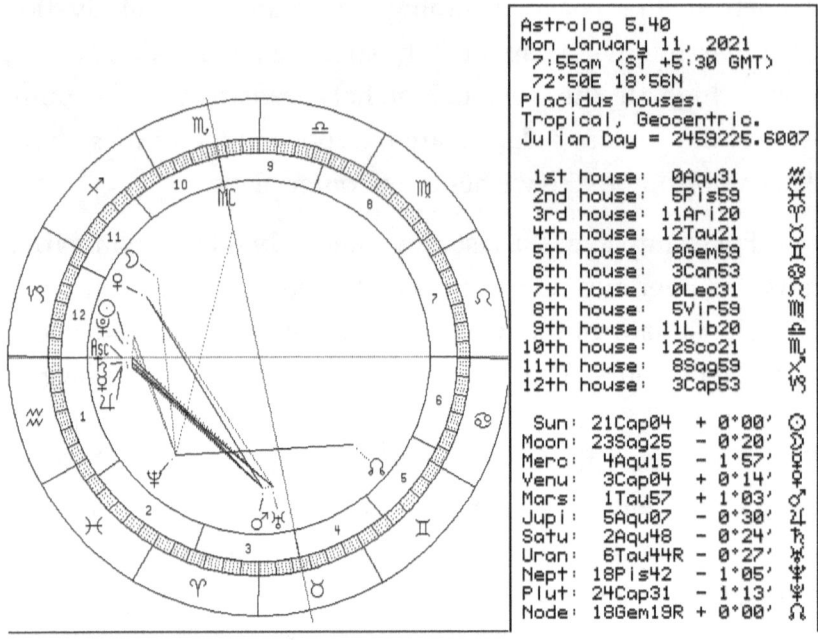

In the chart shown, there are a couple of planets that are conjunct.

Can you name these?

1. Planet Saturn 2⁰48' is conjunct planet Mercury 4⁰16' in Aquarius.
2. Planet Mars 1⁰57' conjunct planet Uranus 6⁰44' in Taurus. Orb of 5⁰.
3. Planet Saturn 2⁰48' conjunct planet Jupiter 5⁰07' in Aquarius.
4. Planet Jupiter 5⁰07' conjunct planet Mercury 4⁰16' in Aquarius.
5. All the three planets Saturn, Jupiter, and Mercury are conjunct the Ascendant 0⁰31'.

6. Planet Pluto 24°31' conjunct planet Sun 21°04' in Capricorn.

The Square

A square aspect occurs between two planets whenever they have an angular difference of 90° between them. Usually, the two planets are two zodiacal signs away from each other. A square aspect can happen between two transiting planets. Then this is superimposed on the natal chart taking their zodiacal signs into consideration to see what effect it might produce. The very square aspect can happen between a transiting planet and a natal planet of a natal chart. That is read differently. The underlying theme of a square aspect is always, "I will and I will somehow".

This intractable nature in us is noticed during the period of this aspect. The square aspect between any two personal planets may be felt but not as strongly as the one between an outer planet and a personal planet. The of a person is so strong to overcome a challenge that the person stops at nothing until becomes exhausted due to frustration. The outcome is felt as an experience gained rather than securing a possible goal. It is better to notice these before they happen and plan a strategy to decide on how far one must go to fulfill a certain desire. But it rarely happens that way. Most people come to consult only after a square aspect has given its much needed experience.

In the chart shown above, both planets, Mars and Uranus are conjunct but they indicate a square aspect to the planets Saturn, Mercury and Jupiter. The net result could be anything complex but the individual will struggle to save himself/herself from an unbearable mental agony on account of the stress produced over planet Mercury. The personal planets viz., the Sun, the Moon, planets Mercury, Venus, and Mars are deeply connected to our state of mind. The mental peace is disturbed if any of these personal planets have a stressful aspect such as, a conjunction, a square, or an opposition with the outer planets. The outer planets have a capacity to overpower the interests of the personal planets. The personal planets always look after our interests first. The outer planets have a pre-determined goal as 'destiny' for us. When there is a clash of interest between the outer and the inner planets, we feel highly stressed.

In the square aspect there is a resistance to oblige from both sides; the seeker on one side and the sought on the other. There are two planets involved and both want something to happen in their favor. Both feel there is something that will weaken their personalities due to losing their stand on some issue. It could be anything like, a certain freedom, a certain personal ambition, or a certain plan to execute a mutually benefiting goal. This is the reason the ultimate desire remains unfulfilled but the struggle continues to occur during a square aspect. Eventually, the 'goal' must be given up and allow retrospection to happen. The experience that has been gathered during the six months of the effect of the square aspect remains invaluable.

The Trine

When two planets are 120^0 from each other or five signs from each other, the angular connection that is formed between them is called a 'trine'. This is the most spoken about and exaggerated to think that it is the heaven that is going to break loose at your doorstep! In fact, heaven does break loose not only at our doorstep but everywhere we go. There is a catch! Because the blessings come from so many directions, we just do not understand a way of taking advantage. It puts us into a relaxed mode.

We all are so used to torment, challenges, predicaments coming and going and even the media prepares us to face these nowadays by frequently advertising bad spells that we overlook the good days coming and passing by. The trine brings the goods of happiness by doing a home delivery of the things that were sought after. But we lose the moment of opportunity; do not realize that this is the period during which if we worked a little more would benefit us. The underlying theme for a trine is, "What a wonderful world! Joyous moments at last. Shall wait for more". The tendency is to lose value for what has been granted easily. It is also very difficult to warn or cause a person to seek opportunity and progress. The satisfaction gained is so much that we all want to rest a while. Only sometimes a previous tough situation during which we struggled leaves us by yielding a happy result.

The trine aspect lets any two planets function smoothly with the agreement between them. The personal planets could be too fast during their transition and a trine occurring between any two personal planets are like experiencing a 'sweet' holiday for a few days. A trine with the fast-moving Moon from any of the personal planets will give happy moments for a few hours. A trine with any of the outer planets from any of the personal planets will result in taking hardships of varying nature amicably. The zodiacal signs have a small role to play here and the characteristics are usually absorbed by the transiting planets. The houses involved in the trine tell us the nature of the likely event.

For example, in the chart shown above, both planet Mars and Uranus in the sign Taurus are trine with planet Venus in the sign of Capricorn.

The other one is planet Neptune 18°42' in Pisces trines the 10th house cusp 12° 21' Scorpio.

1. The characteristics of the sign get embedded in the planets as soon as a transiting planet enters any sign. Both Uranus and Mars have qualities of rigidity, seek comfort in the environment in which they exist, show a liking toward indulgence, and spend money on luxury items, probably an inclination to be a gourmet. All these are the sign of Taurus characteristics.

2. Planet Venus, on the other hand, is in Capricorn, thereby it shows temperance, has a sense of duty, it fears law and order. The planet here has an awareness of its position in society, its economic status, etc.

3. The trine between planet Mars and planet Venus always induces good behavior into planet Mars which is otherwise very brusque. Planet Uranus here acts as a catalyst to promote a connection between planet Mars and planet Venus.

4. You must understand that planet Uranus is a slow planet and its job during any aspect is to pass on information, educate, make aware, show models of freedom and show advantages of living with freedom. If the planet is stationed in a natal chart, planet Uranus has plenty of time to remove inertia from a dormant natal planet and put that to action. If the planet is transiting then planet Uranus cannot be efficacious and instead causes a push & pull effect. All this explanation is when planet Uranus is acting singly.

5. During a transit, if Uranus finds a partner to aspect any planet, like in the above case planet Mars is trine with planet Venus; planet Uranus will accelerate the conversation between planets Mars and Venus. So, there is a better result

than simply planet Mars trining planet Venus without much help from outside. Here, planet Mars gets the education, information, thoughts of acting with freedom in mind, etc., from planet Uranus. Planet Mars also gets a message that it must act with speed.

6. Definitely, because the chart made is a transiting chart, this chart when superimposed on any natal chart, its interpretation will be similar but one will have to pay attention to the houses.

7. When planet Mars and planet Venus have a contact, check the state of planet Mercury. If planet Mercury is badly hurt and humiliated, like in the above case, there is no romance that will bring happiness. It will be more of listening to the sad saga between a male and female. If planet Mercury is cheerful and connected to planet Venus or the Moon, then "Yes"! There will be involvement. Otherwise, it is just a handshake and come home.

8. Trines do bring situations that we do not value and therefore result in a lost opportunity. If it is a 'gift' or some 'cash gain', or anything tangible maybe we will cherish that. To understand circumstances and then ride on them is not in our nature.

The Opposition

When two planets have an angular difference of 180^0 or if they are seven signs apart then the aspect is called an opposition. The opposition does not really oppose any expectation during a struggle. We are burdened to face a challenge and successfully finish it because we cannot bear a loss or a defeat. In the second (a square) the situation is similar but we do not want to change the modality to surmount the challenge. We suffer a constant fear of losing something from our personality or individuality. And it is unbearable to us. That to us is unbearable. In the opposition aspect there is a certain liberty given to characteristics of the signs that are opposing each other. The undesirable characteristics are ignored to the extent possible. Other options are searched and given an opportunity.

For example, the signs Taurus and Scorpio, an opposition between an earth sign and water sign. One is passionate toward power and wealth and the other likes to work and seek luxuries that bring satiety to the senses of our body. There are very few qualities in both to reach any common platform. The only eventuality will appear as a dependency due to inability to achieve through one's own abilities. Since the sign Scorpio is more aggressive all seems to go well with it. The sign Taurus is so much into building, constructing a dreamboat filled with all its 'wants', realizes that its opposite sign has enough plus a lot to spare of everything that Taurus wants. That brings the sense of 'self-worth' into the sign Taurus and it readily forsakes the dislikes it had developed for the sign Scorpio. The sign Scorpio likes the 'holding on to something' kind of nature in Taurus. That looks like security to the sign Scorpio. Besides, the sign Taurus has a variety of other talents to entertain and is a good home-maker. In their personal ambitions, they will always remain independent of each other. But there are certain readymade needy articles available in each other's shops. That keeps them together.

The underlying theme is that, "Why not try other ways, this strategy is not working". This has to be used when any two planets are opposing each other from two opposing signs.

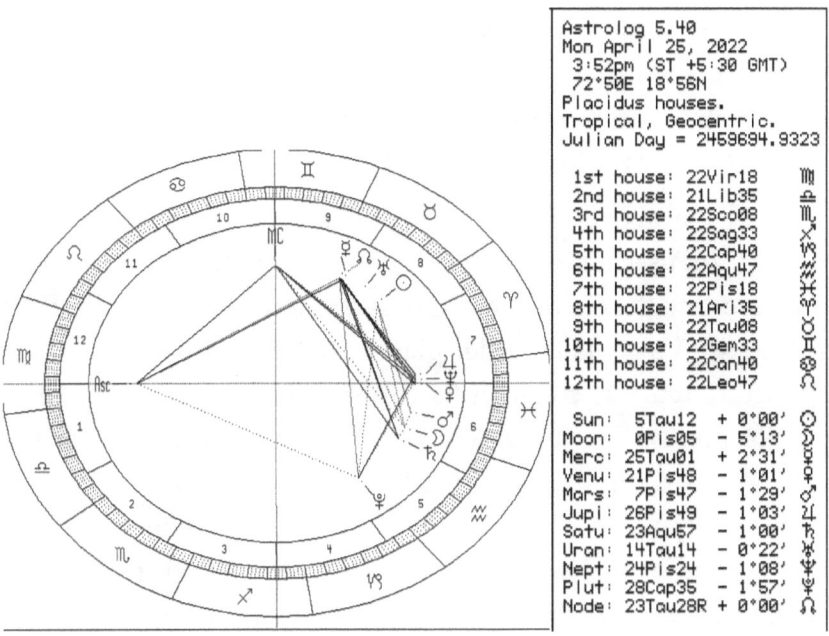

In the chart above there are a few oppositions. Can you notice them?

Notice the Asc, the ascendant, the first house cusp, a sensitive point that has been opposed by planets Jupiter, Neptune and Venus.

What must these be opposing?

These are opposing our very nature. These do not let us be what we ought to be. If the 1st house is our internal makeup, that is our true feelings and thoughts that we carry with us always irrespective of any situation. The Sun is what we want to show to the outside world. That too will have a style and originality. But this quality is subject to where we are and what we do. The Moon is our desire. Even if we pretend that our desires are different does that change our true desires? Never. It is entirely a personal matter. So, there are a few unchangeables and some changeables. The Sun can pretend, more so if any of the personal planets are combust or if a person is born with the Moon either conjunct, square or opposition with the Sun, then the Moon's desires get passed on to the Sun. That background must be remembered each time you see any chart with such positions.

In the above chart, the opposition causes adaptation. If planet Venus causes an opposition, its qualities are forcibly induced into the character of the Ascendant. Here the ascendant is the sign Virgo. Is the ruler planet Mercury being strong? No, planet Mercury is conjunct North Node, square planet Saturn, sextile planets Neptune, Venus and Jupiter and is trine the ascendant. With so many planets to serve, in different ways, planet Mercury loses its own identity. And the planets that are trying to alter the ascendant, our true nature, will find it that much easier. So, Venus will introduce its qualities by superimposing over the Virgo qualities. Planet Mercury being sextile to Venus will always be present in the activities of Venus. Though it is advantageous to planet Venus's needs and talents, but planet Mercury will have to sacrifice its own qualities first. There is a slight chance of planet Mercury retaining its qualities because it is stationed in the stubborn Taurus sign. The sign also belongs to the planet Venus.

Planet Neptune helps to build dreams here for the ascendant and planet Mercury and which is an advantage. Planet Jupiter will increase the intensity of this opposition a couple of folds. That is the preliminary analysis. There were no predictions made. Predictions follow.

Combine the ascendant Virgo with the Venus qualities and check if the Sun or any other planet is supporting. 2nd house, 7th house, the signs Taurus and Libra require attention. If you notice, the 2nd house sign is Libra with Scorpio present in it too. Pluto in the 5th house, the 6th house has a stellium, the Sun is sextile to Moon in the 6th, and the 6th cusp is Aquarius. This goes to show that the person could make finance as a career, there are no health ailments shown, well-motivated with predominantly Virgo characteristics. Moon in the 6th shows the person will feel comfortable in service, with planet Mars in the 6th there will be many skills with hands, and planet Saturn in the 6th will cause a steady working habit. There is an inclination toward the health sector too. Planet Mercury shows higher education is possible and North Node increases the ambition of planet Mercury. Planet Uranus in the 8th is not expecting any planet at the moment and has planet Saturn sitting in its sign trying to keep matters steady. The above analysis needs to be narrowed further. That you will gather slowly with time.

The Sextile

A sextile is an aspect, a bespoke aspect for initiating, hold meetings and doing follow ups. It does not have any great strength to produce anything big. It is good to have personal planets in sextile to each other, if we have an important appointment or a meeting among the project members etc. so try to guess if there is a sextile aspect between planets Mars and Venus, planets Mercury and Mars, or between the Moon and the planet Venus, etc. Please do this exercise. Also, try to notice sextile aspects in the chart shown above.

Chapter-III
The Nodes
Part One

"A word to you about escape. There is no barbed wire. No stockade. No watchtower. They are not necessary. We are an island in the jungle. Escape is impossible. You would die".

Sessue Hayakawa; Colonel Saito in the "Bridge on the River Kwai" to the captured British soldiers.

Before we try to understand the concept of Nodes, first let us understand a few other terms that creep up in astrology during certain descriptions. You will need a certain degree of imagination here to understand certain events that occur during the transit of our planet Earth.

Below, the plane of Ecliptic is shown. All angles are measured with this as reference. If this plane is extended to the Celestial sphere, it becomes the Celestial Equator. *Courtesy: https://solarsystem.nasa.gov/basics/chapter2-2/*

And Science, Civilization and Society1

BOTH ANGLES ARE 23½°

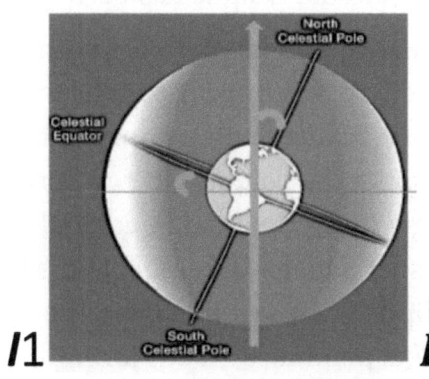

/1 /2

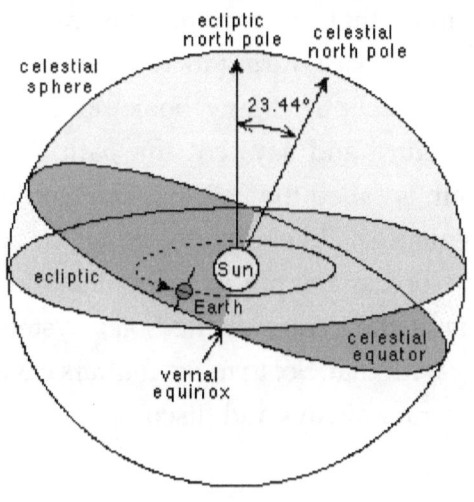

THIS IS THE PLANE OF THE ECLIPTIC.   **SKETCH NO.1**

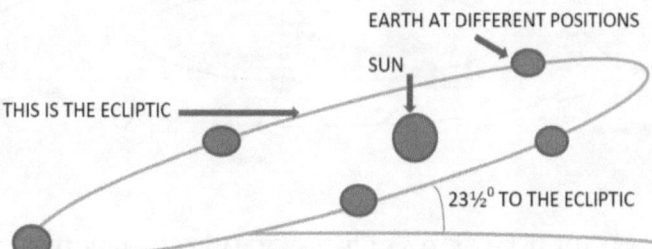

THE SUN IS IN THE CENTRE OF THE ECLIPTIC. BUT BECAUSE IT IS AT AN ANGLE TO THE PLANE, APPEARS RAISED AND THE SUN APPEARS ECCENTRIC IF SEEN FROM ABOVE. THE PICTURE IS BEING VIEWED FROM THE SIDE NOW.

I

PIC I2: The Celestial Ecliptic has been shown in the cyan colour. The Celestial Equatorial plane has been shown in brown colour. Notice the Earth's Ecliptic is parallel to the end circle of the Celestial Ecliptic. Planet Earth is approaching the Autumnal Equinox. Please notice the Ecliptic (shown horizontal) which is actually at an angle to the Celestial Equatorial plane (in Brown colour). The Celestial Equator is parallel to the Earth's Equator. The Celestial Ecliptic is always parallel to the Earth's Ecliptic. The arrow in Pic I₁is pointing at True North.

The first thing that comes to mind is that our planet Earth has a fixed track in space during its revolution around the Sun. This is called the Ecliptic. Many books and articles show an Earth-centric picture and say that the path around the earth taken by the Sun is called the Ecliptic. That could be alright for certain conveniences, liker in teaching or demonstrating purpose. If you look at any physics school textbook it will teach that the Sun is at the centre of the Solar system and there is nothing wrong with that. So, to make matters easy, we will keep the Sun in the center always and discuss.

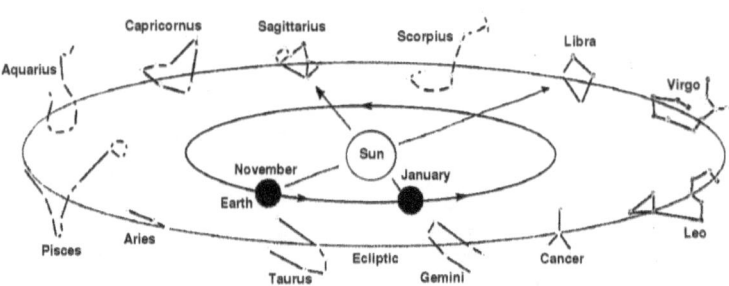

A SIMPLE DIAGRAM TO SHOW THE ECLIPTIC AND THE ZODIACAL SIGNS ON THE CELESTIAL ECLIPTIC. Lots of diagrams available on the net have made some changes for convenience. In this picture, the Sun, the planet Earth, the Ecliptic, and the Celestial Equator are shown flat. This is true for two particular positions only; the Equinox days. It is not wrong. The months of January and November have been mentioned by mistake in the inner circle.

The next would be to know a few facts regarding the speed of the Earth and the Moon when they revolve. The Earth takes about 365¼ days to go around the Sun once and we call it a revolution and a year. Each day the Earth moves about a degree on its ecliptic or its orbit. So, the Sun, which is directly opposite us or directly above us, appears to move in front of the zodiacal sign by one degree. The zodiacal signs are always in the background and are taken to be along the Celestial Ecliptic. The rotation of the Earth is such (around its own axis) that it takes twenty-four hours to go around once (23hrs 56 mins to be precise). What happens is that all the signs of zodiac signs appear above us and go once every day. Some show up during the day (but are not visible) and some at the night if it is clear. But there will be one zodiacal sign that will always remain in the background of the Sun for thirty days and that is what we call the Sun sign. The Sun usually changes its sign around the 21st of each month in the tropical calendar. In the Sidereal system, it changes around the 14th or the 15th of the following month. The date does move to the 23rd of a month toward the end of the year but returns back to the 21st in the month of March. On this day we say that the Vernal equinox is taking place. The length of the day and the night are equal. The Sun is directly opposite the Equator of the Earth and they both are on the same plane. Another such day is the Autumnal equinox on Sept 21st; again, these are as per the dates in the tropical calendar. You will realise that due to precession (explained in the chapter 'The two Systems) the day of Vernal Equinox arrives much later around the 14th of April and autumnal equinox on October 14th, every year.

The Moon takes twenty-nine and a half days to revolve around the Earth. This period of a month is a lunar month and is counted between two consecutive New Moon days and two consecutive Full Moon Days; an average of the two, is a month. The Sidereal way is by actual measurement of the time taken by the Moon to make one complete revolution of the Earth and that is 27.3 days. But the rotation speed of the Earth is such that each day both Sun and Moon pass over us in their respective signs.

Did you ever think, "Why is it that the Sun in spite of moving forward into the next sign rises almost at the same time? On the other hand, our satellite Miss Moon comes to rise fifty minutes late each day? After few days, one can see Moon during the day and set in the evening!!! Please think of an answer now that you have come this far into astrology.

The Moon has almost a zero rotational speed but as much as twelve to fourteen degrees per day of longitudinal speed (could be of celestial sphere or the earth) during its revolution around the Earth. That means every two hours it goes forward by a degree or more in the sign it is crossing. That results in the Moon taking about two and a half days to cross a sign completely. Our Earth takes thirty days to cross a zodiacal sign completely but we cleverly put the blame on the Sun, and we say it is the Sun that travels just a degree every day in its sign. So, what if these speeds are such, do they have any connection with astrology? Do not be impatient please! Nodes are to be understood well. They are being hatched now. Soon these will be born. Twins are difficult to manage.

If Moon travels approx, twelve to fourteen degrees a day to complete its transit through a sign in about two and a half days and then enter the next sign. What happens is that because its previous sign is going to rise before its current transiting sign (on the next day), the Moon will appear to get delayed each day to rise from the East. Did you understand that? For example, let us assume that Moon is in the sign of Libra today at 18^0 at 7:45 pm and is on the east, rising This will be actually seen rising at 7:45 pm from the East. During the next twenty-four hours, the Moon will advance by say, 13^0 in the sign Libra. Tomorrow, at 7:45 pm, the Moon will be in the sign Scorpio at 01^0. The sign Libra takes two hours to complete its rise on the East in the evening (from 0^0 to 30^0). Yesterday, the 18th degree was seen rising, with the Moon placed in Libra at 7:45 pm. Today when that 18th degree Libra rises the time will be 7:41 pm. At 7:45 pm, the 19th degree will be seen rising. This is because of our own planet Earth's motion. The Moon is still 12^0 away from the 19^0 of Libra.

It will take approx. 12 X 4 = 48 mins more for the Moon to rise today. Did you see an answer to the question I had put above? Now try calculating at what time the Moon's rise will be? The answer is 9:25 pm, in Scorpio.

With regard to zodiacal signs, each sign takes two hours to cross our horizon. That means 30^0 of each sign take 12^0 to cross the edge of the earth's horizon. Each day the earth moves (indirectly the Sun) 1^0 in each sign. So, a delay of 4' for the previous degree to rise every day. If 18th degree is rising today at 7:30 pm, tomorrow the 18th degree of the same zodiacal sign will rise at 7:34 pm.

The Sun's rising in the East and setting in the West has a lot to do with the Earth's rotation. There is no change in speed. But you have seen the orientation of the Ecliptic, the passage of the Earth along the inclined path causes the changes. These bring a shade of difference to the Sun's rising time in the morning. But that is not much. The higher latitudes feel the difference more but not around the Equator. As the Sun approaches the Winter Solstice, days begin to get shorter. As the Sun approaches the Equinox the days begin to get longer. Please see the diagrams below.

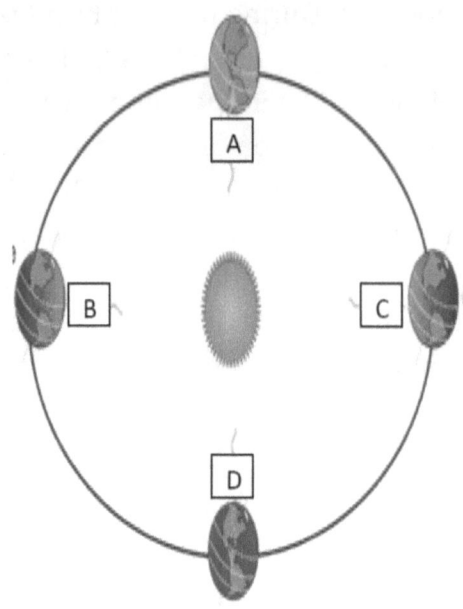

Sketch 2

Points B and C are on the Ecliptic but at equinox time they make contact with the Celestial Plane. When the planet Earth is in this position, it has equal days and nights. These points are called Equinoxes. B is Vernal (March 21st) and C (Sep 21st) is Autumnal. The earth's axis is not tilted toward or away from the Sun during this brief period. Instead, it is along the ecliptic. All these are tropical calendar dates.

Point 'A' is Winter Solstice, Dec 21st. The Earth's axis is tilted away from the Sun on the Northern side. The Northern hemisphere for the most part enjoys the winter season. The Southern hemisphere has summer.

Point D is the Summer Solstice, June 21st. The Earth's axis is tilted toward the Sun on the Northern side. The Northern hemisphere has Summer and the Southern hemisphere has Winter around this time. Given below are views from different sides.

1. View of 'A' Taken from Equinox Point 'C', As in Sketch 2

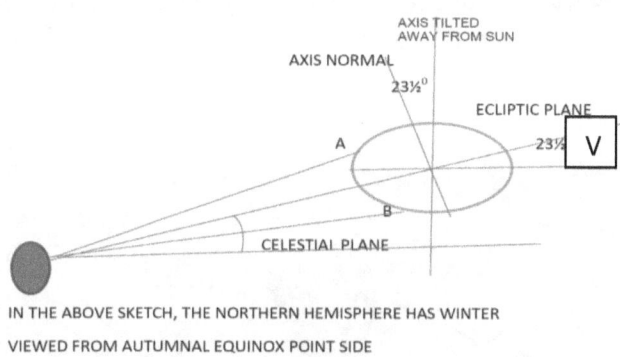

IN THE ABOVE SKETCH, THE NORTHERN HEMISPHERE HAS WINTER
VIEWED FROM AUTUMNAL EQUINOX POINT SIDE

The 'Axis Normal' is always drawn vertically and it connects the true north with true south.

2. View of 'D'taken from Equinox Point 'C', As in Sketch 2

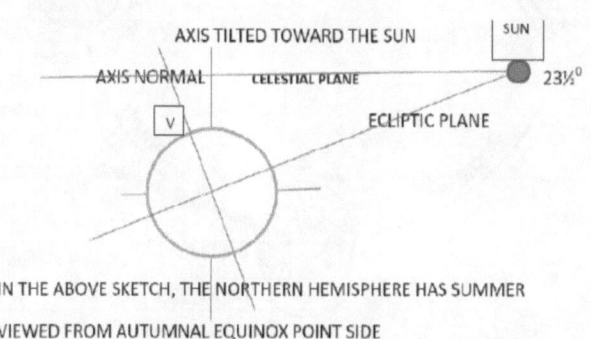

IN THE ABOVE SKETCH, THE NORTHERN HEMISPHERE HAS SUMMER
VIEWED FROM AUTUMNAL EQUINOX POINT SIDE

3. View of Both Equinox Points Taken From 'D', As in Sketch 2

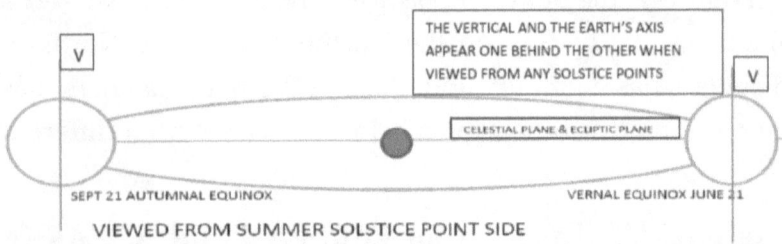

Sketch 3

Observe the white spots in the picture. That is the earth's axis point which will appear eccentric on the northern side of earth.

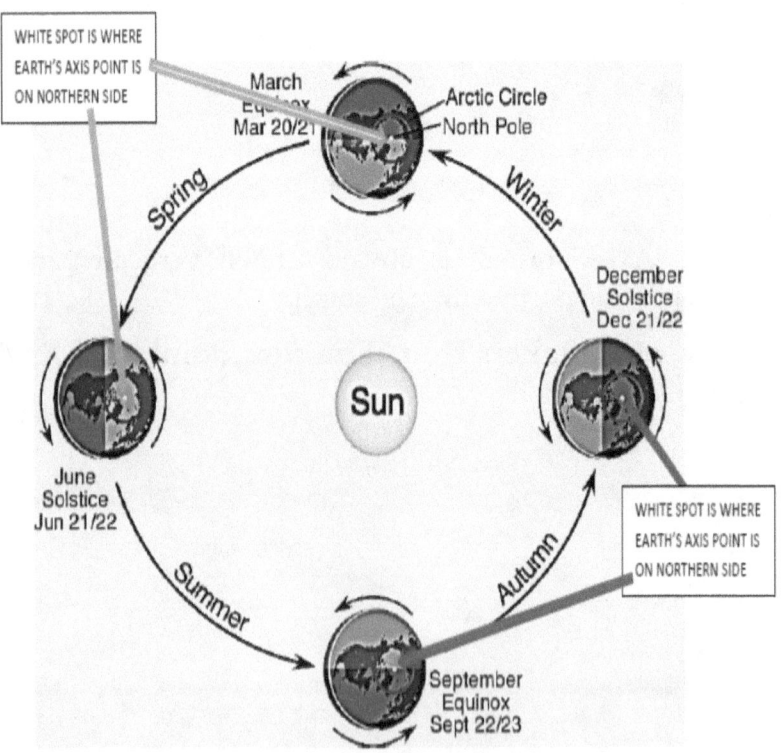

The Orbiting Moon. Its Orbit is at 5⁰ to the Earth's Equator. This Causes the Nodes to Occur.

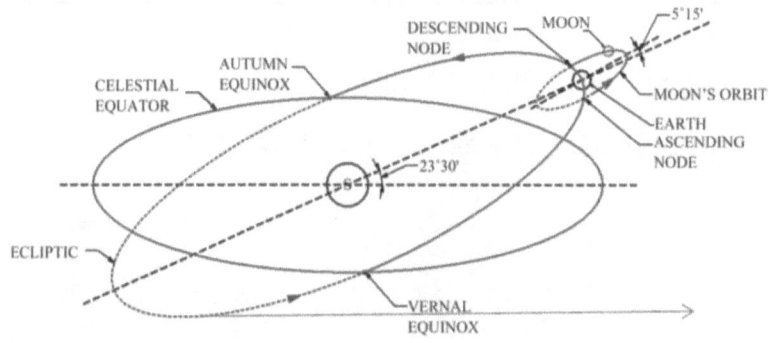

ASCENDING AND DESCENDING NODES OF EARTH AND MOON

Courtesy: Orbital Spin: A New Hypothesis to Explain Precession of Equinox—The Third Motion of Earth; a Scientific paper on astronomical phenomenon of precession by Rama Chandra Murthy Mothe.

In the above sketch of a line diagram, the orbit of the Moon is shown intersecting the planet Earth's orbit; the Ecliptic. Those points have been called the Nodes. Here there is another enlarged view of the Moon's orbit and the Ecliptic.

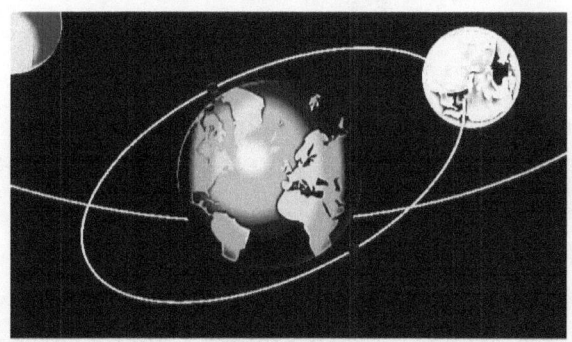

THE ECLIPTIC WHICH IS THE ORBIT OF THE EARTH AROUND THE SUN IS PASSING THROUGH THE EARTH IN THE PICTURE. THE OTHER IS THE ORBIT OF THE MOON

WHICH IS INCLINED AT 5⁰ TO THE EARTH'S EQUATOR. THE NODES ARE SHOWN AS TWO DOTS ON THE ORBIT OF THE MOON. IT IS WHERE THE ORBIT OF THE MOON (EXTENDED OR PROJECTED) CUTS THE CELESTIAL ECLIPTIC, NODES ARE FORMED.

The Celestial Sphere .... Sketch 4

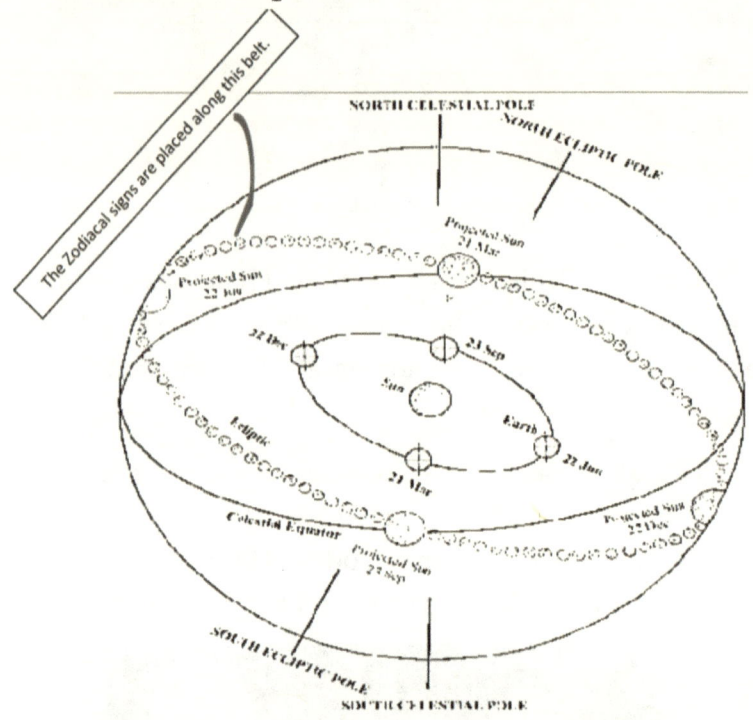

Please notice the Celestial Ecliptic which is a projection on the Celestial Sphere, of the Earth's orbit called Ecliptic when it orbits around the Sun. There is no mention of the Moon in this picture. It would have become a clutter otherwise. For convenience, the Celestial Equator has been shown at the circumference of the Celestial Sphere. Otherwise, the Celestial Equator and the Celestial Ecliptic meet at the Celestial Plane. The zodiacal signs are all arranged on the Celestial Ecliptic.

Notice how the Celestial Ecliptic is at an angle to the Celestial Equatorial Plane.

A picture of the plane of the Ecliptic is shown in Sketch 1 at the start. Such a plane needs to be imagined inside the Celestial Ecliptic. When the Moon's orbit intersects that plane, (once while going upwards into the Northern Hemisphere of the Earth and once while entering Southern Hemisphere of the Earth), Nodes are formed as shown below.

Are you excited? Now that the mystery is out, tell me why do the Nodes appear to be going backwards, in a retrograde motion always?

Part of the answer was given in the description somewhere above! I feel that I am about to reveal another mystery!

SKETCH 5

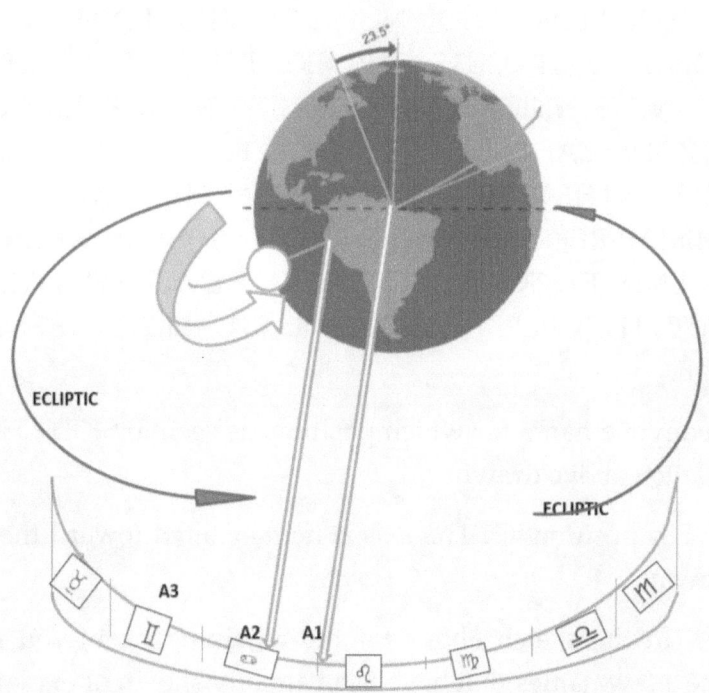

THE ZODIACAL BELT IS ALONG THE CELESTIAL ECLIPTIC. SEE SKETCH 3.

FOR CONVENIENCE, I HAVE CHOSEN THE ABOVE POSITION OF EARTH. THE EARTH IS AT A POSITION OF AUTUMNAL EQUINOX (SEP 21), AS SEEN FROM THE SIDE OF THE SUN. AT THE EQUINOX, THE CELESTIAL EQUATOR PLANE, AND THE ECLIPTIC MEET AND THESE ARE IN LINE WITH THE SUN. ALL IN ONE STRAIGHT LINE. THE DAYS AND NIGHTS ARE EQUAL.

IN THE ABOVE SKETCH, THE ECLIPTIC IS SHOWN AND THE ZODIACAL BELT IS SHOWN. THE ZODIACAL BELT IS VERY CLEAR IN THE SKETCH

THE ECLIPTIC WHEN EXTENDED TO THE CELESTIAL SPHERE BECOMES CELESTIAL ECLIPTIC OR CALL IT THE ZODIACAL BELT. THE ORBIT OF THE MOON IS AT 50 TO THE EQUATOR, SHOWN IN DOTTED LINES. WHEN MOON'S ORBIT CUTS THE ECLIPTIC, ITS POINT OF CUTTING IS INDICATED ON THE CELESTIAL ECLIPTIC OR THE ZODIACAL BELT AS THE NORTH NODE AS A1, A2, A3 (WHEN THE MOON ENTERS THE NORTHERN HEMISPHERE) AND ON THE OTHER SIDE WHERE IT DESCENDS BACK INTO SOUTHERN HEMISPHERE WHERE IT CUTS THE CELESTIAL ECLIPTIC, IS CALLED THE SOUTH NODE.

Can anyone name for which position, as seen in SKETCH 2, is the sketch above drawn?

For position 'C'. The axis is neither tilted toward the Sun nor away.

In the sketch above (or the adjoining page) you must notice a few names that have been already shown or explained.

Let us begin from the bottom. You can see the zodiacal signs that are in proximity to the Celestial Equator.

The curve that is immediately above the band of zodiacal signs is the Celestial Ecliptic on the Celestial sphere. There are three points marked on it; A1, A2, and A3. The zodiacal band spreads itself equally both above and below the Celestial Equator and is along the Celestial Ecliptic.

Did you notice the Earth's Equator? It is in dotted lines. Notice the orbit of the Moon that is at 5^0 to the Equator. The Moon is already climbing its orbit into the Northern Hemisphere. When the Moon cuts the Celestial Ecliptic a North Node is formed; since the Moon is climbing into the Northern hemisphere. On the opposite side when the Moon is descending back into the Southern hemisphere a South Node is formed each time (each month this occurs once). All movements are from left to right. The zodiacal signs are named from the left (West), which is shown from the sign Taurus to the sign Scorpio, in the sketch above. It is only to give you an idea. Normally one can only see three or four signs on one side (in the night sky).

The Moon goes around the Earth from left to right. The Earth too rotates from West to East. Let us assume that the transiting Moon is at 15^0 in Gemini and it happens to cut the Celestial Ecliptic and form the North Node. The Celestial Ecliptic is a fixed imaginary line and it does not move. The Moon during its transit is able to cut the Celestial Ecliptic only while transiting in the sign Gemini currently each month. This will go on for eighteen months. There are 360^0 around the Earth and there are twelve months. If all was normal the calculation will show that the Moon would have taken thirty days to cover the entire 360^0 of the zodiacs. By doing so, it would have returned to the same point for cutting the Celestial Equator at 15^0 of whichever sign. But that does not happen because the Moon takes 27. 3 days to cover the entire zodiacal belt. What will happen then? It will reach this point of cutting the Celestial Ecliptic, while in its orbit around the Earth, a degree or so earlier. It is approximately $1°25'$ every month. This is taken as the movement of the North Node each month but in a reverse direction.

The Moon actually requires 27 days 7hrs and 43 minutes to complete the full distance of the orbit around the earth. Because the Earth also revolves around the Sun and moves further by a degree a day, a certain distance is increased and the Moon takes longer to complete a full circle around the Earth and reach a point from where we began to calculate the time for the orbiting.

I have taken a degree for convenience. It will be a degree and a few minutes earlier. So, in the next month, the Moon will cut when it is at about $14°$ in the sign Gemini. The angular measure of $14°$ is before $15°$ and this point in the sign of Gemini will appear before $15°$ when the Moon cuts the Celestial Ecliptic. The point $15°$ Gemini will lag behind to the right. The new North Node will form and will fall to the left of the North Node that was previously formed, a month ago. Like this, a number of new North Nodes will be formed, all falling a degree or so earlier causing this imaginary point to be moving backward. It takes approximately eighteen months for these imaginary points called North Nodal points to cover an entire zodiacal sign. The intermittent points are interpolated and calculated for the thirty days.

On the opposite side while transiting the sign Sagittarius the Moon will cross over the Celestial Ecliptic again to go down to the Southern Sphere. This time the point is called the South

Node. This will happen after a fortnight. So, the suspense of why the nodal points move backward or retrograde must be now clear. In the sketch above, points A1 and A2 are previous North Nodes that have gone to the right. The new one is A3. But next month the new North Node will have moved to a new position to the left of A3 by a degree perhaps. So, these nodes enjoy a moment of celebration each month of having earned a new longitudinal degree but progressing backward; still can create havoc in our life astrologically.

Chapter-IV

Brigade General Gavin: "He's got to be tough enough to do it and he's got to be experienced enough to do it. Plus, one more thing. He's got to be dumb enough to do it. Start getting ready." Ryan O'Neil as General Gavin in "A Bridge too far".

The Sun
Part One

The Inner Personal Planets

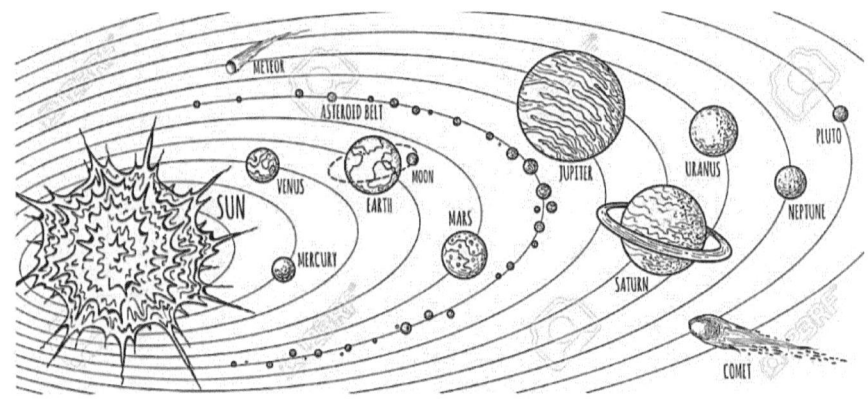

Picture courtesy:
https://www.pinterest.com/pin/332281278767015617/

The above figure depicts the names and their approximate location with respect to the position of the Sun and their order. We begin with the planet Mercury, followed by Venus, the Moon, and the planet Mars. The body of the Sun is also a part of this conglomerate. Each of these has a distinct role to play. Some functions do appear to be overlapping. If observed closely one can always tell the difference.

Before we begin to learn astrology, we must distinguish the functions of an astronomer and an astrologer. If someone reads an article written by an astronomer on the net, any periodical or a book, and gets a chance to hold a conversation with an astronomer, etc., one sees physical evidence of the matter discussed. It is very easy to convince the facts that are disclosed or elucidated. On the other hand, astrology becomes a subject of conjectural thoughts derived and applied freely. One astrologer might not agree with another, what one goes on to predict or summarize an existing situation in a horoscope or the advice offered could be conflicting between two astrologers etc., have become the bane or say, a bone of contention. There is apprehension in the minds of clients before approaching an astrologer. Whether the astrologer has a reputation or has learnt, alone becomes the criteria.

A couple of activities to honour the credibility of an astrologer have taken place and they are continuing. There are universities in the world that have taken up astrological studies, there are few bodies that identify themselves as schools of astrology, there are associations made of experienced astrologers and so on. But what is the common factor that has remained as a 'virus' of disbelief between an astrologer and a client? The client's ignorance on the subject needs to be blamed.

If we introspect ourselves then we will be able to affirm whether or not we have some fundamental knowledge of a subject before we consider consulting with an expert. We do consult a doctor so many times, consult architects and lawyers occasionally, consult a plumber, a carpenter, an electrician, a repairman, a contractor to fabricate and there are plenty of others to place on a list. What is the difference between all of them and an astrologer? Our ignorance about the subject is perhaps the reason. Does it really matter? We all will admit that we have scarce knowledge of many subjects like medicine, surgery, architecture and the nitty gritties of a subject like law, yet we have confidence in ourselves that we will be served well. Why so? The reasons here are plenty but I choose the end result and a role played by an authority to identify such services, set standards and test them periodically. Society's well-being depends on that authority. The authority is liable to take the blame if there exists a flaw that goes unidentified. The subject of astrology has none.

Considering the 'end result' we will admit that a situation or condition may be reached using certain terms and conditions bilaterally. In fact, the entire negotiation begins with whether or not a client will get what he or she wants in the first place. Then there are amendments made to suit a pathway for reaching a consensus. All functions that happen during a consultation with experts in the field lead one way. Client satisfaction needs to be guaranteed and then earning through that has a chance. The astrologers have picked just the last 'fact' well.

The subject of astrology now takes umbrage under the precepts of astronomy. We have all heard, "Whatever shall be, shall be". An astronomer can give out facts that happen in the space above and far beyond our reach, but can he promise us something that is to our liking? No, the astronomer knows this very well. Have you seen an astronomer in the service industry? Impossible! That is why these astronomers are found in either space research centres, as professors in a university, or amidst books researching and contemplating if they have missed a 'link' to identify a phenomenon in space. That is why they have the respect they deserve. The astrologers too need to become like them. The problem arises in this regard as it deals with either limited resources or unreliable work. Many ancient books are difficult to decipher. Either because of the language used or their terminology, the reader feels a need to seek a helper. Certain cultural practices that were existing and followed then had more importance (while using the subject of astrology). The subject consisted mainly of solutions to solve those issues. Today, such issues simply do not exist.

Only yesterday, I was discussing with Mr. Ramamurthy Mothe, a self-taught astronomer and astrologer from Hyderabad, Telangana, has written many original papers and is a member of number of Associations formed by experts in the field of Space research. I felt my knowledge of astronomy appeared minuscule in comparison to his. He was telling me that many scripts on astrology belong to different periods that practiced different traditions. The word 'compatibility' belongs to a modern era that is only about sixty or seventy years old. If one looks back in time, marriage was considered 'sacrosanct'. There was no question of breaking one's marriage. It was as if each one in the family had been served dinner. Everyone had it with all respect and love. There was never a day that one did not attend the dinner because of the interests of someone or something outside of the family. There could be pros and cons on the subject matter and one could debate the merits but, to that period in time that was 'religion'.

The texts reflect this and the astrology of those times dealt with 'tradition', 'morals and ethics', 'diseases that were incurable', 'separation of children from the family', 'men and women of unconventional tastes', and 'death'. You will notice that these subjects were 'taboo' subjects of that period. For that period, it was essential to find someone knowledgeable and discuss to get enlightened on the subject. The astrologers, therefore had a place of knowledgeable and experienced persons in society. These were also very few. The 'subject information' was kept a secret and shared with none. The growth of the subject was limited and only the needy sought it.

Coming to the present age, astrologers have a wide scope to deal and the information that is shared is freely available. My insistence is only on reliability and consistency in the subject matter. There must be enough opportunity to question the astrologer and also update ourselves with the knowledge on the subject. One can never be totally ignorant about something while consulting with someone on mere trust as a foundation. The expert must be humble enough to know whatever 'wrong' was said or advised if pointed out by a client. Only then the malpractice of manipulating gullible clients will stop and genuine knowledge will take over. May I presume, you are ready to read the 'astronomy of astrology' now?

The Sun

The Sun is a star and not a planet. But has influence over us. The Vedic or Sidereal system of astrology uses not only the Sun but even the remaining twenty-seven stars to interpret their influence over us. Thank God! You will exclaim. Those who study that system know how much pain they need to go through. There are very few and people go in search of them and consult them at a place wherever they are available. We cannot find them on the net anywhere. There are differences between the Tropical system or the Western Astrology and the Vedic or Sidereal system. One cannot ignore the merits of both and it will depend on how we were exposed and impressed to initiate an interest in astrology.

The Sun, is responsible for most of our activities, interest, our ways that are unique to us, our looks, thoughts and desires or ambitions. All beginners should go through Mrs. Linda Goodman's book named "Sun Signs", which is available on the internet quite easily. The book was published around 1970 and is still very interesting and applicable as a 'legend' to all future astrologers. That was based on mere Sun signs. Why was that possible? Because, the Sun represents us in all possible activities throughout our life. There could be similarities in some and our 'uniqueness' may reduce. Even then the Sun's location in our chart gets us to 'uniquity'.

If what I have written is true, then why doesn't everyone become rich and famous? The Sun is a crowd puller because it needs attention, admiration, flattery, and recognition, and that is not always out of reality but out of what it wants to do or has already done. Admiration is expected from its associates, colleagues, superiors, spouses and friends. Even the Sun requires a guiding force from someone or something that lies outside of it. If the fact is well understood then you may march ahead into the realm of astrology.

The following are qualities that are picked and adapted by the Sun when present in any zodiacal sign. Even during transit, the Sun would have adapted itself to the qualities of the sign although the transit period is only for a month. What we all must notice first is how far the Sun is into a sign and, second, how much has the Sun shed away those qualities in readiness to enter the next sign. The Sun must be at least 3^0 to 5^0 into the sign, to begin with and must not have crossed the 27th degree of that sign. The same rule applies to the houses too. All personal planets, the Sun and the Moon follow the same. It is useful during observations made in order to foretell something about a person in the present. We must never attribute the full qualities of the house or the sign if the planet is very close to either of the cusps.

In a natal chart, the planets, the Sun and the Moon have a permanent quality embraced into them from the house and the sign they are in. We grow used to that and develop a psyche that some goals are attainable and some are not. Many times, we don't even express happiness or disappointment on account of certain events. We are sure of getting some and not getting many. It hurts only at times when we enter an 'adventure' mode and fail. But that adds to our experience and it is still welcome. Such is the nature of the game in which we seek and we shun. Pay attention to what a person has developed as an advanced sense of his or her own abilities and disabilities. The horoscope is most experimentative if the client is young. You will need to ask, "Have you tried this a couple of times before"? Then you may warn to remain cautious. In an adult's horoscope, one needs to stress on the need to try again although the past showed failures.

With that built into you as background I shall now release the Sun's activities one by one in different houses or signs. The quality of a house and a sign that corresponds to a house irrespective of the sign mentioned in a horoscope remain the same. A writer may use the term 'You' while describing a house in a chart. The same writer will use the term They all' or 'People belonging (or born under) to this sign' when describing the sign and its characteristics. So, keep that in mind. We need to blend if a different sign occupies a house in a chart that is other than the natural sign attributed to a house. For example, even if a sign Scorpio occupies the fourth house in a chart, primarily the fourth house belongs to the sign Cancer and its natural ruler is the Moon. That is where we need to start. Now the connection between the Moon and the planet Pluto tells us the state of the house that is of use to the individual to whom the chart belongs.

The house qualities of the sign Cancer and the sign Scorpio need to be blended.

The Sun in Houses and Signs

1st House or Aries sign: If one understands the planet Mars' nature in its absolute raw form (like the naked ape), then the Sun wants to be like that in Aries or the 1st house. The nature of the 1st house and that of sign Aries are similar. It is a question of assessing 'How much'. If the Sun is aspected by any planet then that planet has a certain power over the Sun. If two or three planets aspect the Sun, then the Sun loses most of its identity acquired out of a house or a sign and puts on new qualities to suit the situation. This nature of the planets is overlooked by many and they continue to attribute the qualities of the house where the Sun is in (or the sign in the house) and wonder why they are wrong with their assessment. There are situations when the Sun is situated in the 1st house, but the sign is Capricorn there. Now what? There are certain pre-dominant qualities that the Sun will adapt from the sign Aries because of the 1st house. Then superimpose the qualities of the sign Capricorn over the few qualities of the sign Aries which it has adapted and continues to survive. Now then, which qualities will the Sun adopt? The easy ones will be considered first. The more difficult ones that are inherent to the sign Aries are avoided. Sometimes, the age matters.

In the younger days, it is advantageous to adapt to the 'child-like' nature of Aries. A couple of years later the sign Capricorn takes over. These basics are to be used each time, for each planet, each house and each sign. As a child, it is difficult to adapt to a Capricorn lifestyle. The Capricorn nature is brought on by circumstances during growth. Possibilities of calamities coming, diseases coming, experience the death of siblings or parents, and extreme poverty are some examples. Sometimes the strict and serious nature of the parents or the guardians or the school teachers, might cause the child to become serious. But it is not natural, but put on for the survival of the self. If the 10th house has the sign Capricorn in it, the child or the person is naturally serious, responsible, answerable, and shows many other leadership qualities with ease. Perhaps it is the eldest too in the family that makes it more caring and shows self-sacrifice toward the family from an early age.

In the 1st house, the Sun has to dissemble a lot. The 1st house or the sign Aries is where the Sun is exalted. What does exalt mean? It means the Sun has the right and liberty to pass on a little extra to the individual whenever there is an opportunity. That makes the Sun even more popular. When I say that the Sun becomes popular it means that an individual will become popular due to generosity. The other qualities that I have mentioned earlier will also hold true, perhaps with a little more intensity. With the Sun in the 1st house be assured the individual hates to see someone ignoring and moving away. The Sun here likes a dress that is noticeable. So, the uniforms come into play, the rank, the festivity, honor are awaited. It is the same with planet Mars here. The difference is that planet Mars really works to achieve a goal and gain recognition. It is not a rank and public image conscious planet. The performance alone counts with planet Mars. The 1st house produces good sportsmen.

With the Sun, only recognition matters. It has an influencing quality to impose and attract attention toward its own achievements. The Sun here could ask someone to do a bit of writing about itself or ask someone to spread the word about its achievements and it never fails to make itself present in front of the higher ups on the right occasions. The Sun works hard if honor and self-respect are challenged and its reputation is threatened. But these happen occasionally. The Sun usually gains access to authority too soon and manages to order others to do the work. On the other hand, planet Mars wants to serve all. One needs to just cajole a bit, humor a bit and Mr. Mars is ready for you.

The Sun is not so bothered about its financial losses in any of the houses for so long, as it is not known to others. If it is revealed then it suffers quietly. The Sun is the only danger to our risky schemes. It loves gambling and takes risks without much work or thought put into it. The stronger the Sun, the more are such tendencies. It has the habit of showing courage where most others fear venturing. For example, approaching a woman and befriend her, take a trip to some place when the weather is at its worst, go into forest alone, go mountain climbing, go on a trip on a boat and cross oceans, and sometimes just to keep a promise made to someone, go out of the way to help are some such activities bordering risks that are life threatening. Many attributes such qualities to planet Mars in a chart. There is a small difference that you must notice that ambition of planet Mars is self-aggrandisement. Planet Mars is happy if it wins an argument, small fights, or proves someone is wrong, gets a certain thing before others, and wins accolades. Aren't these petty? Yes. That is Mr. Mars. Although planet Mars as a soldier, pilot of a jet fighter, or as a Captain of a frigate will achieve bigger feats, you must not fail to notice that '**one**' person in whom planet Mars had an interest in and wanted to impress and win admiration. Perhaps there was a challenge thrown at planet Mars and it was the challenge that caused the heroism. With Sun it is an ambition to get into the Guinness Book of world records. The Sun does not care for any challenges thrown at it because it has an inner confidence that time will tell.

Moreover, the Sun does not regard anyone as high except the superiors. All our superiors are like planet Saturn to us. Planet Saturn and the Sun only exchange conversations, and only here you will notice that the Sun usually replies, "Aye Aye Sir!" Start noticing this and you will catch the Sun or the Mars first, for sure.

The Sun in this house enjoys good health and lives well. All one needs to tolerate is that the people with the Sun in the 1st house are childlike and desire pamper. Usually, they are the only child or the last in a family of three or four and they actually get all the attention. Later, their expectations are not met and that is when they get disappointed seeing the attitude of spouses and friends who do not value this inbuilt desire. The Sun has to learn to live without that doting from others.

Sometimes the planet Mars is combust. That is when a planet is as close as 8^0 to the Sun during transits (8^0 while forming conjunction and later while separating). Then the 1st house loses its importance and all power goes to the 5th house, the sign Leo and the house in which the Sun is transiting during the combust period. In the natal chart to the effect is the same. If under any such circumstances, the Sun is in the 1st house, or the sign Leo is the Ascendant (1st house), then the glory is retained by the 1st house.

All fire signs spend a lot of money wastefully if they are found on the ascendant. They do not hesitate to borrow, take credit and sell some valuables just to prove their spending, to please someone or simply show off among friends and relatives to prove their economic state is normal. With the Sun in the first house, there is an increase in this habit along with a fire sign. With Jupiter's aspect too this habit could get magnified. Planet Jupiter brings that unwanted optimism that money will be generated somehow and so not to worry. Many ends up suffering severely. Please do not blindly believe in Jupiter's aspects that they do good. There is a tendency to increase the aspected planet's desire to the point of destruction. It is better at such times if there is a second aspect controlling the 'short circuit' effect of planet Jupiter. This is true for all the personal planets.

What do we predict from the 1st house?

Effects of New Moon and a Full Moon: A New Moon is a powerful phenomenon that is not understood by many because its effect is spread over a month at least and sometimes stretches over six months. That means any activity, an event, a process or an interest that took birth near about the degree of the New Moon in our chart takes predominance over everything else but its dilution over that long period does not let us feel or realize it. If it happens to form any of the harder aspects with our personal planets then we put great efforts to fulfil our wishes. If it doesn't then the interest quickly dissolves and we try to forget a wish fulfillment. This is the reason we must remain conscious of our activities and thoughts around the New Moon Day. One should consider a range of ± five days around both the New Moon and the Full Moon days.

It is also important that the New Moon occurs somewhere close to the starting cusp of a house. If it happens toward the ending cusp then what was due to start will see its end soon. The planets in the natal chart take support of the New Moon and activate themselves and their aspects promote an inherent interest to materialize. Remember that the planets in the chart are all dormant. They need time to rise and act. The planets transiting is active and wherever they fall in the natal chart, immediate activation, followed by their effect can be felt. What we read in the periodicals about weekly or fortnightly or monthly predictions sometimes come true if they have double effect; one because of the transits with their aspects and the other due to their aspect on our natal planets or the Moon and the Sun. This theory needs to be applied each time to transit aspects.

The Full Moons have a strong effect on closing certain issues. These must happen toward the closing cusp of a house and not the starting cusp. If these happen at the start of a house, the closing could stagger but not close well. Sometimes minor things begin accompanied by a lot of hope but soon fizzle out. The aspects formed during the Full Moon are strong for about four days before and after the occurrence of a Full Moon. Once their effect is lost the closing loses its importance.

The transiting planets too should be strong wherever they are during transit. If there are hard aspects between themselves their strength diminishes. The trine and the sextiles give a comfortable feeling of having received something but more often we do not take notice of these or feel due to lack of preparedness or it is not wanted so badly. Successes are felt with a New Moon or a Full Moon when these have a direct aspect without interference.

In the 1st house, a New Moon has a powerful effect because the Sun is anyway strong and adding to that the conjunction of the Moon makes it stronger. The Moon is our carrier of desire and is now passed on to the Sun for realization. The Sun's 5th house and the sign Leo in the chart, and the Sun's natal position all stand to gain during a new Moon or a solar eclipse. Some aspect's support will tell which house and which planet is involved in completing the act. For example, in the chart shown below, planet Pluto is aspecting planet Mercury with a trine. It is a sure sign of some success in the dealings done at work cleverly. Although planet Pluto puts pressure on all inner personal planets to perform and seek power through their ability, here the planet Mercury will perform without showing any resistance.

When a New Moon occurs, the Moon surrenders its interests, desires, goals, and ambitions to the Sun. The 5th house becomes loaded with both Sun's and Moon's agenda. The 4th house gets neglected. An exception to the rule is when the lunations happen in the 4th house or the sign Cancer, please consider the ruler of the 4th house and the sign on the 4th house cusp. During lunations, these houses and the signs do bring value to one's home. These are connected to the same 4th house direction or 4th house fulfillment of emotional desires and seeking 'unconditional love'.

Here is a sample chart to take an example of a situation in the 1st house.

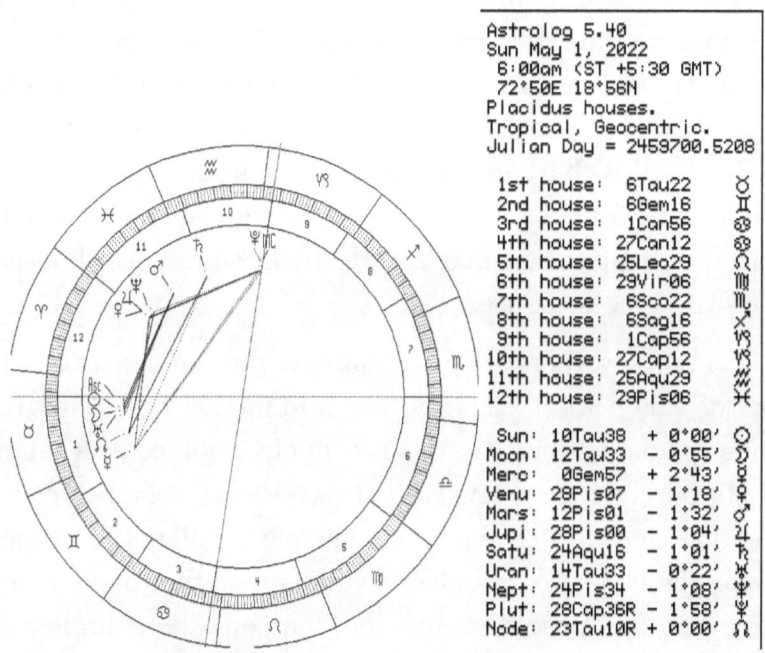

We shall notice the salient features of the New Moon during transits. The observation needs to be superimposed on a chart that is taken for analysis later.

Before we even start, remember to notice what will happen to the 4th house on a New Moon Day. The Moon has let go of its power over the Sun. The 3rd house with the sign Cancer in it will suffer. With it, planet Mercury will suffer too. But the 4th house gains its importance because of the sign Leo in it. It is an indirect gain of the 4th house alone. It is an eclipse too. So, the gains of the 4th house are much higher. The only planet Uranus is conjunct to the New Moon and the Sun. Planet Uranus rules the 10th house and is placed in the sign Taurus, in the 1st house. But just the planet Uranus conjunction cannot do much, its job is to impart knowledge and experience, the time is too short for it. Keep in mind that the New Moon and planet Uranus are both in sextile to the planet Mars. Planet Mars from the 11th brings fresh information and knowledge regarding friends, one's purpose towards community and society, to bring in reforms, and pass on the experience of its transit through the 10th house to the Moon. The Moon is in the house of self and it is Mars' natural house. The current owner of the 1st house is planet Venus for this chart and planet Venus is in the sign Pisces and on the threshold of 12th house with the sign Aries in it. A lot of starts can happen here that include the 11th house, 10th house, 1st house and the 4th house.

I will say, there are possibilities of putting in a lot of work for one's own good, planet Saturn is in the 10th house, it is now under planet Uranus. Uranus is actively involved as a catalyst to support planets Mars' intent. As Venus conjunct planets Neptune and Jupiter, the time available for planet Neptune to make planet Venus visualize a situation so that plans will go according to a procedure may not happen. Planet Jupiter will increase this haste game and cause planet Venus to turn impulsive. As the conjunction of planets Venus and Jupiter increases planet Venus' worth, there will be monetary gain. But when planet Venus moves into the 12th house within the next 24 hrs., that money will be wasted away. The 12th house also stands for intoxicating activity, hospitalization, seeking escapism, etc. if planet Mercury is stressed then there are more chances. Planet Mercury is trine to planet Pluto and might be not stressed so much but is occupied with taking certain decisions. Planet Mercury is also in the 1st house and is involved in 10th house needs because the planet Pluto is currently transiting the 10th house. The work is regarding one's responsibilities, one's status in society, and what one wants to show the world as capable. When you superimpose these on anyone's chart, there will be differences, that you must manage. I have given the transit meanings. You must apply using these, if applicable, to do a guess work for that person. Remember always, transiting aspects and the planets are more active. The planets in a chart are dormant. These need to be initiated and that requires time. Fast-moving planets do that quickly; just for a purpose.

Let the Sun be in any house or for that matter any of the personal planets, unless these get a jolt, a taste of suffering and failure they cannot give the beneficial result. One needs to ask if the client has suffered in any way before in connection with the planet in a house. If yes, then further improvement causes benefits probably in the mid-twenties or mid-thirties. Only planet Jupiter gives a birthday shower and moves on. The rest of the outer planets bring misery and leave. These weaken our composition so that we work toward rebuilding it. Even our will gets devastated.

The inner planets have a spoiling nature and build indulgent habits. These are the ones that are responsible for our death. So, watch out for the inner personal planets or bodies such as the Moon and the Sun for weaknesses. If all four of the personal planets are affected frequently, there will be a period of suffering. Great happiness usually means indulgence that could happen or could be already taking place. The Sun is very easily carried away by circumstances. The next in order is planet Venus, planet Mars, and then planet Mercury. So, notice these early.

2nd House or Taurus sign: The 2nd house belongs to planet Venus. This planet Venus is sensual rather than more companion-seeking planet Venus of sign Libra. The planet Venus here is self-reliant and is more interested in earning money for its own security than showing dependency on others. The idea to work, putting in effort consistently and buy the luxuries of life is very appealing to planet Venus of Taurus. The Sun has to imbue these qualities to survive. There are plenty of talents to choose when the Sun occupies the 2nd house in a natal chart. But there will be a limitation with speech and voice; unless planet Venus is placed strongly in the chart. There is an obsession to look strong, huge and muscular. Weightlifting and training fascinate the Taurus Sun. The connoisseurs of food, drink and wine belong here. The singers, musicians, dancers, voice artists and the wealthy are found in this house too. If the Sun wants to be like the planet Venus, then it needs to be strong by its position in the chart. A weak Sun cannot and it chooses a select band of people who belong to a lower class, religion or poor economic status. The Sun loses track of its dignity if weak and the quality of association suffers while seeking the much-aspired attention, admiration and glorification.

The Sun is weak when located in the 11th house or the 7th house the signs Libra and Aquarius, but that are still manageable. If any of the outer planets or the North Node aspect the Sun, then also it is weak because it loses its independence and thereby its vitality. If an eclipse occurs with a hard aspect to the Sun in a natal chart, the Sun is always under instructions and command of this phenomenon. The tantrums, whims and fancies of the Sun increase. The Sun starts to pretend and demands attention and false admiration. The North Node increases the Sun's need to be important. If other planets pose difficulties, then the Sun has trouble living with it.

The 2nd house stands to bring awareness in self-worth, self-earned income, family status, well-being of family members and speech quality.

Self-worth is assessed through the performance of the self in various activities. At school through studies and later in college too, it is judged through performance. In the twenties, the self-worth gets proven from the Sun's ability to win over friends, to get invited to parties, to be considered as handsome by some and get certain importance out of choosing a career that will enable it to earn well. This is true of the Sun, even if it is present in the sign of Taurus anywhere in the chart. The self-worth is assessed through the sexual performance too. There is a lot of experimentation with casual sex, choosing different partners, sometimes there is compulsion and obsession attached to that (hypersexuality normally, if planet Mercury is weak then through anxiety), and mostly the relationships have a short life. The Sun is just trying to prove itself that it's worth its mettle.

In the job zone too, a similar experimentation is possible. The Sun needs to be strong in this house or else one loses sight of morals and ethics in order to assess self-worth and earnings. Towards the family, the Sun here is very possessive and caring. Hard work comes naturally but that is towards the family and its job, real estate appears interesting, agriculture, horticulture become hobbies, cooking, dress-making and mathematics are very interesting to pass times here, and investments into stocks to earn is a common venture with the Taurus sign.

The self-worth can also be identified by observing spending habits in a person. The stronger the Sun is, the more the tendency to spend on luxuries (Taurus sign and 2nd house). Frequent parties at home, giving away expensive gifts, although the Sun has good taste in most items of luxury, it will over do. The self-earning capacity is good if the planet Venus is strong in the chart somewhere. Venus is strong in 2nd house or the 7th, signs Taurus and Libra. The sign Pisces has more compassion attached and earnings come through talents, legacy, auctioning antiques, marriage, healing arts and the occult. These will be passed on to the Sun in the 2nd house to benefit. The aspects from other planets do play a big role and they can change a situation drastically.

With an aspect from planet Jupiter to planet Venus, increases the strengths of all houses where planet Venus has influence. Whether that is good or bad needs to be assessed. Sign Taurus is extremely excitable when aspects to planet Venus happen, or aspects to planets in the 2nd house or aspects to the ruler of the 2nd house. The sign Scorpio has been attributed with a lot of clandestine activity, sexual abuse, etc. No one thinks that it is the sign Taurus that is capable, whatever the sign Scorpio is afraid of.

Imagine if planet Venus is combust and the Sun is in the 2nd house. This will benefit the individual a lot. Only the 7th and the 12th houses, signs Libra and Pisces will suffer. Taurus will not suffer. The Sun represents the father, the elders, the boss or any superior who is influencing our life at that time. So, depending on that we must ask and then tell. In the natal chart, it could definitely represent the father, but later on, it changes. With any planet getting combust, the 5th house, the transiting Sun's position and the sign Leo will benefit. The planet that gets combust, its own house and sign suffer. The sexuality that I described above will be passed to the 5th house too. The person will enjoy sex as a tool of entertainment and seek surfeit.

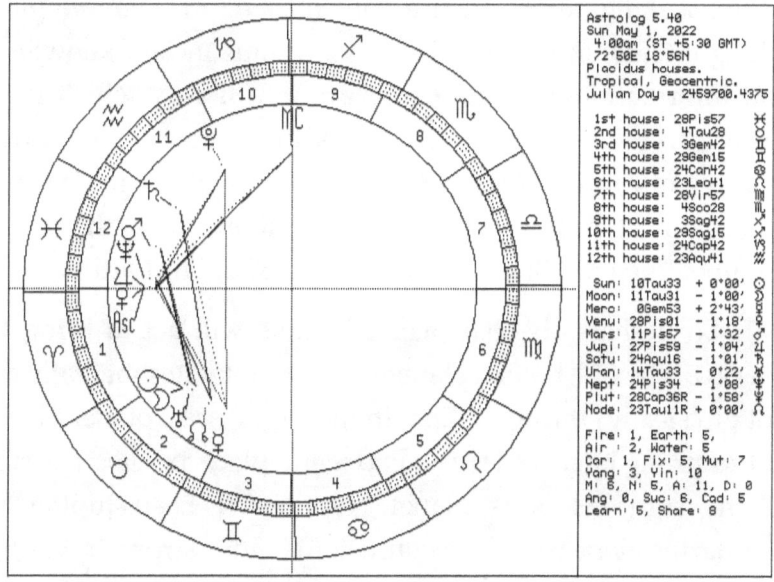

Observe the chart and write a few lines on the present state of the 2nd house.

It is a solar eclipse in the sign Taurus. It is at 10⁰ and it is occurring around 5⁰ into the 2nd house. All New Moons are starters; eclipses are stronger, especially if they happen within the first 5⁰ of any houses. Planet Mars aspects the eclipse and planet Uranus acts as a catalyst. Planet Uranus always uses the personal planets or even planet Saturn for that matter to convey its message of knowledge. Planet Mars is the ruler of the 1st house and it is going to start something from the sign Pisces on the 12th. What could these be?

The 12th house is secretive and deals with giving up on materialistic values. It also brings recuperation and rehabilitation for healing purposes. It can take one far away, if need be, for seeking relaxation or simply escape the tirades of a superior at work who causes work pressure. Apparently, this house causes a lot of wasteful expenditure. Usually, mental health treatments (all water sign houses and signs have this issue), seeking advice from a person living in a remote place, taking interest in subjects that have certain ancient knowledge and information, and the books are in a library which is not easily accessible. The person wants to venture with a strong resolve into unknown territory and live seeking mercy from others or completely independent. Remember the movie 'Rambo, The First Blood'? Like that, Rambo; The Outlaw.

So, I shall say that planet Uranus will act to bring the effects of the 12th house (planet Uranus motivates mentally and not physically) through Mars. In the sign Pisces, planet Mars is not so strong but could try well to seek a place to relax. The ruler of the sign Pisces is planet Neptune (I keep Jupiter for Sagittarius alone to reduce confusion), and is strong in the sign Pisces. There is no contact between planets Mars and Neptune now. So, from the 12th house planet Mars will incur expenditure but will find a lot more hidden information during its venture. The North Node is square, planet Saturn in the 11th, causes planet Saturn to release its boundaries in order to spend money and a few talents if any. With the aspects of the North Node all planets release their boundaries in order to oblige. The North Node does whatever it has in its mind and operates from the house it is transiting. The 2nd house is for self-worth, family welfare and a house to indulge. It is possible that this person has a family function or a promise to keep for the family and therefore finds an opportunity. But will feel the expenses once after the return. Whenever planet Saturn releases its boundaries, expenses happen, and the money is freely used. After a few weeks, the aspect from the North Node will separate and planet Saturn will regain its hold on the securities, all expenses, and losses will come to light. We feel terrible.

Observe planets Venus and Jupiter which are conjunct so close to the ascendant. This aspect will have a planet Mars effect to it like, impulsiveness, insist on enjoying, spending on luxuries, dress, travel, etc. The good side is that the aspect allows the funds to flow too from a source like earnings, savings, or simply by selling stocks or property.

So that was a simple analysis for that period. The solar eclipse effects last for a year. The lunar eclipse effects last for six months.

What do we predict from the 2nd house?

Generally, any planet transiting the 2nd house causes a need to spend. That is an easier way to feel satisfied and happy. That causes inner confidence to build which we call the self-worth building exercise. Although, this is not an ideal way to go, perhaps it is the quickest. The outer planets cause us to take a new direction to earn and will not allow spending. By spending, we show our self-worth and self-earning capacity. With the presence of the outer planets our self-worth, self-earning capacity falls. Our self-confidence is lost. Regarding the outer planets and their effects, I have devoted a separate chapter to that.

If a New Moon happens to fall here, certainly we begin a new job, a new project to make ourselves secure and feel good. If there is an aspect to the lunation from any planet, then the characteristics of the house and that of that planet get passed to the New Moon. The New Moon will then initiate an activity related to that effect. If a Full Moon happens here then there is a gain towards which some effort was being put for a while now has the possibility to reach us. Usually some lump some money, a gift arrives. If there are eclipses something of a higher order can happen.

If planet Jupiter or planet Venus is passing through this house a happy event like a wedding, birthday party, dinners, and association of rich people (much higher in status) happens. If planet Mercury is transiting there could be a deal set up for a business or a company in which you may be involved. The longtime spending planets have a different purpose and these cannot be linked to any predictions as such. These outer planets change our attitude year after year to set us on a new course to achieve. Plenty of events happen during those transits.

For planet Venus to deliver, it needs the best of guides, coaches and tutors. It can bring expressions if it has been hurt badly by the outer planets. It will earn well if the value of money was taught early in its life. With planet Venus, nothing can build in the middle age or in the late fifties except a few artistic talents. As planet Venus primarily seeks a companion throughout, if the planet is not exposed to its talents, then it sees no point in pursuing these.

Planet Venus in the sign Libra learns to work sedulously. Planet Saturn is exalted in this sign and leaves plenty for planet Venus to focus on how to apply itself well to get results. The best mathematicians had the planet Venus in Libra or Taurus. Planet Venus is not just about love and romance; neither is planet Mars. These planets need a distraction, something to make them weak and only then do the primal desires alone remain for survival. Do not just declare romance seeing planet Venus in the 5th or 7th houses. Planet Venus has to fall down from grace first, so for the Moon, and so for the planet Mars. If they are ready for that in the absence of any superior purpose then you may declare anything and it will be always true. Only the Sun takes time to fall from grace. A weak Sun anywhere looks for outside support to feel good and appear well and keeps countenance. It has low self-esteem and that is redeemable. The Sun in the sign Libra and Aquarius are weak. But will do nothing disgraceful.

3rd house or Gemini sign: The 3rd house has a number of functions to do with our mental abilities and wants to seek people to sell or listen to our ideas, give us a placement after interviewing us, let others know our opinion and ways to deal with neighbors, maintain our relations with siblings, maintain our memory ability and habits such as reading, writing, publishing (although more from 9th house) and teaching in general are all controlled.

There is a strong desire to be in front of the public through speech and talents that use hands. Most radio and television artists have a strong 3rd house and a gifted voice. What the 3rd house cannot produce is an in-depth interest. It loves to remain on the surface of everything but hates to be involved and claim superior knowledge. A jack of all, so to say. It can do plenty of talking to express something but none of that comes with an intention to love someone. It is very superficial. The stronger the planets therein, the stronger will be planet Mercury, with any aspect from planets like Mars and Jupiter to planet Mercury or the ruler of the house, with the Sun in the 3rd house with the planet Mercury combust and a stellium of planets that contribute to the house if present in the 3rd house, the person is constantly wanting to say something without waiting for a turn to come or without even bothering if others are interested. Such extreme desire may be easily noticed. The stronger the 3rd house, the greater the anxiety level which later reaches a stage of developing mental disorders.

The Sun in any house loves to seek validation from others for its deeds, activity and achievements. Sometimes, others too get fed up with flattering these achievements because not all are worthy of comment. In the 3rd house the Sun wants validation on a daily basis. It is a house of self-esteem. For that, it searches its friends' circle, someone new who does not know its nature well, or anyone gullible enough to listen to the self-proclamation and unintelligent talk. The weaker the Sun gets or the planets present in the house, or the weak ruler of the third house, and if planet Mercury is weak, then, the need for validation goes up but finding listeners becomes difficult.

For the normal strength 3rd house Sun, there are plenty of academic achievements possible. 'Normal' means the ruler of the 3rd house and planet Mercury should have no aspect to weaken them or increase their ability very high, like with an aspect from planet Jupiter. Any magnifying aspect to planet Mercury in a chart brings mental disorders. It starts to think of its state in the future and also the possibilities of achieving that state. The worry factor becomes constant and predominant. These result in anxiety to begin with and later increase to depression, bipolar disorder and schizophrenia. If everything is normal with the 3rd house, planet Mercury and the 3rd house ruler, the person with the Sun in the 3rd house or in the sign Gemini will show abilities that he or she can learn quickly, learn many languages like linguists, enjoy travelling and show an ambition to increase knowledge, write and spread the knowledge. Even with friends they become the most likable and are invited to most parties. They are favorites in the academic circles too.

The sign naturally has planet Mercury's ruler ship. If planet Mercury is aspected by outer planets, eclipses, or the nodes, naturally the strength of planet Mercury reduces. This is followed by a habit that is cultivated mainly to fulfill basic Gemini sign desires. The superficial side increases. The people with such weak Mercury begin to see everyone with a purpose and once it becomes clear that the other person's interest has diminished, they feel a crisis within and start looking out for someone new who is gullible. Remember the qualities of planet Mercury.

The Sun in this house learns to be ambidextrous. One could even be a magician; a card player who is very sharp to notice others expressions and decides how much to bid. Could be an avid reader or a writer. All air signs and their houses like 3rd, 7th, and 11th are poor wealth producers. Their intelligence is unmatched but these signs and the houses do not know their way into the money market or the job market. These signs and houses need others attention and that lets others notice their exploitable ability. After this, there is a good chance of earning wealth. Usually, this takes time. The air signs bring wealth quite late. After the age of 50 or so the period of comfort begins. Otherwise most lead a mediocre lifestyle. In fact, there are more stories of losing wealth due to optimism, carelessness, indiscriminate behavior, etc. attached to the air signs. To earn popularity and fame through talent is their god given gift. So please bear in mind these 3rd house abilities and apply them. If the ruler of the 3rd house, planet Mercury or planets in the 3rd house have an aspect from the outer planets then the push taken could lift them earlier on with a certain hardship or a loss. We shall see some charts later to notice these.

What do we predict from the 3rd house?

During transits, if we see a focus on the 3rd house, usually an attempt to make a contact is to be expected. The contact could be through an e-mail too. The 6th house is usually a letter or a mail with a bigger purpose. Information is passed confidentially. The reason for receiving a mail in the 3rd house could be an attempt to pass knowledge, information or let someone know a secret or their ability to seek a job prospect. After this short travel, an assignment to write, publish or speak is possible. There could be siblings visiting, a family problem requires solving and this requires a lot of research and therefore asking people, searching the internet, etc., could happen.

The 3rd house rules instruments and equipment for communication. These get importance during that extra activity period. Generally, the 3rd house involves contacting friends, certain associations or bodies like radio and television, or a job as an announcer, etc. What others dream about working in the media industry, these get with their hands down. So, remember these.

Talking of success with Sun in the 3rd or even planet Mercury in the 3rd is that a failure in a career is necessary earlier in life in order to rework in the field of interest and succeed. There are plenty who choose a field under the advice of someone elder in the family. Later they realize that they would have fared better if they had chosen something else. The 3rd house has a quality of Gemini's duplicating habit, repeating a certain function, keeping plenty of alternatives on the side, this dual sign wants to adapt to something new always. It feels happy when it is behind the scene rather than boldly facing a situation. Quite the opposite of sign Aquarius. One might say that these 3rd house kinds are difficult to trust or confide in.

Please do not forget that they are more focused in what they are interested in and not so much in you. This inquisitive sign is very curious about people and their affairs. But not in the people or what are their feelings towards their friends including themselves. What they do or did and why they did something somewhere is of no concern to these 3rd house types. It is more of a statistical or a diagnostic type investigation. So never try to win over by a self-revelation assuming that you are building trust. Feed them with new information that is hard to get otherwise. They will turn into glue and you can't remove that sticking gum.

4th house or Cancer sign: When the Sun is either transiting or placed in the natal chart in this house, the Moon's characteristics are taken up by the Sun. During transits, the Sun stays for just thirty days but the Sun too turns moody; changes its intent every two and a half days. The Moon takes about two and a half days in each sign and the Sun too has to accommodate that. So, there is no one set of activities for the Sun but multifarious ones. Some could be easy and some difficult. If the transiting Moon is stressed due to some aspect, then the Sun too will suffer. These are the first rules to remember when the Sun is in Cancer or the 4th house.

The Moon's desire is always to look for 'unconditional love'. The second is showing attachment to all the living and non-living matter. The third is similar to planet Mercury's habit of turning into a vagabond or preferring to lead a Bohemian lifestyle if under stress. We all prefer to travel and stay in isolation to recover from a stressful lifestyle. If we are hurt badly, we prefer detachment from all. The Moon is the cause for letting memories weigh high and let us remember persons who have come and gone in our life. It is also responsible for storing the memories in the heart perpetually.

Always remember that it is planet Mercury that starts to imagine a relationship in the head (our brain) and works out plans to succeed in seeking a mate and getg into a relationship. We are always mentally in love at the beginning. If we are not consumed by someone who repeatedly reminds us of their existence somewhere, no relationship is going to take place. Planet Mercury has to do it plenty of times until it is assured of a future. Only after the planet Mercury decides to rest the relationship enter our heart in the form of permanent memory. When we say 'heartbroken' we actually mean our Moon is broken. During the stay, the Moon feels so comfortable that it thinks there is no need to work out any scheme for itself to save a relationship.

This is 'trust'. Did you ever have to work out a plan to ask something from, your parents, siblings, relatives, and some friends? Never. Once the heart is accommodated by someone, the trust been automatically built up and 'tricking one's way' is just not required. All these become the Sun's job here. But the Sun is not used to changing so frequently to the whims and fancies of the transiting Moon in the heavens. The Sun finds it difficult. Even in the natal chart, if the Sun is found in the 4th house, once every month the Moon will visit that house and remind the Sun about whatever is going on in the Moon's mind. The Sun has to respond to that. The 4th house has stronger effects of the Moon on the Sun.

The interests of the Sun in order to gain affection, validity, attention and admiration make it a clinger. It cannot cling to all but a few; the Sun has fewer friends here. It is more homebound than outdoors. Professions that permit hoarding and hoarding, professions that permit feeding and caretaking are admissible. Large families are preferred here. Parents are well cared for. Overall, the love that was once generated is protected.

When important events need to occur at home, one must observe the 2nd, 4th, and the 9th houses and see how strong these are. Sometimes we do get clients who come asking about a child's marriage. First, check the three houses if any good planet is going to make a long stay. Then check the child's entire horoscope for certainty. I usually check the position of planet Jupiter and if those planet aspects any planet in the houses mentioned or their rulers. Next check for a New Moon or a solar eclipse in the very houses mentioned above.

The 4th house Sun has an uncanny ability to provide variety in its work. This one is not a 'Jack of all' type like the 3rd house Sun. In order to create an interest in all its associates, family, etc., it can think of numerous ideas or ways to excite them. The best chefs have a strong Sun here or at least a strong 4th house. The Moon is exalted in the sign Taurus. This Moon produces wealth out of nothing sometimes. It is never short of money. Usually, it is found in persons born into a rich family. Poverty is seen if planets like Saturn, Pluto, Neptune and Uranus are in the 4th house. If the personal planets have been weakened in the 4th house, then the childhood too would have been subjected to poverty.

I can safely say, this Sun has caretaking as its concern, wherever it is placed or in whichever profession. Doctors and nurses are common if their 6th house or the 12th house indicates any healing aspects. The 8th house looks deeper into the body through an incision, hypnosis or studies the psyche. With any connection to the 4th house, the work carried out by the 8th house has care and concern attached to it.

What do we predict from the 4th house?

As soon as you see a number of planets active in the 4th house, perhaps lunations, an outer planet transiting (that usually is very long) or the ruling planet or the Moon becoming strong during transit. Sometimes the 4th house is strong in a natal chart and that strength does not diminish due to a few transits of personal planets. Our analysis must be focused on what the person considers important in the present.

The 4th house looks for 'unconditional love' perpetually. There is no end to this search. If it does not find in living beings it starts to get it from inanimate objects like equipment that offers comfort or entertainment or pleasure. Television set, a repair tool kit, a motor car, mobile phones, a house, a bed, a kitchen, a study room and a few others that lead one to isolation yet keep the pleasure coming in the required doses. Planet Saturn in the 4th house causes us to seek happiness out of inanimate objects. The 3rd house also has an interest in the list that I mentioned above but its interest is from showing that it is keeping abreast with the technology. Only the use of it matters and there is no emotional attachment towards anything. They normally do not feel the loss of any of these so much. They just go out and buy another to replace. The 4th house accent is on emotional attachment towards everything. They just hoard, hoard and hoard until someone at home goes insane seeing the junk. So, you must bring these facts in your statement of prediction.

In most situations, the 4th house activity has to do with, a family function. The entire family will be involved in a plan to successfully complete the celebration. The 2nd house, 6th house, and the 10th house too indicate such camaraderie but with a difference in purpose. There is a possibility of parents requiring attention, the house requiring attention, house repairs, and painting could be due, simply putting, the desire from the heart is to go out shopping and buy something beautiful and feel the pleasure (attachment to things).

The exceptional case with all water houses or signs is that if there has been a trauma of some kind, like sadness due to bereavement, heartbreak or there has been a loss of interest in everything that one used to find pleasure in, then isolation is sought and travel ensues. There during travel, the person recovers and the feelings of the heart are set right.

The 4th house is directly opposite the 10th house. Transiting planets like the outer planets have an opposing effect to the 10th house cusp. There is usually a change of scenario at work place. One might change a job or suffer a transfer, face difficulties due to the organization, not performing well or one's own bag of tricks to achieve something fails miserably. That becomes a cause for anxiety. The decision to change depends on how brave is the person. In the 4th house, the Sun caters through diet, clothing, a secure home, be a care taker, a provider and then exercises a motivation to get things done its way. It never uses force or harsh speech. If weak, there is too much clinging and nagging.

Some of the deep-rooted qualities of Cancer come out when the outer planets are either stationed permanently or these transits pass through the 4th house every couple of years. Even their aspects to any personal planet in the 4th house will have a similar effect. Planet Saturn will take 2½ years in each house it transits, planet Uranus takes 7 years, planet Neptune takes 14 years, and planet Pluto takes about 17 years to complete a transit through a house made of thirty degrees. These bring in radical changes but gradually. You will read about these in the chapter on outer planets. But learn to differentiate which planet brings what change.

Let us take an example chart and see what can happen with a Cancer Ascendant.

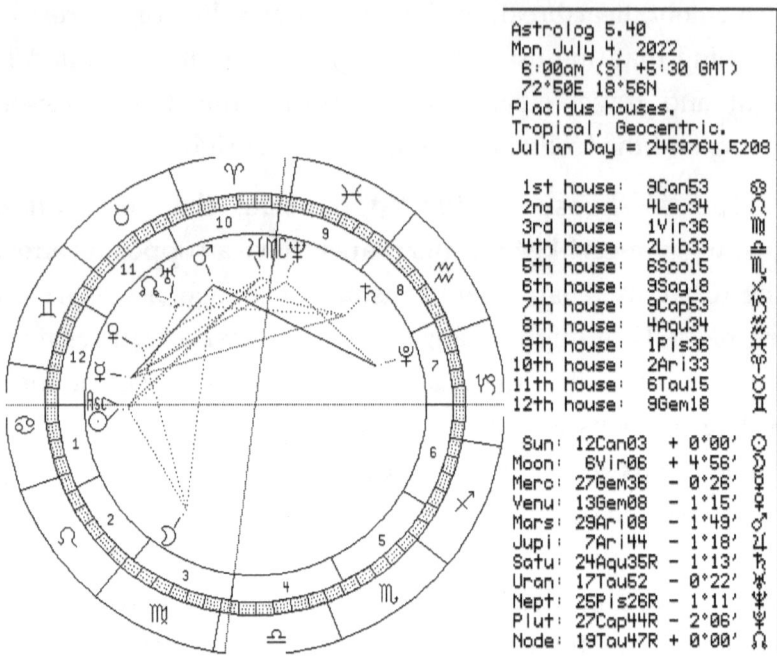

Assume the above chart is a natal chart of someone. Our preliminary job is to assess the Sun and therefore start looking for the ruler Moon and its aspects. The aspects formed by the Sun and the Moon and the ascendant will matter if the fundamental nature of the person needs to be assessed. In a Cancer ascendant or a Cancer sign anywhere else in a chart, will look for anything that can wreck the emotional side of a person. If that is healthy, rest is solved.

The Sun is sextile to Moon in Virgo, an orb of 6^0. The Sun is a square planet Jupiter in 10th house Aries. The Sun is close to the ascendant and is therefore conjunct with the ascendant. If the Moon gets connected to the Sun in the sign Cancer or even otherwise, the Moon's desires, intent, want all get passed to the Sun and it takes over those responsibilities. It is a sextile aspect and therefore it is like getting reminders if a job is not done. The other hard aspects like conjunction, the square, the opposition are compulsive to the Sun.

The trine is a comforting one and no stresses are felt by the Sun in fulfilling the Moon's cravings. Notice the square aspect of Jupiter and this will increase the intensity of the sextile aspect of the Moon from the 3rd house with the sign Virgo. This becomes a writer's, communicator's and all other 3rd house characteristics becoming predominant. Planet Jupiter in the 10th, with Sign Aries becomes a dynamic force causing the Sun to be more pro-active in its pursuit. Its ruler, planet Mars will tell what the Sun would like to show to the world that he is good at something and ask for a value. Planet Mars is in sign Aries but in the closing degrees of 28^0. So weak and we say it is anaretic. Anaretic planets are in their last 2^0 of a sign or even a house. These planets cannot deliver; instead, they either back off or do something to contrary to what they usually promise. If the 10th house lord is weak, then the planet Jupiter will take over and increase the sextile aspect intensity from the Moon.

The 6th house has planet Jupiter's rulership. The 6th house is empty, planet Mercury is its natural ruler, is aspecting a trine with planet Saturn in the 8th house, planet Neptune squares it from Pisces in the 9th house. Saturn brings jointly involved finances, other people's money handling, and thereby earning. Passive income is desired here. Planet Neptune in the natal chart allows planet Mercury to dream and visualize its dealings, transactions, nature of work, kind of people to associate and even what education and knowledge to attain before involving itself into something. The square brings urgency like, "Unless I have tested and tried certain things, I shall not entertain". It is a good aspect to have in a natal chart. There is a sextile aspect from planet Mars to planet Mercury. This constantly reminds the planet Mercury to actively seek whatever it wants to achieve and be quick. So, in conclusion, 3rd house, 1st house, 10th house, and 12th house are all active. Healing, writing, and working in an advisory capacity or being a consultant suits the chart.

Wherever the Moon ruled Cancer ascendant comes into the picture, our nature has an effect of constant change due to the Moon's transition through other houses each month. The ascendant controls our inner nature, the Moon controls our desires, and the Sun controls our external appearance and outlook. As the moon changes its house every two and a half days, our nature is subject to change too when the ascendant has the Moon in it or the Cancer sign on it. Do not forget that the 4th house is motivated by the 8th house. In this chart, the Moon is the benefactor.

The Moon brings wealth on account of its nature to hoard. It likes to keep the family together. It earns through legacies because of its caretaking nature. Loves children and provides home and security to all. It enjoys travelling to fulfill desires that give freshness to one's imagination on seeing new and different things and people. It enjoys travel by land or water. The Moon in 4th house will want to change its living place frequently. It will either move from place to place or simply redecorate its home. The Moon and our brain are connected to help visualize the future intuitively. If the Moon is weak or badly stressed then we lose that ability and we become erroneous in our judgments. False fears, hallucinations, and delusions can increase with stress when placed in 3rd or 9th house.

5th house or Leo sign: It's Sun's own house and it is its natural ruler. All qualities of the Sun are attributable to this house. In the presence of other planets, those house qualities change and selected preferences are brought forward towards certain interests of this house.

The 5th house has more to do with the outside world than the inside of the home. The children aspect is the only function that is carried out within the home. The house stands for motivation. Not only for the self but for others too. All houses that are 5th from any house in a horoscope are motivating houses for the 1st house. The 6th house is a motivating house for the 2nd house. The 7th house is a motivating house for the 3rd house. The 8th house is a motivating house for the 4th house. So, if any planet is transiting 5th house, it will automatically motivate the 1st house. That means, whatever the 'self' wants it is achieved through the 5th house. There are good things and bad things included here. A lot depends on the mold of the character that is represented by the horoscope.

If the Sun transiting the 5th house is strong without any bad influence or temptations then most activities conducted will be good. If the natal Sun is placed in the 5th house and is strong enough then too good character will be shown. Both of these, natal and transiting Sun will do the job of motivating the 1st house. That apart the other functions, events will not become too risky for the individual. Gambling and risk taking are two functions that belong to the 5th house and sign Leo qualities.

The weak Sun needs to show some qualities that will win admiration. The Sun cannot take up certain challenges when weak. It withdraws and earns attention and admiration from something else. Then certain other habits will also follow.

The house has an education, training, travel for pleasure, designing, and originality attached too. The enthusiasm shown takes the person to good heights of popularity. Even transiting Sun or any personal planets causes some good events and goes.

I have always felt happy whenever planet Jupiter transited the 5th house. I had to face tests, had to travel, educate myself higher, and teach students, in all such activities I felt happy. The inspiration was obtained from the 9th house too. Together the two houses helped me. So, when you need success in any house, please check the movement in the motivating house. In my case, the 1st house of 'self' was motivated by the 5th house of 'activities'. The 5th house in turn got motivated by the 9th house for higher learning and adventure.

What do we predict from the 5th house?

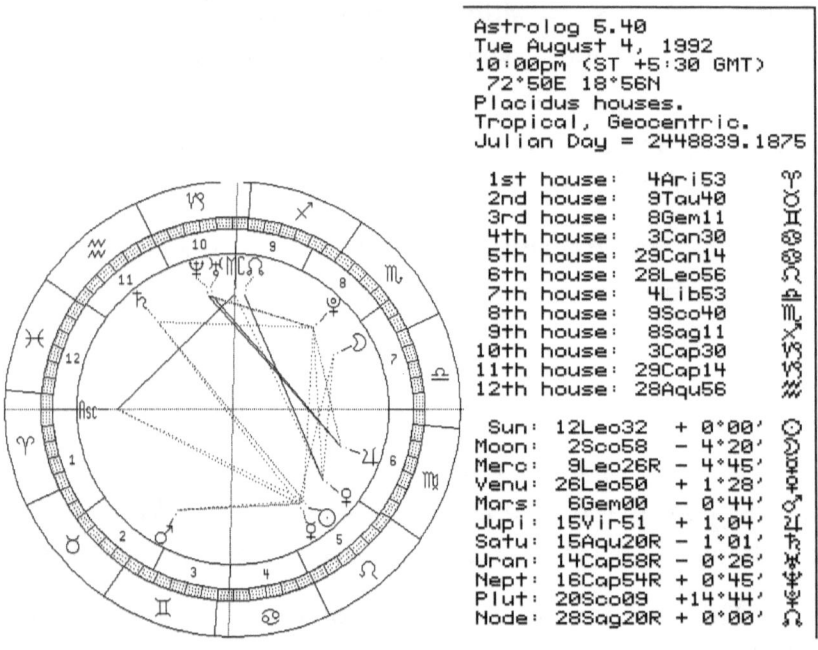

Let us take a chart for a short discussion.

The Sun is in the 5th, planet Mercury is combusting with it. But the entire power is given away here due to the 'combust' situation will go to the Sun and its sign Leo. Planet Mercury will lose its power and houses 3rd, 6th, sign Gemini and sign Virgo become helpless. Here, the 3rd and 6th houses carry the same signs that belong to planet Mercury. This is a natal chart of one of my clients. Unfortunately, even planet Jupiter is in a weak house. Planet Venus will benefit tremendously because of the 5th house benefiting due to the 'combust' of Mercury.

Planet Mars is also weak because it is in the Gemini sign but in the 2nd house. There could be some face saving due to strong Venus. But, nothing apart from that. The ascendant lord is not as strong as it should be. The sextile aspect between the Sun and planet Mars is also encouraging. Since the 5th house is lighted up, with Sun, there is also a stress causing aspect from Saturn, opposition from the 11th house. When the aspect comes from the 11th house it is usually about friends not cooperating but also advising against whatever the Sun has in mind. The 5th house normally motivates the 1st house; here it can do a half-hearted job when planet Mars is also weak.

Planet Neptune is trine with planet Jupiter, which will help planet Jupiter to plan well after dreaming about those first. When planet Jupiter is weak, in the 3rd, 6th, 8th and 12th, it can benefit the house but not any other house that is aspected by it. Here the 6th house will benefit but any other planet placed far from it cannot. Continuing about the 5th, the Sun loves entertainment, gambling, cinema, theatre, learning, teaching, sports and even love affairs. Planet Saturn's aspect causes the Sun to think if all that it is interested in, is going to benefit. So, a lot will be cut off. Regular habits will be developed, health consciousness is high, and therefore will benefit wherever sincerity is demanded. Planet Mars being in the 2nd house and sign Gemini, this person will develop two independent interests of work. Pluto in the 8th encourages passive income. The two outer planets Uranus and Neptune in the 10th house show (aspect planet Jupiter in the 6th) that the person will run an ancestral business. The sign on the 10th house is Capricorn and the planet Saturn is in 11th. So, there will be superiors running the business, this person will be subordinates. The person took sports as a hobby and did well for himself. He did well at school, but not in college as he became distracted by cricket. So that was a method of analysis.

If there is New Moon occurring here and is coincident with a planet or the Sun or the Moon, then that planet will be predominantly playing a role in initiating something new. Most periodicals that I have noticed write about a new love affair beginning! It always depends on where is planet Mercury in the natal chart. Planet Mercury needs to be with the Moon or planet Venus in the natal chart. Only then an encounter with the opposite gender after a period of conversation or interaction will result in planet Mercury recalling the event a couple of times later. A desire could take birth, followed by a plan to have another encounter. That might result in an affair in time. Otherwise, it is difficult. In the above horoscope, even if planet Venus 26^0 (toward the end of the sign and the house), is in the 5th house, it has no aspects from planet Mercury. But it is in the sign Leo where the planet Venus likes to show off and attract. But beyond that? If you see the Moon, it is in the 7th house, 2^0 in Scorpio and its ruler is Pluto in the 8th. Pluto is square to planet Venus with an orb of 6^0. This aspect can give rise to a relationship with a 'conscious power' awareness attached. It can work sometimes. Usually, these end up as one of the two individuals becoming possessive with a fear of losing the other. There can be a difference in economic status causing one to believe that the future is bleak and therefore one need a lot of time to reach a position of commitment. Planet Pluto brings emotions initially that are strong but with time there is an increase in power playing a role to control the other. It is not a healthy combination to have. But it can happen. Here the Moon has the desire to look for partners or companions constantly. Early marriage is possible.

6th house or Virgo sign: This house too belongs to the planet Mercury but here it is dead serious about anything it does. When the Sun transits this house or is stationed in the natal chart if the angular measure for the Sun is between 3^0 and 27^0 in the 6th house, the person shows diligence, methodical application, one takes care of health, develops good regular habits, concerns one with the law of the land, consults a medical expert, gets a measure of the health condition through tests, builds friendships to mutually benefit, has a desire to serve others and desires to show perfection in everything.

The 6th house has both friends and enemies. The Sun if strong can keep away enemies or simply ignore them they cannot do any harm. When weak the Sun is led astray. The 6th house is a house for regular habits and one shows dependency too. So, addictions are possible if the Sun is weak. The houses 5th (for fun and entertainment), 3rd (thoughts and self-portray), 1st (self and self-aggrandisement), 12th (to be lost and away from the material world), 9th (in pursuit of freedom and strange personal beliefs regarding everything), 8th (experimentation with human nature and therefore the subject of psychology) are all houses for addiction of some kind or the other. These only increase if attention is not brought to them consciously.

What a lovely long list! All this holds true provided the Sun is not distracted or weakened or given additional responsibilities due to one of the personal planets getting combust (planet Mercury here). So, the number of 'real' and 'efficient' Virgos is very small. For that matter, this is true for all houses. We are all dragged down by distractions. Only a few manage to focus well on their goals and achieve them well. How many CEOs, top businessmen and toppers at the universities, top doctors, engineers, and lawyers do we run into our life? Unless we belong somewhere after working sincerely towards a goal, there are opportunities created for such association to build. So, the numbers of horoscopes that we get to see are also going to be of the mediocre type people mostly. But our own study should see somewhere in a horoscope that shows promise of high achievement.

The reason I brought up the topic of 'high achievers' is that the Sun in 6th house or the sign Virgo is capable. Although, my own experience of the Virgos has been the 'shabby' and the unkempt types! That was due to the difficulties faced by the Sun in their horoscope. What they managed to do was get themselves a spouse to clear their mess so that they could manage their ambitions, goals, and desires. The Sun in the 6th house must have a use for everybody. The service attitude must be shown towards running the family as a unit. It will not be like if one of the family members works only for the self. I personally think that the earlier 'joint family' system was invented by none other than the Virgos.

What do we predict from the 6th house?

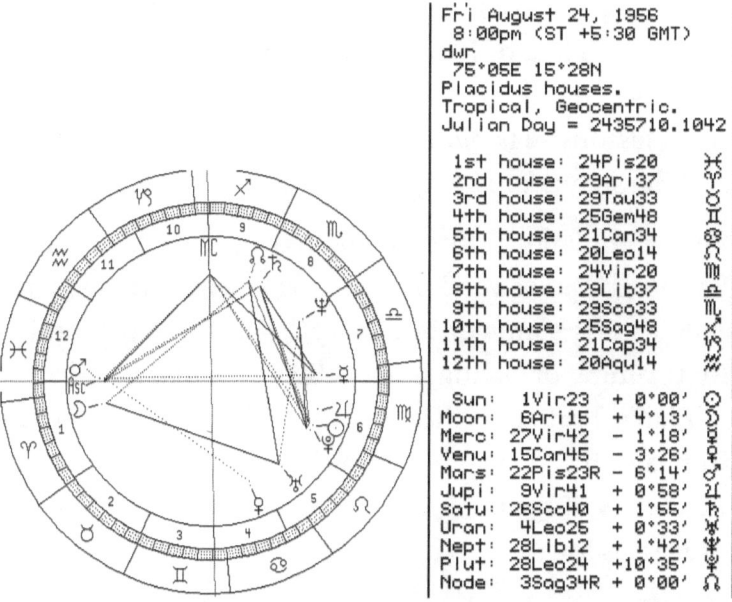

```
Fri August 24, 1956
  8:00pm (ST +5:30 GMT)
dwr
  75°05E 15°28N
Placidus houses.
Tropical, Geocentric.
Julian Day = 2435710.1042

1st house:  24Pis20
2nd house:  29Ari37
3rd house:  29Tau33
4th house:  25Gem48
5th house:  21Can34
6th house:  20Leo14
7th house:  24Vir20
8th house:  29Lib37
9th house:  29Sco33
10th house: 25Sag48
11th house: 21Cap34
12th house: 20Aqu14

Sun:   1Vir23   + 0°00'
Moon:  6Ari15   + 4°13'
Merc: 27Vir42   - 1°18'
Venu: 15Can45   - 3°26'
Mars: 22Pis23R  - 6°14'
Jupi:  9Vir41   + 0°58'
Satu: 26Sco40   + 1°55'
Uran:  4Leo25   + 0°33'
Nept: 28Lib12   + 1°42'
Plut: 28Leo24   +10°35'
Node:  3Sag34R  + 0°00'
```

The 6th house has diseases, enemy activity, law and police involvement, habits for health, systematic work, regular habits, gain from selling other's needs through a shop, being in service to others, friends, daily work as one would go office.

In the above chart, the 6th cusp is in the sign Leo, the planets Pluto and Jupiter are conjunct to the Sun. Here these two planets are not to be considered combust. These planets have enough strength not to be overpowered by any other body in astrology. The same is true with North Node too. The ruler of the 6th is in 6th house and that is a good sign. The ruler of the 8th is square to planet Saturn and is conjunct the Sun. The Sun is constantly made aware of the power it holds. The Sun cannot afford to relax when it is so close to the planet Pluto. Planet Jupiter increases the tension between the Sun and the planet Pluto. This person always feels that 'power' must be attained at any cost. Usually, at the beginning of their career (6th house), these people suffer and experience abuse too. That makes them consciously seek power. If the Sun suffers then the father of this person could suffer too. It could mean an early death to his father. Planet Uranus trine with the Moon shows early detachment lessons. The Sun needs to seek power using its 5th house and the sign Leo. The sign Leo is partly in the 5th house.

When the planet Saturn is squared by the planet Pluto, planet Saturn is made boundary-less permanently. If the planet Saturn attains this status of boundarylessness, the person has difficulty retaining or saving money. Someone else has to do it for him. Planet Pluto specifically wants planet Saturn to lose values for law, the police and punishment. So, there will be close encounters of breaking the law at least in early life when the awareness is low.

If you observe, the Moon is strong in Aries as planet Mars is on the cusp of the 1st house. Because of Moon the planet Venus is strong. Planet Venus and planet Mars are trine shows that planet Mars is well behaved. Planet Mars is in a water sign making him quiet. So, there is a good support to Sun, planet Venus has no other aspects except planet Mars. The ruler of the 1st house is planet Neptune placed in the 7th house; the sign is Libra.

The natural ruler of 6th house is the planet Mercury, which is in the 7th house and this is a connection with the planet Venus. This allows affection toward the opposite gender to blossom. In the 7th house, planet Mercury can pursue law as a career and it has the Sun's support from the 6th. When planets like Jupiter, North Node, planet Saturn, planet Uranus and planet Pluto transit over the Sun, and planets Jupiter and Mercury (7th house) big career changes occur toward improvement. When 6th house is stressed, the planet Mercury is under pressure. So, mental anxiety could be a problem. So, transits, New Moon, and Full Moon need to be observed.

The person had a high ambition to join the army. Since he had a younger sister, his mother objected to that as they needed a responsible person to run the house well. Planet Saturn is in the 9th very close to North Node. The 9th house Saturn insists on playing a father's role very early in life. It is not comforting place for Saturn to be with the North Node. The North Node makes planet Saturn boundary-less and brings a feeling of crisis because once the planet Saturn becomes boundary-less, it releases its hold. One of the holdings is the father or some dependable person like a guardian. Such 'people' go out of hand like how one spends money and loses, in that way. Normally only money is lost during any outer planet's transit over planet Saturn. This guy struggled and passed the Chartered Accountancy examination and is an independent practitioner today. This horoscope is a perfect example of why a person cannot save money. North node in the 9th brings the association of the learned, well-placed and high achievers' type.

Chapter-V

"You are the twelfth in a long line of governesses who have come here to look after my children since their mother died. I trust you will be an improvement over the last one. She stayed only two hours". Captain von Trapp (Christopher Plummer) to Maria (Julie Andrews) in the "Sound of Music".

The Sun
Part Two

7th house or Libra sign: By now you must have picked up the method of how to connect the nature of the Sun with the characteristics of the house and the sign. One must learn to do the same with other personal planets too. When you combine it all, you will have a ready analysis of the client's personality. Then slowly get down to predictions. Do not be in a hurry to announce a great result too soon. You might get disappointed.

The sign of Libra is where the Sun is debilitated. That means the Sun is helpless in the 7th house. It needs to be salvaged in order to make it survive. On top of this if there are tough aspects like the conjunction, the square, the opposition from the outer planets or even the planet Mars then the Sun suffers from inferiority. In such case, a Sun cannot seek people above its class in society. It prefers people from the lower class. I am not advocating a class system to be used for assessment but we all realize that there are difficulties to mingle with superior cultures, superior backgrounds, superior educational status, etc. I was once accused of being 'racial' and 'discriminating' in Durban, South Africa by a taxi driver one day. The difficulty came when the driver asked me to show him directions to the destination; I was still new in the city. He too had a GPS on his mobile phone so I asked him to use it instead of asking me to give directions. That brought a conflict and I had to convince him that my father was dark looking too and back home there were plenty of dark looking people and some of my friends too were dark. I began to wonder why asking him to use his GPS set him on a conflicting route with me. I concluded that there could be a difficulty within him that does not give him comfort while taking orders in spite of being in the service industry. Such disturbance arises in the Sun, when naturally weak and it is unable to maintain dignity.

There is hope for recovery too. If the Sun finds admirers among its associates, colleagues, and superiors it quickly musters the courage to face bigger challenges. But that dose of flattery, cajoling and extolling is necessary to pull the Sun out of quicksand. The sign Libra is where the planet Saturn is exalted. 'Exalted' means a feeling that one is above all others and that results in thinking that one is like an elder brother, so some degree of generosity is shown toward others. So, planet Saturn is not so concerned about security here but releases some funds from its holdings. It will have strict instructions given to the sign Libra and the planets therein that one must be traditional, thrifty, and spend where an opportunity gives rise to more new ones. In short, the Librans too are miserly and spend where they think there are opportunities in the future if a certain friendship is cultivated. Planet Saturn always makes us think if there is a return on investment. So, both Capricorns and Librans are alike towards spending.

The other qualities that the Sun will show are looking for a companion in everyone it gets friendly with or introduced to. An affair is easy to break out with a Libran always. Their conversation is usually leading towards that. These types are not so easy to convince unless one is financially secure. But if you see the substrate, most with the Sun in Libra or the 7th house, have a need for a person to reflect on their ideas, plans, etc., so that they serve as a self-assessment tool. If they receive positive feedback, they go ahead with whatever they have in mind. This is where their debilitated Sun is actively pursuing attention to improve its ability. It is again to be stressed that the Sun should not be adversely stressed by any outer planet. That will further increase their difficulties. The Sun here is constantly sending a message to people around, that it is in need of a partner in order to give support to complete a certain plan or a project. That partner is only there to say, "Yes, please go on, you are doing fine". This is how the Sun ropes in people for a final selection someday in the future and that search for a companion end.

After the Gemini Sun, the Libran Sun has a hoard of friends. The sign Aquarius, even though very friendly has very few friends among all the sun signs. The Libran Sun does not indulge much, to waste away money. It will invite you home, serve you dinner and the parents are introduced to you. If you do not pass that test, you better remain away on a far-off island with the local tribes. There is a little 'Saturn' in every Libran Sun, it causes the Sun to think that it is not up to the expectations and an inferior feeling is driven into it. It will prefer something fresh and will not hesitate to start from scratch.

One can find plenty of talents in the Libran Sun. In fact, all the air signs are above average in their intelligence. What they do not know is how to be street savvy and that is why they look for friends, partners, associates and helpers. The best quality this Sun has is, it never fights to just prove that it is right. It will argue for long but give up before you reach the battlefield. Isn't that nice? By making you the winner the Libra Sun gave you the pride to feel good. Tomorrow it is your turn. Just give a listener's ear for some time and it will share its lunch with you.

What do we predict from the 7th house?

Think of cardinal signs as taking a lead to initiate something. The signs Aries, Cancer, Libra and Capricorn, the houses 1st, 4th, 7th and the 10th are cardinals. Their objection to their own style of living as well as others' is that one must not leave anything midway if one is serious about achieving something. That gets everyone else into a conflict with them. There is a lack of emotional lock as soon as these signs notice a lackadaisical approach from their family, mates, colleagues and even their superiors! On the other side, people generally have a liking, fondness and a sense of togetherness when they seek their friends for various reasons. This bonding is always under a survival test if the association is with the cardinal signs. That leads to a constant search on the part of the cardinal signs for suitability of their purpose in life. So, they all get called 'selfish', 'self-serving' and 'materialistic'. I call 'materialism' as greed.

You will wonder how signs like Cancer and Libra have been dragged into this scathing criticism! One needs to associate closely for months together in order to experience where the friendship is heading. Cancer sees its future in 'security' terms only. It hates to take a chance. The sign Libra sees balance and equality. It cannot belong where the balance is inclined. Moreover, the planet Venus if well placed and safe shows a capacity to be self-reliant first and then seek its mate or friends. Traditions and social norms matter a lot to these. The status of the people sought must not appear in any way inferior. The demands are more or less like those of the sign Capricorn. The reality is that both these signs suffer and repent regarding their selection later. What they forget is that planet Saturn loves to put more responsibility on their shoulders too soon. The two signs yearn to come out of this (burden) so badly that they literally fall into the hands of deceivers or apt to say the Librans misjudge. Yet their façade remains calm and their internal miseries are not known to anyone. They realize somewhere during their late thirties that they better learn to live with serving the family by putting in much more than their spouses. The signs Aries and Capricorn have much in common too. While Aries tries to create a false sense of confidence in others by overstating (boasting) its achievements, asserting over its ability to transcend all fears, it under looks what it attracts naturally. All the cowards, the undecided, parasitic, over-dependent, flatterers and the sycophants are in its bag. The sign takes a life-long contract to rehabilitate such people. It takes great pride in such activity. Even the sign Pisces, Aquarius and Leo lag behind by at least a mile in comparison if we consider 'restoring' or 'reinstating' activity. The minions gathered by the sign Aries drain them throughout their life. Even if the sign changes its coterie of followers the newly sought are no different. To the world, the sign Aries always appears to be a leader because of this fellowship of dependents. But have you noticed any time if one Aries is admiring another Aries?

The sign Capricorn has a great desire to rise above all and feel safe, grand and attain a recognized status on account of the miseries that it has gone through. It vows never to be near that. It identifies the needs of the people around very fast. It then camouflages itself and caters to the needs of a 'belief system' that co-exists with all the people around whom the Capricorn wants to hobnob with. The 'belief system' identifies what is visible and what is audible. Because it is a career oriented, success tasted after repeated failures kind and loves any form of recognition, it manages to gather. That emptiness haunts throughout but it is its chosen meal. The more these signs, Aries and Capricorn see success the more they walk into trouble territory.

That leaves the sign Cancer to be the best Cardinal sign, isn't it? Yes, from a comfort point of view comparable to the sign Libra. For its own comfort, it collects 'wealth' and 'people'. Perfect as a political party, isn't it? If it could only have control over its moods, memories and thoughts it would have been a covetous sign for all other ones. One needs to wait for the tides to change like the seafarers or else their boats will hit the rocks! That is what life is like with water around and a Moon above.

So, the occurrences like transits, lunations and aspects during transits require the above background before any venturing into predictions is attempted. I find it very difficult. I have now learned a little to know how opportunistic these cardinal signs are. All of them use subtle ways before they drag anything into their territory. Let us see another example and try to interpret it.

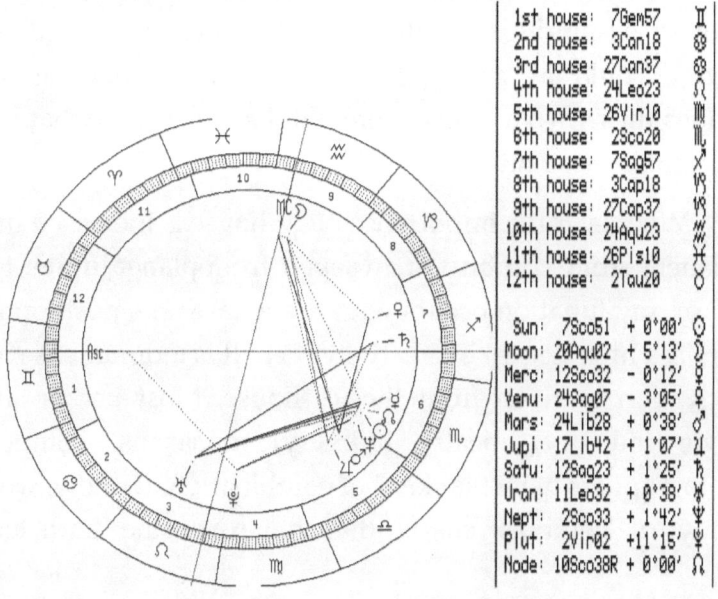

This is a natal chart and we shall focus only on the 7th house first and if need be, the other houses too shall be paid attention.

Ascendant Gemini, the ruler is planet Mercury, placed in the 6th, combust, conjunct North Node. The Sun takes the power of planet Mercury, the 5th house, 6th house (because the Sun is placed in the 6th) and the 3rd house, with the sign Leo there, gets the benefit. Fortunately, both the houses (naturally ruled) the 3rd and the 6th are restored to power in this example. Only the planet Mercury's own signs, the sign Gemini and the sign Virgo will suffer. When planet Mercury is combust, all its territories become weak. The 1st and the 4th houses suffer. Mental abilities, personal ambition, the self-confidence, and all suffer due to the 1st house losing strength and the desire to seek 'unconditional love' will suffer due to the 4th house losing power. What should come naturally to you will have to be sought from outside if available. Usually, there is a tendency to show in front of others, how miserable and how helpless one is on account of circumstances. This attracts sympathy as well as a covert assumption on the part of others to think that the 'victim' could be asking for an intimacy displaying favor. Besides these two aspects, there will be a few more that I shall not elaborate too much.

Whenever the importance of 5th house is increased due to a planet getting combust or an aspect from planet Jupiter to the Sun or any lunation occurs with the natal Sun's position then, there is a high degree of creativity seen. It is more intense if any motivation is given from the 9th house. Most people in the movie industry, theatre industry, musicians, composers, photographers have that kind of combination. Usually, we find plenty of combust charts that have become addicted to television and movies or music. But they cannot pursue any of the talent required beyond a hobby level.

The very next thing to see is whether any addiction is present. Check the sign Pisces, 12th house and the 8th house for that. If the 4th house is disturbed and the person is unable to find any 'unconditional love' then too addictions are possible. Water signs are quick to catch addictions because emotionally they are very disturbed. The earth signs and the air signs except the signs Taurus and Gemini maintain temperance. If the 6th house is stressed then we may have to include the sign Virgo too. The fire signs too do not get addicted but there is a desire to show that they can entertain people. There they get into such habits. But they usually come out of it.

If you observe the Moon, close to the 10th house, is trine to planet Mars in the 5th. The Moon besides its regular desires has a few others to its credit as it gets closer to the 10th, likes more of attention, importance and glamour when in the company of people or at work. So, will work towards that consistently. Jupiter is also trine to the Moon and will magnify this desire. The Moon in Aquarius is unconventional and unorthodox. Since it is at the closing degrees it has shed the qualities of the 9th house to take on the qualities of the next house. The 5th house desires are passed on to the Moon too. There can be a number of associations with people, risk taking and gambling tendencies and a desire to get entertained frequently should be expected. Planet Jupiter too increases this desire.

Where the 5th house is overly exaggerated and unrestricted, there is recklessness. Indulgence cannot be controlled. The Sun too is given extra powers taken from planet Mercury. So, possible failure in judgment may be expected. The 3rd and the 6th houses show our mental abilities. This person could do well in 'sales and marketing', anywhere that has an opportunity for competitiveness and a task achievable through meticulous work, paying attention to details, etc. Even the 3rd house qualities may be used in any profession to help promote a company's products or interests. Selling health products, health awareness, etc., can also succeed. These two houses (3rd and the 6th) have the influence of the Sun and become hyperactive.

The North Node is always responsible for increasing the desires of the planet that is close in conjunction, square and in opposition. A trine with a North Node is manageable and so is a sextile. The hard aspects create a crisis of a calamity or a famine. The person goes boldly to seek entertainment (because 5th house is under focus on account of the Sun's proximity to the North Node). One can easily expect, the marriage is most likely to suffer. The 6th house always has 'service to others' in mind and not to 'rule over'. Even in romance, these people appear as if they are doing a favor. The 5th house can also bring pleasure out of travelling. The purpose is to just have fun. There is no work attached. The 3rd and the 9th houses have a purpose to serve. The 12th house too has a purpose of running away to seek relief type quality to it. One would have restoration of health in mind, simply to find a place unknown to many to get to do what one wants to. The sign Pisces is well known for 'getting lost' through inebriation because it has a capacity to absorb the pain, the injustice and the emotional barrenness in people that are taken as unrequited love.

Let us pay attention to the 7th house now after eavesdropping on other houses! The 7th house has Saturn trine Uranus in the 3rd and planet Venus sextile planet Mars in the 5th. Planet Venus in the 7th house reinforces the need for a companion in a dual sign of Sagittarius. The sextile from planet

Mars shows there are frequent interactions with people and with each a constant reminder is sent about a romantic interest or involvement. All personal planets, the Moon, and the Sun have connection with the 5th house in this chart. With planet Saturn the game is different. Planet Venus generates a lot of associations with people who are well placed in society with a certain amount of power. But planet Saturn has a habit of critically viewing all companions selected by the individual.

This placement is always complaining about the companion showing utter dissatisfaction much after legally possessing the person of its own choice. There is a difference in the economic status of the partners or the differences arise in terms of endearment. This planet has eyes set on the earnings of the partner throughout. The desire is to rise above in status as compared to what it was before. It does not see the difficulties of the partner to show sympathy or any understanding. It is a self-harming position yet protects the marriage until death. Any divorce will be expensive on account of court and lawyer's fees. Planet Saturn in the 7th is the strongest sign of keeping the marriage unbroken. Whether happy or not is a different matter. Both to enter into a wedlock or come out becomes difficult since the planet Saturn is a protector of all legal commitments and transactions. In between, the planet Saturn goes retrograde, aspected by outer planets or sometimes lunations happen to make hard aspects to the natal position only then planet Saturn becomes weak and releases hold on our securities. Usually, our reserves get used up during such time. We feel happy for a short period but as soon as planet Saturn recovers after a couple of months we feel the losses, suffered due to the expenditure. With these in mind, one must consider the transiting planets next and apply them to the chart. Otherwise, the true meaning is never conveyed.

8th house or Scorpio sign: The 8th house stands for power gained on account of one's standing in society. It is also a house for unearned money. Strange! isn't it? It means the money that was earned without putting in any daily labor. There are plenty of opportunities for that. In trading, it becomes the demand and supply situation that permits a certain value to go up or down. It is the same in stock exchange dealings. What about earning through talents? Then there are plenty of others like banking, insurance, the occult, consultancy, and many service industries. The house represents joint ventures for mutual gain. What one needs to understand is that this house is a gain over whatever takes place in the 7th house. Once in a while, there is a transformation after realization. Usually, Full Moons closely aspecting a planet in the natal chart, any outer planet aspecting similarly, or the ruler of the house aspected by planet Pluto or planet Saturn, bring a reality to the surface.

This holds true for all houses. The 6th house is a gain over the happenings of the 5th house. We were motivated and educated in the 5th and we begin to work on a regular basis as indicated by the 6th house. The 4th house is a gain over the activities done in 3rd house. We become frustrated over our own superficialities in the 3rd house and the 4th house teaches us the value of taking care, giving relief and seeking unconditional love. If my 2nd house is weak, whatever I did to myself to bring changes, improvement, gain knowledge, experience, get trained, earn myself a good name, etc., are of no use to prove self-worth or increase self-earned income or any good to the family members (like wife and children). The previous house becomes a house of waste for the next house if that next house has less capability. There are plenty of occasions when the inner personal planets including the Moon become combust. All the ownership houses thereby become weak. During transits, these happen for a couple of days and if found in a natal chart they are (that is the weakness) permanently present. The individual slowly grows used to it when he or she finds out that certain attempts, trials, hard work or even perseverance do not help to bring the results they want. They realize that they have to completely forget certain expectations. When you read charts, this fact needs to be remembered well.

The exception to the Sun in the 8th or the sign Scorpio is that it avoids attention but does not mind admiration. Close friends are few and business contacts are many because it looks like it is enjoying unsolicited power while hobnobbing with them. There is certain secrecy attached to it too. The subject of human nature appears like a mystery to it. It wants to experience that more. Many with the Sun here study psychiatry and psychology and reach the doctorate levels and still continue to do their research. There is also a desire to look deeper into a person that interests them. The investigation, diagnosis, and surgery are all part of that same curiosity, and these subjects are pursued. An ordinary placement could only consider money to be the chief source of power and this Sun goes all out to achieve it. Once again only like-minded people are welcome here. If you are waiting to retire and earn joint savings from various sources, then you cannot be called 'interesting' by a Sun in 8th or a Scorpio sign.

What do we predict from the 8th house?

The usual prediction includes small attention given to how one would earn through the other's investments in your work. It can be any industry, self-run business, giving money on credit, earning interest, etc. the greater attention is paid to what way one's secret dealings are revealed to the public or in which business will a person invests and earn gains, like the stock market. There are earnings through talents, occult and expenditure coming out of a forgotten payment or any unexpected event. The 8th house is all about seeking or feeling a power gain on account of a deal. Let us assume that a New Moon occurred in the 8th house, quite close to the starting cusp. The 8th house would probably have invested or taken an order to manufacture or do some service. The job will have all the needed importance and the earning amount will be high too.

There will be a small exposure to occult practices, and application of human psychology where necessary can also happen. The 8th house benefits out from the work done in the 7th house previously like new agreements, meeting new contacts, any work related to law and court matters, etc. Let us see a chart and see how we can apply our information.

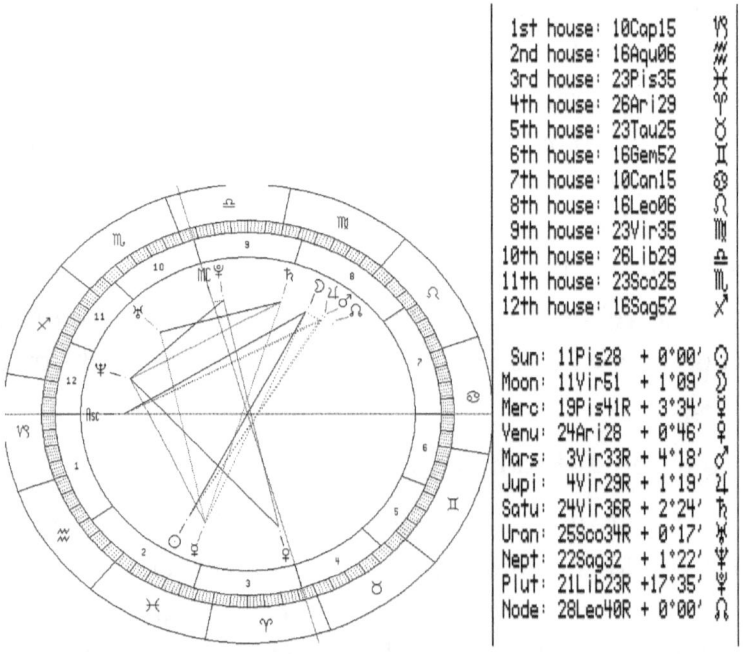

This too is a natal chart to show what the 8th house could produce.

Ascendant is the sign Capricorn; the ruler is planet Saturn and is placed in the 9th house in the sign of Virgo. The natural ruler is planet Mars and is conjunct to planet Jupiter and the North Node. The North Node is in the sign Leo but conjunct to planet Mars in the sign Virgo. The Moon and the Sun are opposing each other. The Moon is in the 8th house too, conjunct from a distance, as I see that the orb is around 8^0. Planet Mercury is retrograde and is approaching the Sun with an orb of 8^0. I consider this combust. The other factor one must consider is the speed of the Moon. It is separating from the conjunction with planets Mars and Jupiter. The effect is too little. Planet Saturn is opposing planet Mercury, planet Neptune is trine planet Venus. Planet Pluto is opposing planet Venus in the sign Aries. Planet Venus is on the cusp of the 4th house.

In this horoscope, the 8th house is laying a lot of stress on earning income through servicing the needs of customers with a focus on power. This is done through specialized services. Notice, that planet Venus is in its fall (Aries), it shows one is much concerned about money and dignity. The services offered here could be occult services as well as serving personal needs. A second aspect of planet Venus is seen from the planet Pluto. The 3rd house apart from all other qualities mentioned earlier indicates the extent of greed. Pluto's messages to the planet Venus are always about keeping power and remaining influential with whatever talents and abilities possessed. The pressure from Pluto in this case is quite strong as the 8th house is also focusing on earning. Planet Venus is being weak, the 2nd house and the 7th house both suffer. Since planet Mercury is combustible, the Sun takes its value to brighten the 5th house of pleasure and entertainment. The 2nd house gets the benefit too along with the 8th house.

A lot of stress is on secret earnings or perhaps underhand dealings. The need being money, planet Venus not so bothered can result in association of disrepute people. This is what I wanted to highlight. The 9th house Pluto brings in powerful contacts, help from the law and police to venture into plenty of nefarious activities. The Sun too will insist on fulfilling its wishes from the 5th house natural rulership. There is a constant urge for getting pleasure, spending on pleasure, addictions are possible (Over emphasized Sun in Pisces), a weak Mercury is quite stressed whenever a crisis occurs and looks for a hideout to release itself, etc., are common here. Although the horoscope shows plenty of money, plenty of anxiety which requires outlets to keep one calm. Over-emphasis on 5th house, poor planet Mercury's state is likely to bring mental disorders here. The 8th house has plenty of opportunities in the occult field. But planet Mars placed next to the planet Jupiter brings a lot of overheads. The Moon too is placed here that causes desires.

But Moon has passed its desires to the Sun due to the opposition. Whenever the Moon and the Sun are in hard aspects, the Sun takes over. There are plenty of mental dissatisfaction issues when the Moon transfers its desires to the Sun. The Sun functions more on a platform for displaying ideas and thoughts. The Moon's desires are not met in that mode. The Moon relies on the Sun and the 4th house affairs, the house with the sign Cancer affairs, all suffer. In this chart, the 4th house and the 7th house will suffer on account of the Moon; the Sun will try to raise the standards of the houses that have their own interests like the 5th, 3rd and the 6th houses. These houses allow business, communication abilities, and systematic working abilities. But mental stress due to both planets Mercury and Venus along with the Moon are very serious. Do not forget planet Saturn opposes the planet Mercury too. Saturn's restricted influence becomes a cause of a lot of anxiety related problems. With all said and done, planet Mercury has retention power here. Its houses are in good health; though planet Mercury could be suffering.

9th house or Sagittarius sign: This house is fundamentally a very capable house from many aspects of astrology. Basically, it takes care of our health, our interests, our freedom, and our beliefs about the social structure around us that we call by various names like religion, tradition, and the mores of society. From here a trine to the 1st house and the 5th house is possible. So, you know now what to expect. This house inspires or motivates the 5th house. If I say, that the 5th house is gullible then look into the 9th house. If your 9th house is weakened or the planets are weakened or if the Sun here is weakened then it will motivate the 5th house likewise. In astrology, two negatives do not make anything positive. To me always, the 9th house is a driving force in all of us to do good, achieve goals, and reach fulfillment. The house lets you study too. The higher knowledge beyond what a 3rd house can provide is provided here. The Sun here has a good time mingling with all types of people who have great achievements to its credit. These people are very rare to get hold of and see their horoscopes. I have seen only one. All the 'greats' are produced here, provided there are no blemishes to the house or the planets. Although the Sun is said to be dignified, exalted in Aries or the 1st house, I always felt an unspoiled Sun is dignified in the 9th house.

The nature of Sagittarius is difficult to gauge from what it is displayed. They could be nomadic and scholars both. They could be philanderers and advocates of education, health, scientists, astronomers and astronauts simultaneously. It is because the sign Sagittarius is one of the dual signs along with the signs Gemini, Virgo, and Pisces. The dual signs have adaptability and see no point in holding on to their beliefs for the sake of reforming society. On a personal level, their beliefs are different but they do not let these interfere with their associations. The Sun having achieved a certain status learns to accept others and their achievements and remains tolerant.

Most of such achievers too do not pay much value to dogma, or religious beliefs but consider reform is necessary to have a holistic approach to life that brings harmony than dispute. In this Sun there is curiosity and a desire to mingle with foreign culture, the unusual kind like the tribes, history, archaeology and such things become interesting. If you ever wondered how a civilized and educated got involved with a person of disrepute or a person of different culture entirely then it is their 9th house that is responsible. Planets like Jupiter, Mars or any of the outer planets present here could cause an interest first from a curiosity point of view and then an involvement takes place.

The sign Sagittarius by nature looks for more freedom than the sign Aquarius. The sign Aquarius will only say, "Let it be, I have nothing to do with the kind of lifestyle the other chooses to". The sign Sagittarius on the other hand goes beyond and says, "I don't care what others think but I like that weird character because that is more mysterious and I feel that I am solving something".

What do we predict from the 9th house?

Let us take an example where all the personal planets are intact and are not weak. Most of the previous cases had some problems or the other.

A Walk in the Park: For Beginners -Tropical or Western Astrology ☆

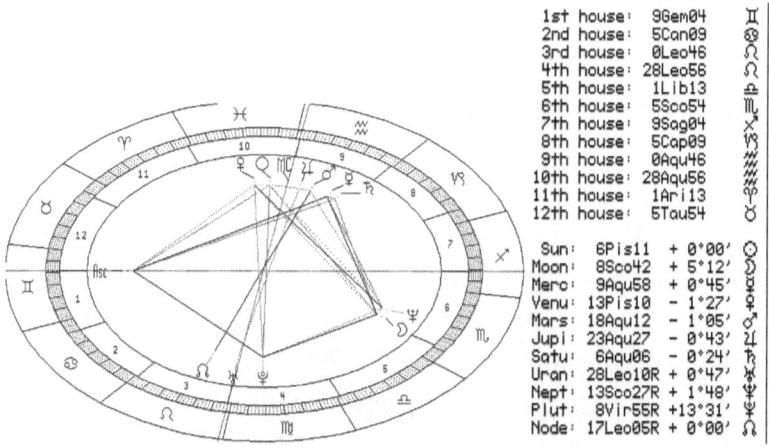

In this chart, the ascendant is the sign Gemini; its ruler is planet Mercury, stationed in the sign Aquarius in the 9th house. Planet Saturn is conjunct planet Mercury, and the ruler of Aquarius is planet Uranus. This is in the Anaretic degree in the sign Leo, conjunct the 4th house cusp, a very sensitive point. Planet Jupiter is directly opposite to the planet Uranus in the 9th house.

The 9th house has a connection with the boss, the people in the hierarchy of the company and many others from other branches of industry who may be considered stalwarts. So, planets like Mercury and Saturn who are directly connected with what we do, and what we need to know are directly told to us if we choose to become their protégé. Planet Saturn is so close to the planet Mercury causes planet Mercury to be on the edge always seeking information and retaining it. Frequently, planet Mercury will seek an escape route for a hideout.

The North Node is stationed in the 3rd house, the South Node is stationed in the 9th house, conjunct planet Mars. *Whenever you see a South Node conjunct a planet, the South Node uses that to pit against the North Node. It does it in a very unassuming manner. It first lets the planet Mars to obey the North Node which has mostly gratifications in mind. The success goes into the head of planet*

Mars and it starts to overdo. That is when the South Node strikes with one of its lunar eclipses on the lap of planet Mars. Mars is rendered destroyed. I have seen South Node on planet Saturn in charts where initially an opportunity to earn wealth comes and the person thinks that this will go on forever. Spends it all recklessly and is left with none. The planet Saturn has control over our possessions, land, savings, gold and our relationships too, if they provide us a secure feeling. If the control is lost due to the Nodes effect, we start misusing and losing all. You must check North Node's transiting position and aspects if any with the personal planets to tell the period.

It is better for this person to be cautious and not get brave any time.

The Sun is in the 10th house, the sign is Pisces, and is opposed by planet Pluto. *The Sun is restricted and pressurized by planet Pluto to constantly seek power at the place of work. Planet Pluto's influence is such that it does not want any planet to wait for any opportunity or fear the law. The Sun tries to find a midway and walk. Frequently the opposition (Why not try a different way?) causes stress because the Sun, which has been thrust with responsibility cannot take a path of inconvenience to self. Venus is combustible and planet Venus too takes the pressure from planet Pluto. Whenever planet Venus or planet Mercury is stressed or combust, intoxicating oneself can become a relief. Moreover, the sign Pisces is in the background. Currently, in the 2nd week of May 2022, there are three planets in Pisces, planets Venus, Jupiter, and Neptune. The first solar eclipse took place on the 30th of April and the lunar eclipse is on its way.*

Regarding planet Venus, it is combusted and we cannot avoid it. The 2nd house and the 7th are lost to the Sun, the 12th and the 5th are also lost to the Sun. The Moon is the ruler of the 2nd house, manages to save the 2nd house. The Moon is in trine aspect to planet Venus/Sun. The honor of the 2nd house is saved. The 5th house is well *fed. Because the Sun is being made powerful by Venus, the sign Pisces and therefore the 12th is saved too. Only the 7th house is at the mercy of planet Jupiter which is in the 9th. The sign Aquarius is unconventional in habits and practices; the 9th house has its own set of beliefs regarding religion, social practices, and tradition. Planet Jupiter is also in opposition with planet Uranus makes the married life a little loosely tied. The partner needs to be more flexible here to show tolerance to such difficult minded mates. The attitude of the individual is quite similar to colleagues at work, friends and others. So, conflicts are common with such.*

The Moon and the planet Neptune are conjunct in the 6th house in the sign Scorpio. Planet Venus is combust and the Sun is trine with both the Moon and planet Neptune. Planet Neptune is the ruler of the 10th house. *The Moon holds grudges and dreams of future gains, items to hold on to as security, but secretly. All the Moon's activities regarding health, work, children, home, parents, etc., are not for anyone to know. Planet Neptune builds dreams with the Moon repeatedly about what needs to be acquired or possessed. The dreams could also be connected to what the Moon wants to attach itself with. The 6th house Moon has fewer friends and fewer dependable people. The Moon needs a strong planet's support its fulfillment of desires. The Moon is connected to planets Mercury and Saturn on the 9th, planet Pluto on the 4th. The moon seeks its pleasure and fulfillment from foreign cultures, seeking knowledge from distant cultures and backgrounds. Planet Pluto from the 4th house brings power to the Moon through real estate, legacy, etc. So, Moon is well placed.*

A lot of activity is seen between the 6th and the 10h houses, the 4th and the 10th houses, and within the 9th house. Planet Jupiter increases the intensity of planet Uranus which is on the 4th house cusp. The 4th house cusp is a sensitive point that holds our inner secrets. The sign Cancer has plenty of past activities to hide. Planet Uranus feeds the 10th house of our public image and our methods to project that image. Here, the image is projected of a low-key person, who enjoys the confidence of the superiors and therefore becomes the doyen of power, and chooses to work wherever the person wants. The job of planet Uranus is always to pass on information and knowledge in order to make the person independently seek whatever is wanted. It does not like dependency. On the cusp of the 4th house, the person acquires 'secret' knowledge given in confidentiality. This is passed on to the planet Jupiter. Planet Jupiter in return increases this habit of seeking secret information in the planet Uranus.

10th house or Capricorn sign: By now you must have noticed that I am neither referring to the Sun frequently nor am I giving details of when and why the Sun could become weak. But you will remember the previous mention of it and that is sufficient.

The Sun in house number 10 is now in the house whose natural ruler is planet Saturn. Planet Saturn has control over the Sun in matters of money, law, order, responsibilities, and becomes a subordinate to someone in authority. The Sun does not get authority early in life. The other issue is that the Sun learns planet Saturn's ways rather late. The Sun is not quite used to working or living with scarce resources. If Sun is living merrily in Leo or in the Sign Aries in this house or in Capricorn the Sun learns what is poverty, blame, responsibilities thrust with limited power, less independence and always short of cash. To come out of this struggle, Sun takes very long and somewhere during the mid-fifties learns the ways to feel free even amidst a crisis. The authority is gifted, cash flow improves, the burden on the family and other members reduces and the Sun feels that he is very young still and can take more work and responsibilities on its shoulders. There is a saying that, "A Capricorn ages reversely". Many Capricorn Sun people start new ventures, learn new games to play, develop reading and writing habit (provided the 3rd or the 9th helps) after the age of 58. They even look younger than others of their age. It is the freedom they feel they have earned. The stress seems to have gone somewhere. Although they manage to build a good number of associates in their field or profession, their personal friends are few. They would have developed plenty of skills by then, and that helps to keep them busy either teaching or as consultants. People usually trust them and seek counsel.

Like Sun in the 1st house, in the 10th house too, the Sun is fond of uniforms and patriotism. There is much more ambition in the 10th house than the 1st house. One cannot specifically say which profession would suit the Sun in the 10th or the sign Capricorn. The Sun develops a dependency of others on itself so much that people do not usually let it go. Being Saturn ruled, the Sun has a penchant for money and rewards and it prefers to go in search of that.

What do we predict from the 10th house?

It is a house that inspires the 6th house of regular hard work (sign Virgo). The sign Taurus motivates it (2nd house) by showing the rewards. All seems to go well if one has working personal planets, the Sun or the Moon in the 10th house or in the sign Capricorn. The motivating houses should be strong houses; that is a pre-condition.

The 10th house usually brings fame if the Full Moon is well aspected and comes close to any of the planets in it or outside and aspects them. Not a South Node eclipse but the North Node eclipse. If planets like Saturn are transiting the 10th house, do not expect a better job but expect there will be a struggle to keep the job. Planet Saturn causes difficulties in what is likely to be performed in front of people to show what one is. That is how one gets fame, popularity or acclaim and recognition. Seeing the difficulty, we all struggle and face whatever crisis we have to. It is easy to predict the negative. Start with, "You shall not get this………for the next two and a half years!" Just recently I did that to a girl who worked in our office. The planet Saturn had just entered the 7th house and her query was, "When will I get married"? You all must have guessed my answer. Exactly after two years and a couple of months later, I did receive a call telling me the date has been fixed! So, in the case of planet, Saturn certain predictions are easy. What planet Saturn causes is a feeling of inferiority, incapacity, inadequacy in qualifications, difficulty with movement (travelling for work) or an illness that further demotivates us. Then it says, "The game is afoot"! If you happen to win, that is usually after the planet leaves that house, you feel great. After such hard work will anyone leave and go? So, the rewards earned when planet Saturn leaves a house are the ones we keep for long. No one ever forgets to say, "Bye old man, next time be my guest and not as my mentor". The other outer planets stay for too long and their effects are occasionally felt unless their transit is directly over our personal planets.

Let us see a chart and you start before me. Then compare how close were you or could you add a little more.

A Walk in the Park: For Beginners -Tropical or Western Astrology ✯

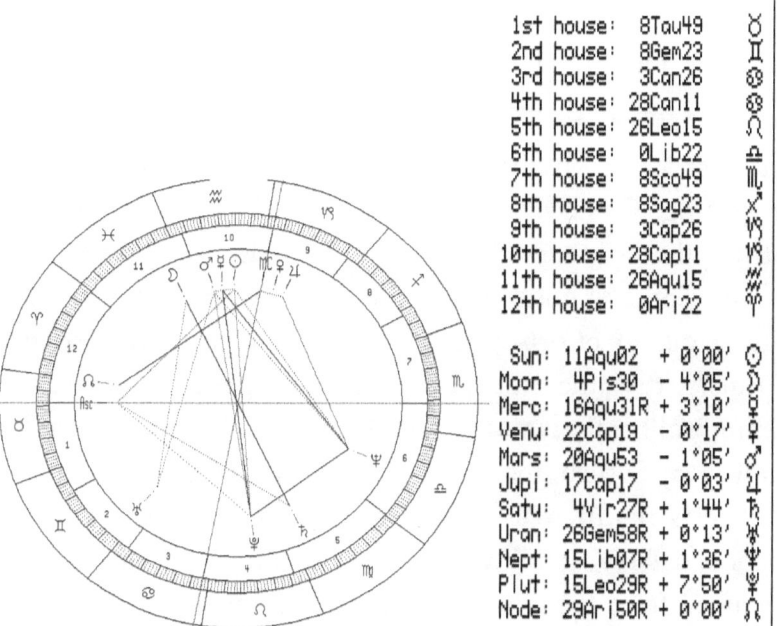

```
1st house:   8Tau49    ♉
2nd house:   8Gem23    ♊
3rd house:   3Can26    ♋
4th house:  28Can11    ♋
5th house:  26Leo15    ♌
6th house:   0Lib22    ♎
7th house:   8Sco49    ♏
8th house:   8Sag23    ♐
9th house:   3Cap26    ♑
10th house: 28Cap11    ♑
11th house: 26Aqu15    ♒
12th house:  0Ari22    ♈

Sun:  11Aqu02  + 0°00'   ☉
Moon:  4Pis30  - 4°05'   ☽
Merc: 16Aqu31R + 3°10'   ☿
Venu: 22Cap19  - 0°17'   ♀
Mars: 20Aqu53  - 1°05'   ♂
Jupi: 17Cap17  - 0°03'   ♃
Satu:  4Vir27R + 1°44'   ♄
Uran: 26Gem58R + 0°13'   ♅
Nept: 15Lib07R + 1°36'   ♆
Plut: 15Leo29R + 7°50'   ♇
Node: 29Ari50R + 0°00'   ☊
```

The Ascendant is the sign Taurus, with its ruler in the 9th house, in the sign Capricorn, with planet Neptune square from the 6th house, in the sign Scorpio. The houses 2nd and 7th are unaffected and are safe.

Planet Mercury is combusted and conjunct the Sun, planet Pluto is opposing both from the sign Leo, from the 4th house. Planet Mercury is highly stressed. This person used to stutter and carried a lot of mental pressure throughout. He rose to a position of authority fairly early in life and had good administering abilities. The 5th house definitely got its attention from a bolstered-up Sun. A 10th house Sun, Mercury and even planet Mars are all aware of how qualified they are and constantly increase to remain abreast of progress happening in their field. Since the 5th house is powerful the education and training side improves. The 5th house although belongs to planet Mercury's sign, has not suffered. The 6th house has planet

Venus as its ruler and planet Jupiter is placed in conjunction. So, the 6th house too is quite strong.

Planet Saturn is opposite the Moon in Pisces, 11th house. That restricts both the 3rd house and the 11th house from performing. This is a second blow to the 3rd house. It not only restricts the characteristics of the 3rd house but brings more anxiety. The 11th house has future hopes and wishes, friends, gaining out of efforts put into the 10th house, etc. Bringing reforms, getting the support of people in superior positions, and gaining politically is not possible. When the Moon is affected this way by Saturn, there is a great need to earn money and a sacrifice is required to be made. Usually, one has to forego personal desires, inability to take care of children or the mother, stay away from the wife for long, etc. All these are the Moon's sources for attachment. Planet Saturn disallows that.

The 5th house Saturn restricts the fun from the 5th house. Romances could be brief if not totally eliminated. The children need more attention but won't get it. It is a life-giving house but does very little. Everything that planet Saturn produces from here is a wife who appears very uninterested, lacking the spirit and incapable of providing the cheer required in life. The desire to go for fun and frolic may be present but planet Saturn restricts or places hurdles. Since it is a planet Mercury supported reinforcement in the Sun, friends and associates have a good educational, and professional background. The general attitude is more to serve everyone than just trying to be a boss. The true desires of the Sun are never fulfilled.

Planet Mars in Aquarius or any air sign has a low libido and a lot to talk. Planet Mars turns into an entertainer rather than a bold leader. He can gather support because it talks of ideals and reforms. Here, with opposition from Pluto, it is under pressure to seek power and hold on to it. But it is of no interest to the person. One might rise on the corporate ladder but will not use that to gain more control or earn power. This person will love to be a subordinate to someone in power and seek favors.

That's a brief analysis. Further predictions are possible by seeing the transits of all planets, lunations and nodes.

11th house or Aquarius sign: The Sun here allows an individual to be of service to the community, society or work in groups for the benefit of the needy. The Sun could be in any profession but it has a political bent of mind. It uses the power or that body of people in order to fulfill its future hopes and wishes. Until that power is attained it works as a social worker or serves charitable institutions. Again, I reiterate that as an air sign or the 11th house that has plenty of intelligence to handle any branch of career. It is most happy when it gets to serve the people. It has no other ambitions of attaining a top position of authority. All air signs are inefficient when they are in a position of authority. As they find it a desolate place. These signs like to be among admirers. The Sun here looks for popularity in whatever it does. So, you will find these signs active where there are people.

The Sun here does not have prejudices towards any religion, type of people, any culture, etc. But there are a few differences between the sign Sagittarius and the sign Aquarius although both identify with freedom of thought and freedom of expression. The sign Aquarius has an agenda to bring reform to the people in whom it has an interest. Sagittarius has an interest in solving problems for the people and bringing a solution. Aquarius says that we all need to change and adapt to a new set of conditions and then we can have better standards of living.

Sagittarius has multiple problems to solve. It keeps itself busy there and does not force any reforms onto people.

What do we predict from the 11th house?

From this house, we get to see if there is any gain out of the work, we put into the 10th house. Seeking new friends or losing some, our plans to improve a certain group, organization, or community begin to take a shape and work for us. We can also see monetary gains out of popularity, our status, some new venture and an ambition to prove our self-worth. See, the position of this house, it is 10th from the 2nd house. What we try, what we prove to the outside world, how we change our attire, our looks and thinking matters most to earn from this house. So, it becomes easier to tell the client what to work on.

Also realize, how certain houses help certain other houses for a succeed. The 4th house of seeking and giving 'unconditional love' is a success in the 7th house. The 7th house of a good partner, spouse, friends, respecting the law, and seeking a balanced approach to life and not showing greed helps our 10th house of public image and profession. The 6th house focuses on consistency and methods. It becomes the law, it becomes the doctor, it becomes the servant. So, connect houses as and when you can, to bring a fresh thought. Simply looking at one planet and its aspects won't let you go far.

Here is another charter for study.

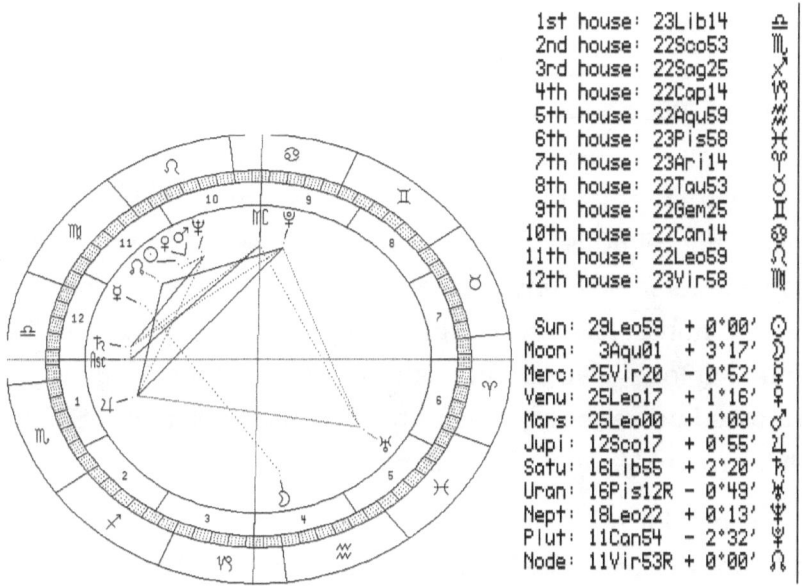

```
1st house: 23Lib14    ♎
2nd house: 22Sco53    ♏
3rd house: 22Sag25    ♐
4th house: 22Cap14    ♑
5th house: 22Aqu59    ♒
6th house: 23Pis58    ♓
7th house: 23Ari14    ♈
8th house: 22Tau53    ♉
9th house: 22Gem25    ♊
10th house: 22Can14   ♋
11th house: 22Leo59   ♌
12th house: 23Vir58   ♍

Sun:  29Leo59  + 0°00'   ☉
Moon:  3Aqu01  + 3°17'   ☽
Merc: 25Vir20  - 0°52'   ☿
Venu: 25Leo17  + 1°16'   ♀
Mars: 25Leo00  + 1°09'   ♂
Jupi: 12Sco17  + 0°55'   ♃
Satu: 16Lib55  + 2°20'   ♄
Uran: 16Pis12R - 0°49'   ♅
Nept: 18Leo22  + 0°13'   ♆
Plut: 11Can54  - 2°32'   ♇
Node: 11Vir53R + 0°00'   ☊
```

Let us restrict ourselves this time to just the 11th house and avoid red-herring.

Ascendant is Libra, planet Venus, the ruler is with the natural ruler of the 1st planet Mars in the 11th house and in the sign of Leo. Further, the Sun is in the 11th in the sign Virgo. The Sun is in the Anaretic degree 29°. Both planets' Mars and Venus combustible. Fortunately, the power to the 11th house was restored because it has a Leo sign. The Sun is in the sign Virgo so this 11th house is powerful.

Planet Venus' natural houses 2nd and 7th will suffer. Let us see if the current ruler has any strong aspects. Planet Mars is the ruler for the 7th cusp. The remaining portion of the sign is Taurus which is ruled by planet Venus. The 7th house is now weak. Whatever the Sun provides to the sign Leo will be gained by both planets Venus and Mars. The person will get married since there is a good connection between the rulers of the 1st and the 7th. The marriage could face the test of compatibility for a long. Planets Venus and Mars if together in a chart, bring passion towards anything that interests us. It is not just seeking romance everywhere. The sign Leo is demonstrative and therefore there is a lot of expressions. The 5th house brings artistic interests like acting, singing, music, painting, drawing, and photography, etc. all become sources of income. Taking risk due to the 5th house emphasis and the passion shown by the planets Mars and Venus can also become a source of income. The 1st house has planet Jupiter there and it gives all the optimism one wants. The natural ruler planet Mars is on borrowed power but will help the 1st house to be brave. So, the job taken up definitely has risk involved in it.

The North Node too is in a good house, 11th. It helps to fulfill the desires of the 11th house. There are no adverse aspects. The aspect from planet Pluto to planet Jupiter is a trine. Planet Pluto gets a lot of support in the 9th house affairs. Planet Jupiter is given impetus to take on challenges throughout a person's life. This person will take big ventures into hands and meet the targets successfully. The 9th house has contacts that are much above our status and they offer help to build our projects. It is also a house for our beliefs regarding the norms of society, tradition, and religion. Foreign travel to learn higher knowledge from different cultural backgrounds, publishing books, and even teach people. It gathers power through the 5th house activities and motivates it.

The Moon also shows 11th house desires to be fulfilled from the 4th house. The person has plenty to seek from home. Planet Saturn is in the 12th in the sign Libra, where it is exalted. In the 12th house planet, Saturn is weak. It feels as if it's foundationless and without much hold on anything. It likes solitude and has an interest in matters that are abstract. In a natal chart, the person stays aloof and uses the time to concentrate on subjects that are difficult to understand by normal standards. It reaches the point of highest qualification and works to advice people. Power and authority are desired but it soon learns that it has more power using its special knowledge than any money or status. Planet Neptune is sextile to planet Saturn and that helps in building visions for the future.

Planet Mercury is in its own sign, Virgo. The intellect is very good. My usual interest is to get into the study of law and medicine. Because it is on the cusp of 12th, this planet too prefers to seek isolation. I have a strong feeling that this person will accomplish something extraordinary in life.

There are two houses that interest me and these are both working houses, the 6th and the 10th. The 6th has the sign Pisces, its ruler is Neptune and is connected with Saturn who is the ruler of the 3rd. The 3rd house is a serious house now and not the usual chatter box or playful or simply a matter-of-fact type. Planet Mercury in the sign Virgo is strong. The 10th house has the sign Cancer on its cusp and the Moon is stationed in the 4th house. The sign Aquarius is much known for learning and practicing professions that have a lot of research work involved. The Moon is trine with planet Mercury. Lastly, I want you to pay attention to the water signs that are involved. The water signs are always healing signs. Under the circumstances, this chart has a great promise to produce a doctor with superior degrees. Even reaching great heights and achieving fame.

12th House or Pisces sign: The Sun in this house wants to be aloof most of the time. It could want relaxation from the outer stressful world, it could be seeking treatment or it is involved in understanding a subject to solve a certain mystery. All water signs and water houses have a certain mystery about them. These signs live to either solve or simply hold to them as precious. The 12th house goes a little beyond and maintains mysteries and secrets that are unknown to us. These are either revealed for us or by us and that turns out to be like a power bestowed on us.

The 12th house is definitely a healing house and it does by shunning us from all other involvements. Sometimes we do not even know that we have been deliberately removed from the maddening crowd. We repeatedly try to get back to our old activities or ambience only to be pushed out again because the 12th house if active wants us to take a short holiday into the unknown. If we realize that, we decide to go into isolation and seek salvation.

Both the 6th house and the 12th house produce healers or doctors. The sign Aquarius and Sagittarius are equally strong in producing plenty of doctors. A few are from the other signs. What makes the sign Pisces special is that it understands the patient far deeper than all others put together. It appears as if the healer could see you through and find whatever you needed. It has deepest understanding of human nature and it serves with compassion to bring you back to normal. If the sign Virgo is going more by the book, the other two signs, Aquarius and Sagittarius prefer sophistication and modern medicine. I missed the sign Scorpio which beliefs in cutting into the body; is quite conversant with human nature.

The sign Pisces gets stressed mainly on account of going deeper into understanding people telepathically or intuitively. That exhausts its thinking ability. Its compassion towards all, gives an opportunity for its own exploitation. The Sun now is vulnerable and has little chance to recover and it takes shelter in intoxication. Pisces is one of the addictive signs of the zodiac. It does not have to be drugs alone. There are plenty of others that one can get addicted to. But it needs ways to release itself from mental stress frequently. I once knew a healer and also a tarot card reader. I happened to read her chart and I wanted to know what she was addicted to. The 8th house had three planets plus the North Node. She did not admit to anything. It just happened that day that I was in her house sitting in her drawing room and she opened her cupboard in front. There I saw there were at least fifty different fragrances of perfumes, deodorants, and colognes sitting on the shelf waiting. I again said, "Aren't you addicted"?

Its interest in occult subjects, horticulture, gardening, pets, space, adventure into remote places, ocean searching for new species appear more and more amazing if you happen to listen. But their sob stories make you wonder if 'compassion' toward all did any good at all.

What do we predict from the 12th house?

Let us take this final example and move on to the next.

The chart shown below has a stellium of planets in the 12th house.

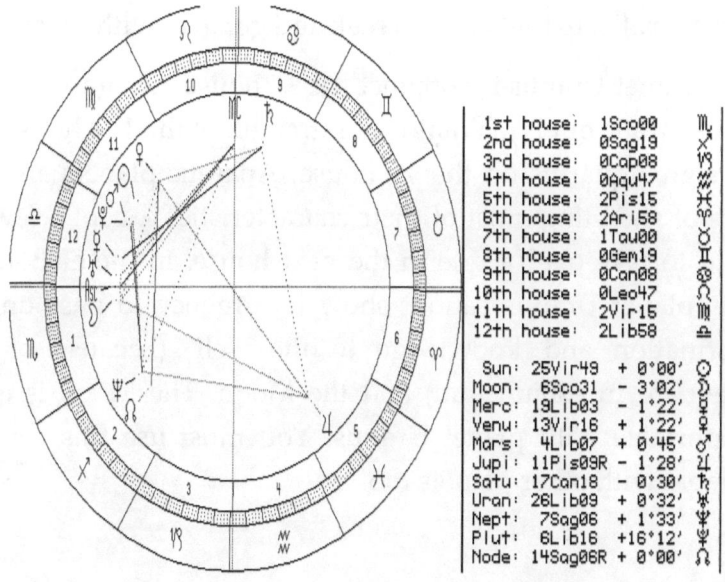

The ascendant is just 1^0 Scorpio, the ruler is planet Pluto in the 12th house, conjunct planet Mars, and sextile planet Neptune. Planet Mars is the natural ruler of the 1st house and is close to the Sun and combusts.

The Sun takes the power from planet Mars (to be courageous in this case) and passes it to its own houses like the 5th, 10th and the 11th. (5th and rulership houses)

The 1st house loses its power on two counts; planet Pluto is in the 12th and helpless, and planet Mars is combusting. The 6th house loses its power partially. Planet Mercury is not weak in any way except that it is in the 12th. But planet Mercury is stressed under the square aspect with planet Saturn. A stressed planet Mercury has long-term retention memory but not short-term memory. The recall is good but not so much like the recognition type. Planet Venus is stationed in the sign of planet Mercury. That makes planet Mercury quickly involved in the activities of planet Venus, thereby causing a craving that planet Venus has to enact for planet Mercury. This is retention memory. It is disturbing when hurts. In the 12th house, there is no material help that one can seek and get over with ill feelings.

Planet Uranus is conjunct the 1st house cusp (ascendant). It is Anaretic but it maintains the strength of the 11th house and the sign Aquarius on the 4th house. Anaretic planets are in a state of shedding most of their characteristics except a few, in order to take over a role in the next house. In the elaborated case, planet Uranus cannot show its urgency to pass on the information and knowledge to the 'self' (because of the ascendant in conjunction) and the Moon. The Moon is quite comfortable with planet Uranus. You must use this concept suitably with other planets too.

Around $29°$ are taken as anaretic for the outer planets because they are slow. For the fast-moving inner personal planets, around $27°$ to $28°$ if taken will serve our purpose. Even if they enter the next house, the first two degrees are a preparatory period for the planet to assume a new role. For the slower planets, $1°$ may be taken. For the Moon, there is a carry-over of the previous house characteristics into the next during the first $5°$. The initial $5°$ may not be committed to the new house entered by the Moon. One may consider the rule with signs too within a range of $\pm 1°$.

The Moon is conjunct ascendant. Planet Jupiter and planet Moon are trine. This increases the intensity of the conjunction. Could make the person moody but at the same time very imaginative in activities that require an initial visualization to get a mental picture of a finished product or a scenario. It helps in planning and designing if required in any profession.

Planets Mercury and Saturn are square to each other. When planet Mercury is the square planet Saturn, planet Mercury has to discipline itself. Although intelligent in Libra, the sign Libra is whimsical and indecisive. Planet Saturn controls and restricts and puts money making in its head. The knowledge of law appeals to planet Mercury. Loss of power due to planet Mars getting combusted is the only problem this person will suffer from. That courage can come if its mate someday has a strong Mars to influence this person. Planet Mercury performs better after the first Saturn return around the age of 28 years. Usually, these people are late bloomers.

The North Node and planet Venus are square. Jupiter and planet Venus are square to each other.

Planets Neptune and Mars are sextile. Planet

The 12th house has a few good things to tell but all material appears lost. The planets have difficulty grounding themselves in order to have control over other planets in the chart. The 12th house therefore, faces a constant situation of 'lost battles'. In order to recover, it goes into isolation for recovery, getting lost in a state of unconsciousness, or taking proper healing. It has an interest in the supernatural, ancient theories, to diarize events, writing mystery novels, and the occult. The sign Pisces is on the 5th cusp and planet Neptune is placed well close to the North Node. Planet Jupiter is in the 5th house, the Sun has additional power and that goes to the 5th house. Overall, a working house is the 5th house at the moment.

If the 5th house is a working house, then let us see if planet Mercury is useful or not for all practical knowledge, education, and later in jobs.

Also, the 11th house too appears like a working house here because the North Node from the 2nd house squares the planet Venus, planet Jupiter opposes the planet Venus. The North Node compels planet Venus to work towards self-earned income, to be placed well. Planet Jupiter increases this aspect intensity. So, planet Venus is the breadwinner. Planet Venus in the sign Virgo loses its usual companion search but gets involved in improving working skills reinforced with knowledge and qualifications. It is very compassionate and service minded. It can work physically for long hours. It has skills that require meticulous preparation, an ability to concoct and prepare medicines, and even prepare recipes. It can work in restaurants, hospitals or pharmaceutical companies, food industry, hotels, etc. Even the Moon is well placed with planet Uranus and will gain knowledge and information, will appreciate all that is new in technology and turn modern. The 4th house is strong too. 5th house is definitely going to lead the way into the entertainment sector, movies and television, courage factor gets added to the house because planet Mars is combust and the Sun takes courage to its houses.

Chapter-VI

Abraham Lincoln: "A compass, I learned when I was surveying, it'll……. it'll point you true north from where you are standing, but it has got no advice about the swamps, deserts and chasms that you will encounter along the way. If in pursuit of your destination, you plunge ahead heedless of obstacles, and achieve nothing more than to sink in a swamp……what is the use of knowing true north?"

The Moon

The body of Moon appears calm and is a delight to watch in the night sky. Very few know that the same Moon has powers that can have influence over us on a daily basis. The Moon can shift the oceans and cause tides that can rise many feet high. It is on account of the Sun that these tides are controlled and kept manageable on this planet. If the Moon could cause such havoc on the planet our bodies are miniscules in comparison and may undergo plenty of changes from within. I wished that the changes happened on the external side too; we would all be playing personas like actors on a stage daily. Perhaps it is its speed that does not leave enough time for greater changes. The Moon's 12^0 to 14^0 of longitudinal movement in a sign daily, can be daunting enough; has to encounter other planets too and exchange its energy a couple of times. No wonder then it leaves the exterior of all of us undithered.

Let us understand what does the Moon control and what will benefit us from its transit. "The Moon has control over our mind" say a lot of books. Can anyone define the mind? Is it our brain? Our emotions or imagination? Leave it, we are walking into the Moon's territory of utter nonsense. We all need a hope to live right? These hopes are created repeatedly in order to survive. The animals do not live on hopes but on instincts. Perhaps the pre-historic man lived on instincts alone. We have evolved into an advanced state of mind. The state of mind does drop occasionally but with each daylight hitting upon us we seem to become optimistic and continue to do whatever best we can. It is that 'optimism' that is required to churn us out of a whirlpool that we get into during these tidal changes. That is why planet Jupiter is working for us. The Sun throws light on new issues so that the old ones are forgotten. It is the few who are still stuck in their maelstrom and never seem to recover; perhaps they had no one to cheer on their way in and then out of bedlam.

So, our imagination capability is in the hands of the Moon. The next is accumulated wealth of any kind that we ought to have received is also under its mercy. It is not lottery money or money earned at the gambling table. It is what you were gifted because of an 'unconditional love' that was shown in the past to someone with no expectation of receiving anything back. It is something that had no expectation but you would have liked it too if you received such 'unconditional love' from someone. Legacies are passed on only because of what is remembered of a person for the deeds or care shown and remained unrequited. Some are due to simple love and nothing more. All these are treasures hoarded in a small cabinet that the Moon carries. Besides the insurance plans, fixed deposits, imprest accounts, ownerships of houses and land become part of the Moon's controlled assets. If the Moon is stressed or weak just forget about ever laying your hands on any of those that I have mentioned. If it is in association with planet Saturn you will see wealth more on paper than liquid cash. Liquid cash will just flow out as water from your grip. All the outer planets do not let the Moon function in its natural way. The Moon is forced to giveaway its attachments one by one and survive without. With exceptions when the Moon is strong under the aspect of planet Jupiter, if the Moon is placed in the 2nd house or the sign Taurus.

The attachments that the Moon holds on to are plenty. Our job, spouse, children, parents, the home, the car, the pets, siblings, neighbours and friends are all part of its repertory. Think of how do we attain these? It is with unconditional love and not by clinging. Clinging too is Moon's quality when it starts to feel a dependency on someone or something. Then it begins to complain and nagging begins in a relationship. There is a difficulty in handling the Moon because most of the Moon's effects are internal to us. There could be fears developed within us, showing over reliance on others, plans to build financial security, etc., are our hidden intents or weaknesses. The Moon's desire to seek attention (just like the Sun) is quite different. It achieves without saying much but through plenty of affection and care. Do we say nurture? Then that is its territory. It expects the same in return but also realises is difficult to receive from all. Is it clear now, why we become sad due to the Moon?

Let us see what Moon truly changes into in each of the houses of our chart:

The Moon in general represents the females that come into our life and the Sun represents the males. Both these bodies represent our parents and the elderly. The mother is definitely represented by the Moon. If the mother has made a strong impression the male will search for the same very qualities of the mother in the woman he wants to marry. The female will look for the Sun's qualities in her man whom she prefers to marry. There is a small danger here like a 'hidden clause' of an insurance policy. Suppose, the father represented by the Sun is abusive, the girl has a false feeling that she has seen it all will show a tendency to seek a person who has such hidden qualities in him. It is a feeling of showing familiarity and feeling comfortable. This quality is developed unconsciously in us. We attract the character that we dreaded but accept with sympathy. A similar thing could happen to men too on account of the placement of the Moon.

Aries

In the sign Aries or if the Moon is in the 1st house, the mother is active and dominant and if the Sun is found in Aries the father is dynamic too besides being dominant. As children you will be quite familiar with how the cats and dogs fight from an early age if both your parents belong to the sign Aries. With just your Moon in Aries, you will see that your mother is frequently shifting or changing the furniture around the house. She is happy outdoors and working somewhere or else she would like to be amidst her friends planning activities. You too will be doing the same since you are sure your mother will not object to her seeing similar activities performed by you. Thus, you emerge a brave child and also fond of outdoor sports. She will not pester you to study so much but will not tolerate your laziness. Meals will be cooked at moment's notice and served. She will do the dishes too after that. She is thrifty as well as someone who can do a year's shopping in a day. But do not make her listen to your old stories again and again. She has less patience for old stories being repeated and she dislikes daily chores etc. Be with her you will be lucky to go on a holiday every summer.

The Moon in Aries is a spender like the other two fire signs; may not be on luxuries so much but on activities and sports. A few that I have seen spent on dress and shoes but very little on make-up. You are excited with almost anything held in your hand and you want it too. This is where the Moon is disappointed usually. How can we have everything? There is generosity toward the siblings too. The Aries Moon never complains against the siblings but quietly tolerates. It needs the siblings to play with, how would it spoil the relations? Aries Moon is the best sibling and a friend at all times.

When the Moon is placed in the 1st house, irrespective of the sign the person has a special charm and is considered photogenic. If there are aspects from any outer planet the charm becomes universal. With Moon in Cancer, Taurus, Scorpio in the 1st house, there is charisma and the people are very attractive.

Taurus

When the Moon is in the sign Taurus or the 2nd house, the placement provides accumulated wealth either as legacy or as gratuity. If money is saved in some fund regularly it is well received when the need arises. The person has a good voice, and speaks well too. There is a special sense of a connoisseur present in the Moon and that is a good source of income if used well. The self-worth, self-earning capacity is natural to this position. The Moon is in exaltation here and I always wish that it is not badly aspected. The only aspect I dread is that of planet Venus or that of planet Mercury with the Moon. It weakens the self-control of a person when dealing with the opposite gender. With planet Mercury the thoughts recur constantly and yearn to seek encounters frequently with that one person; the smooth talker to build a relationship. With planet Venus the Moon yearns for attention just like planet Venus. Planet Venus is naturally capable of dressing and decorating oneself in any way possible and always. Not everyone is capable of attracting attention either. So, planet Venus is quite content in whatever it manages to under normal circumstances. With the Moon, the desire turns into compulsion and later obsession. When it receives less response, it gets hurt badly too. Then mental disorders develop. Both planet Mercury and the Moon have a capacity to hold as memory in the head. Planet Venus (natural ruler of the 2nd house) is the 'baiter' and the culprit. If there is any combination present then it is sickening. If by chance there is an aspect from planet Saturn to the combination then there is a relief. Planet Saturn sows the seed of class difference in any relationship like a spanner thrown in a turning wheel. The economic-status thought becomes a relief under such circumstances when a person is totally consumed by another. Otherwise, one only can warn and send away the client.

In the houses 2nd, 3rd, or in the signs Taurus and Libra a situation might arise as explained above. In the houses 3rd, 6th or the signs Gemini and Virgo one might get mentally affected due to loss of dear ones or break-ups. When the Moon is strong either due to positioning in 2nd, 4th, or the signs Cancer and Taurus the attachment to things and people is very strong. People who are in a relationship with such must not play with the other's feelings or flirt. The damage could bring in a calamity to the Moon.

The 2nd house is motivation to the 10th house. With the Moon, we tend to project before the public what we are good at and do it well to earn well. Not everyone is born rich but they all become one with the Moon in this house or the sign.

Gemini

The Moon is more interested in writing or diarizing its thoughts and ideas in the 3rd house or this sign. The house does represent talkativeness but not without the help of the planet

Mercury. The Moon could use poetry, music or seek the media to communicate more. It turns into a good listener if you say something of its interest. Very affectionate but gets bored if the topic is not of any interest. The Moon loves journeys, the environment, and its siblings. It is not fond of electronics but will keep them as an item of possessions. It has plenty of outlets to its imagination in this house and the sign; the Moon becomes multifarious task master. In none of the houses does the Moon works hard or engages one to do hard work. One has to see the house that is motivating and the planets therein to decide who will execute the order from the Moon. Sometimes the aspects come from other houses and they too get motivated. Since the Moon is an imaginative body, it causes us to think to visualize, pre-meditate, plan, and design much before in readiness. Planet Mercury executes it when the Moon is present in the 3rd house or the sign Gemini.

The Moon is adaptable (dual sign) and duplicates everything in order to ward off a crisis. Two marriages, two houses, two children, and perhaps two cars will make it feel secure. Now is your imagination working overtime? Yes, two lovers too!!!

The mother here is the one who brings forth the idea of duplicating everything. She could be an outdoor woman working or running a business. She could be letting her children be looked after by a maid or a governess. The children get used to the spare keys for the house, alternatives to all appliances, even food is cooked and kept frozen in separate containers so that the children can always find food. The Gemini child gets used to different people coming and going as guardians. The mother's absence is well substituted.

Cancer

This is home for the Moon in the 4th house. It learns the importance of mother first and the family in general. The Moon learns everything from the mother; the household chores, cooking, stitching, decorating etc., and tries to emulate. The Moon grows remembering its past and as an adult wait for a similar situation from its mate where it can serve or simply look after in a similar way. If it is a male then there is an expectation from the wife to be looked after and run the house like his mother did. This causes tiffs frequently as such expectations are never met to the full.

There is an insistence that abundance in everything is always present. The Moon is highly insecure in the sign of Cancer. There is every chance of becoming anxious over even a small crisis at home. The children are pampered to the extent of spoiling them. The Cancer Moon loves to feed in a variety of ways. Overall, the Moon is interested in mysteries, the past, and the occult for its own pastime. There will be plenty of secrets to hide too. The 4th cusp is our point of concealment. Whatever we love to hide is at this point. This point is directly opposite the 10th house cusp which is the point of display to the world. If any person's planet like Saturn, Neptune, Uranus, and Pluto fall on the 4th house cusp, we feel like revealing ourselves to them. It is as if they hold the key to our Pandora's chest. The North Node falling here during its transit causes us to fulfill these secret desires. The South Node causes us to lose interest in pent up desires. If anyone's personal planets, the Sun or the Moon fall here we are comfortable with them because they do not try to elicit any secret.

Leo

In this house the Moon is fond of close relationships and wants to appear grandiose too. This desire takes it to the stage and perform the personae or characters for satisfaction. It needs to tire itself from its own desires. It is also hard to tame and control. The mundane lifestyle is simply not interesting here. It likes the show business much more. One must realise here that no one ever becomes an actor or a performer due to chance. The desire has to be very strong. The survival in a world, full of performers who all have a certain degree of establishment and a following, is not easy. If one gets quickly exhausted in a disability to transcend the hurdles like, from 'not being liked at all' to 'not even welcome for an audition' appear insurmountable too soon to many. The 5th house is always the motivating house for the 1st house of 'self'. This Moon here, a couple of planets here, strong aspects to planets in 5th house, are the only survival mechanisms if you ever want to reach the stage and seek success. Also, the 9th house needs to motivate the 5th. The 9th house leads us to the doors of people who are superior to us. The rich, the powerful, and the famous keep on appearing in our life. We might have failed in our attempts but there is light shown again and again at the end of the tunnel. So, the 9th leads to a situation of being invited like how in the Japanese legend of the Straw Millionaire, the poor man becomes wealthy by selling straws.

Besides dramatics, the Moon wants everything extra-large. Plenty of children, plenty of holidaying and gambling followed by a large house are essential here. Do you have enough to spare or are you a daily wage earner? Make sure your name resembles somebody who is well known. If you do not possess any of these keep a long rope ready or simply stay away saying this is poison. Risks excite this Moon. It takes long to hold on to any mate for a life time.

Creativity interests this Moon more than any other work. The 3rd house habit of writing short stories becomes writing big novels. It loves audience and a fan club. The good side is if the 9th house, the motivation house is well served the same Moon builds different interests. Teaching and learning become the passions instead of stardom. But it will still try to experiment with original ideas.

It all starts with the mother; who is more powerful than the father in all the fields, if tested. The child has seen the family set up where the father was a mere provider and the mother brought the best of things home. Her circle of friends and family were from astonishingly high society. The adult now wants to recreate. If the 9th house is strong with planets like Jupiter or Saturn or even Pluto then there is enough opportunity to mingle with people belonging to higher echelons, the learned, influential etc. But these individuals (with the Moon in 5th house or the sign Leo) are best if seen on stage or on the screen.

Virgo

The 6th and the 10th houses are where the Moon is in a poor family or simply a serving mother who suffers most of her life. The poverty state must be faced so that the Moon contrives to come out of it. The sign Virgo is all about meticulous work and reach perfection and serve. There are health issues here and the person is aware what delicate health issues are and can cause crisis at home. These people get their small doses of knowledge of medicine throughout their lifetime on account of experiencing illnesses or seeing other family members suffer. The Moon here has enough experience of medical treatments either because it is born in a family of doctors or due to association. The children suffer too. The person with a 6th house Moon is made aware that the family needs a breadwinner at its earliest. The struggle begins early in life. Except for the habit of achieving perfection which is naturally built in as a virtue, for everything else the Moon causes the individual to seek a job very early in life. The legendary Virgo who did not marry on account of so many reasons and said, "Shall be alone if I have to but shall not seek a family", had the Moon in Virgo and not the Sun. The Moon fears calamities and crisis situations a lot. Most phobias are due to the Moon. These fears keep the Moon away from commitments or take any bold step,

The person has interests in athletics, word games, literature. Many interests are common with the 3rd house. Both these houses are competitive. They excel when tested. Many sportsmen have strong 3rd and 6th houses. It is just that the person lives through crisis; the person is well prepared yet anxious always. If the 2nd house can be somehow motivated from here, then the Moon can achieve good amount of wealth. If the 10th house has good aspects to the planets, then the 6th house Moon can recover fast. The Moon is happy working with hands on experience as a chef, as a hair-dresser, as a nurse or sometimes even as a doctor. Healing arts, showing compassion toward animals and provide relief are some of the rare qualities that Moon possesses to seek happiness.

Libra

The Moon can only cause desires; to possess and attach itself to a thing or person. The Moon is shy and secretive of its instincts. The Moon in Libra struggles to find its mate because the Moon has no means to express. It can visualize what sort of mate it is interested in and it needs to motivate the 3rd house and its planets or get motivated from the 11th. Also, the sign

Libra is where the planets Saturn exalts so the focus is on security too. So, check the 11th house for motivating the 7th house, and check the 3rd house to check which planet will work for the Moon on its behalf. This is planet Venus' house and the Moon sooner or later is likely cause a mental involvement with someone or the other seeing wealth or the looks.

Just as in the 2nd, and the 5th, the Moon encourages talent for popularity. It develops expression of the self for seeking attention in this sign. Here too it can create using the imagination. It is happy with friends, in business partnerships, and the spouse. The Moon here is not a spender in this sign.

The mother is the first experience of planet Saturn to the Libran Moon child. The childhood has a lot of hardship added partly because the bread winner earns very little, or could be the only person earning a salary and the household has many dependents. The planet Venus of the Libra sign does not appear anywhere near the horizon at that time. It is only after the adolescent age the relief is felt but the stress is always on get educated and start earning. Many a times a Libra Moon takes up part time jobs while attending college until a suitable job prospect arises as soon as college education ends. Higher education to these children is rare. The talents of the Libran Moon do show up if there are enough signs of motivation and planets to cooperate and act on behalf of the Moon.

In the years to come the earnings go up but the desire to develop talents remains unfulfilled. The Libra Moon vows to develop talents in its children instead among other things. A lot is devoted both financially and personally to the well-being of the family. A Libra Moon is a lot different than a Libra Sun. The Moon and planet Saturn do not get along well. With the Sun, the Planet Saturn can only place hardships for a while. The Sun surmounts all hurdles and hardships in time. The Moon has to wait till one of the personal planets comes to succor.

Scorpio

After the sign of Leo with Sun in 5th house or in the sign itself if there is any sign for revenge it is the Moon in Scorpio. Not so much the Sun in Scorpio or the Sun in the 8th. The Moon here carries deep wounds and as usual its memory is stronger when hurt. It cannot rest in peace until it avenges and never forgives.

This fear of disappointment followed by atonement is well known to the Moon; the habit of seeking revenge. That is one of the reasons for not getting too close to anyone. You may even include the spouse here. Relationships never succeed with this Moon. It will pretend to be fond of something or someone for a while until its motives are met but after that one sees this Scorpio or the 8th house Moon no more. It is away trying to fetch something somewhere but very far away.

The mother here has a lot of fears built-in for strange reasons. She fears social life or social contacts because she thinks others might know her true value. A lot that goes on in the family is kept a secret and the children learn that soon. They are given to think that it is safer if outside contact is kept to a minimum. This habit becomes second nature to someone with the Moon in Scorpio or the 8th house.

It is quite similar to planet Venus in Scorpio or in the 8th house when it comes to relationships. On one side is secretiveness and on the other is a safe distance. Planet Venus is not interested in any revenge but it is afraid of betrayal from the very beginning. It is very hard to contain this planet Venus in a relationship. It is better to let the planet Venus lead and take over. That way it has more assurance. Perhaps it earns an insurance endowment with the responsibility thrown into its lap. The Scorpio ascendant is also afraid of betrayal. It involves its mate into false activity for the sake of saving face later. It can always say, "I was only interested in friendship and nothing else". In all these the common denominator is fear of a loss of face and trust. The Moon too comes under the same banner but as I said before, it uses the other planets to serve its purpose; from the aspects of personal planets or the planets of the 4th or the 12th house.

Beware! Wear your armour much before you decide on accosting a Scorpio or the Moon of the 8th house.

Sagittarius

The Moon in the 9th or the sign Sagittarius is very desirous of knowing other cultures, visiting other countries to know their culture and history, seeking people with authority from high places and winning their confidence are its passions. This house is a recovery house after suffering in the 8th house. The Moon of the 9th house be a doctor or otherwise has plenty of home-medicines under its belt to treat itself or others. Some of these people are very good doctors. Besides, it is efficient in seeking, higher knowledge, mastery over difficult subjects, an entirely different belief system regarding religion, the society norms, and the legal system. Here the attachment theory of the Moon changes to freedom from attachment. In the 9th house there is not much room for materialistic objects except artefacts collected during research work, moon rocks if one happens to find, some precious stones, and some ancient books that have been passed on. It is once again important to see the motivation from the 1st house excites 9th house. Also, what does the 9th house motivate in the 5th? The 5th house also contributes to learning and experience and not just love affairs or entertainment. The motivating house ruler could be in some other house. If from that house an aspect to the 9th house is coming then too the 9th house gets benefited. Remember the Moon needs aides; if the aides come from the motivating houses so much the better.

The mother here is very inspiring as she inculcates the thoughts of independence and seeking knowledge through various sources. She could be a mother of many children or someone who has friends from different backgrounds that lets her children mix freely. She could be a learned woman herself or an autodidact. She loves to tell stories and take children on holidays to strange places. The zest for travel in children comes because of the mother who is very fond of travelling. In many cases the adolescent children live away for their schooling and later college education. She hates clinging and dependency from the children.

The Moon has a desire to overload oneself with educational qualifications. It has lots of stories to tell from its reading habit; both real and imaginary. This narrative ability allows writing letters that are voluminous, writing books that are thick and wordy; may be used as pillows at times! Exaggeration apart, people seek this person with the 9th house Moon for taking counsel. This Moon is always ready to do service to community like the 11th house Moon for free. The visitors come at any time and leave; some even stay a couple of days to the annoyance of the spouse. But the Sagittarius Moon welcomes all; it has a story to tell one and all.

Let us study a horoscope from a simple motivational point of view. A lot has been said so far and I felt that I should demonstrate through an example.

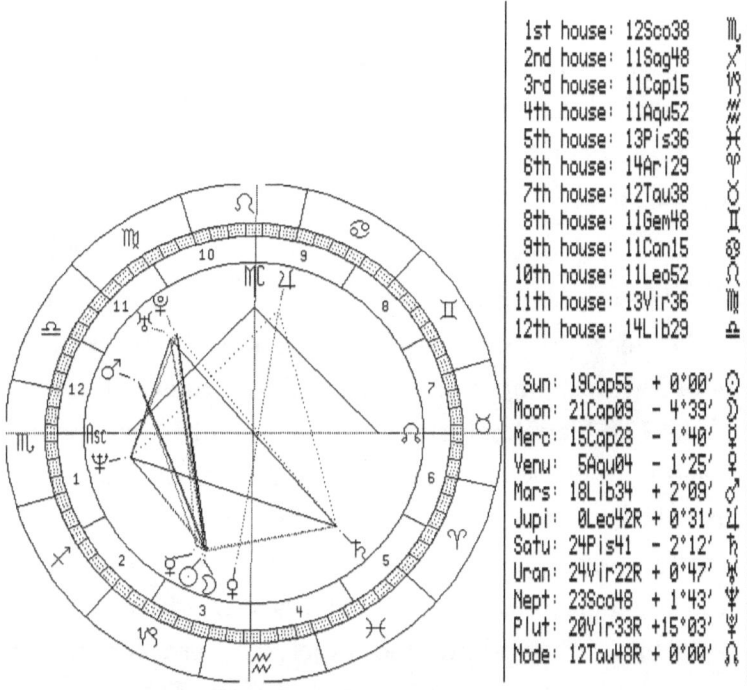

Let us take the fire houses; houses 1st, 5th, and the 9th.

The 1st house cusp is Scorpio at 12⁰. The ruler is planet Pluto in the 11th house of hopes, gains and wishes. The 1st house has planet Neptune at 23⁰ and is the ruler of the 5th house which has the sign Pisces on its cusp. The 5th house has planet Saturn at 24⁰ and it appears that planet Saturn is responsible for motivating planet Neptune. Planet Neptune builds dreams in the natal chart and makes it into a habit. The person visualizes a trend or an event and lays a foundation.

When the opportunity arrives, it becomes convenient to pursue the dream. Usually this takes a couple of years. Planet Neptune can build dreams in planet Saturn and not vice-versa. Planet Saturn will constantly remind of the expenditure to planet Neptune and nothing more. Planet Neptune is more powerful than planet Saturn. The dreams repeat and get consolidated and finally planet Saturn is forced to release funds and fulfilling of the dream occurs. Both Uranus and planet Pluto oppose the planet Saturn from the 11th. That weakens the position of planet Saturn. That means resources will get exhausted soon.

There is a sextile relationship between planet Pluto and planet Neptune; both are slow moving planets and therefore will take years to manifest. The question of planet Neptune (ruler of 5th house) motivating planet Pluto (ruler of the 1st) does not arise. The planet Saturn can only motivate someone who is obsessed with work of any kind. Here the person is a Capricorn (a workaholic and a perfectionist) who can only think of work and nothing else. The fire houses are not for work in the first place. They increase our high spiritedness in whatever we do as adventurers. If we show too much concern for a lack of resources, the cause for motivation is removed.

The 9th house ruler is the Moon and is combust (New Moon Day) and has no strength; it has been passed to the Sun. the Sun has 5th house as naturally ruled house and the 10th house of the chart has the sign Leo in it. The 5th house activities are all restricted because of planet Saturn. Any little risk or adventure and a lot of expenditure ensues. The planet Saturn makes us realise that we spent too much. What really happens is that the repressed desires come out whenever the planet Saturn is weak or stressed temporarily, and a lot is spent in a fear of a dearth of opportunity to enjoy and entertain oneself. So, it becomes a spurt of spree.

The connection between planet Saturn and the Sun comes into use in the 10th house, which is again work related. The 3rd house also benefits in the work in so far as communication area is concerned; connectivity, sincere will to approach others in order to pass on ideas and benefiting from them, are some of these qualities. Planet Mercury is also combust here and its power is also given away to benefit the Sun. Once again, the same three houses get lighted and the benefits come. Planet Mercury's travel bug comes through the 5th house. There is a romantic expectation out of each travel venture. There is a liking toward escapade than just entertainment. The 9th house is not really motivating the 5th house much. There is a trine within an orb of 6^0; but planet Jupiter in Leo is at 0^0 is considered weak. Planet Saturn is the greatest hurdle here in the 5th house. A success through a love affair is not possible.

Let us take the air houses. Only the Sun has power here and the other two bodies are combust. Just like the Moon, planet Mercury too is working through our head and needs the help of other planets. The 8th house (Gemini sign) and the 11th house (Virgo) have lost their power. So not much help to the 7th house. But the 11th house is benefited by the powerful Sun from the 3rd house. This person will work hard for future hopes and wishes and money gain will happen using a lot of will, taking help from the 10th house's hard work (Leo sign of the Sun). This will benefit the 2nd house. People have to put up with constant boasting about achievements the subject of conversation must revolve around them; due to over-emphasis on the Sun in the chart.

Let us see the Earth houses. There are no planets here. The only connection is that of a square between the planet Mars (in 12th house) and the Sun in the 3rd house. Planet Mars is a ruler of 6th house and the Sun is the ruler for 10th house. This is a struggle to put in consistent work and there are chances of giving up on account of stress. The 6th house is a house that denotes health decay on account of working regularly. Because planet Mars is in the sign of Libra but in the 12th house, the person works with spurts of energy and never consistently. There is an opposition between planet Venus and planet Jupiter that increases Venusian desires and brings about relationship issues. So does planet Mars from Libra. These two planets are not internally connected in the chart. These need to be externally connected (through transits); only then there is a chance.

That completes the motivation story.

Capricorn

This is the 3rd of the Earth signs and ruled by planet Saturn. The Moon in the 10th house or the sign of Capricorn has to face poverty for sure in its childhood or its adolescence. The entire family relies on this Moon of the 10th house to do well and earn for the family. There could be an exception here if there are elder siblings who have already taken the burden but even as a last child it does not experience any pampering from the mother. It realises that either it must look outside for some love or completely separate from the family in search of it. Most Capricorn Moon children leave home early and return to meet and spend some time with them and return to their base. Many are in the Services and some prefer a foreign country. They will not ignore their family. They do regular remitting of funds but prefer staying away.

The mother here appears strict and reserved. She is not experienced much or exposed to the outside world. A few could be working mothers too. But her sole purpose is to get the children to be self-reliant from the financial angle. That's the difference between the 9th house Moon mother and this one. The children are provided with whatever that is considered as minimal subsistence, minimum education, all basic needs met without much ostentation, going on holidays is provided too with some sacrifice from the mother. The child grows amidst guilt and remembers all the hardships as to be a bane on its poor mother. In fact, these children deserve an opportunity to gain access to higher education. Since the money is scarce, they manage to do that later on their own account. The Moon is not comfortable until it comes out of the clutches of poverty in this house or the sign.

Usually there is a family run business like, a shop, some land, some trading business, repair workshop etc. But the children lack interest in that. So, the Moon in Capricorn brings a good share of legacy to the children of the family. That is accumulated wealth coming from the Moon. The Moon is in its fall but the loss is only in keeping a public image. The Capricorn or the 10th house Moon is shy and feels inferior to others because of its background. It is a different story during its fifties. It will appear brave and bold. The early ages are full of worries and fears. If the Moon is in Cancer (or the 4th House), or is in Taurus (2nd house) the person is usually well off from the beginning as these signs are blessed to be comfortable. There is a lot of self-confidence from early ages. It is a different story with the Moon in the 10th house.

A thing that a child is taught from very early years is not to cry or show emotions outwardly. This is true in the case of all earth sign Moons; the Moon in Taurus and the Moon in Virgo. The child misconstrues that, to show false emotions could be alright. That leads to living a false life which takes shelter under displaying everything that is acceptable to the outside world and wanted by all to be appreciated. The Moon in earth signs grows with a fear that if anyone knows the truth it will be outcast. There is fear to experiment, a fear to venture in the open, and a false respect is developed toward elderly. These

Moons do not mind but feel comfortable doing everything behind the scenes.

Likewise, the Moon in fixed signs is taught never to be stubborn; Moon in Taurus, Leo, Scorpio, and Aquarius. Although people with the Sun in fixed signs look very stubborn, if you ever run into one, these people use it to display and create a fear in others so that no one goes against their wishes. You must never forget the qualities of the Sun. The Sun loves to put on and perform a drama if it has to attain or seek something. Never fear that stubbornness. Retaliate with a similar attitude or demeanor that you shall not budge. You will see the difference.

Aquarius

The Moon in Aquarius or the 11th house has a lot of concern about others than its own self. It loves friends and well-wishers to get popular. Its talents are plenty besides it is also very sincere in knowing something. It is not superficial or shallow while doing its research but goes in to depths to know 'that' something. It is liked by all for its generosity. But it has a tendency to put down demands or condition on others to suit itself. The fixity of their Moon is unbearable to others. Many oblige but many don't.

The Moon here wants to be a leader for its ideals and reforming nature and goes far to fulfill its goals. It loses many friends on its way and makes few here and there. It remembers to meet them all after achieving its goals and all others feel proud about its achievements too. After all, friends mean a lot to this Moon. Now after achieving all that it wanted to, it will give you a, "I told you so" kind of look! The others realise and admit to their failures but definitely they would have never been able to work with a single purpose like this Moon in Aquarius or the 11th House.

The mother is very influential because she is highly educated and capable of influencing the family members. She plans the future of all the children and their academic performance means a lot to her than any other activity or talents. She does not like her children to freely mingle with the children in the neighbourhood. She also acts hard to please and makes certain that they obey. These conditions cause the child with the Moon in 11th house or the sign Aquarius to wonder what is really wrong with their friends because the mother does not like some. They continue to mingle and play and they quite enjoy it. They put conditions on them because the mother is putting in plenty regarding everything and become annoying to their friends. This habit continues but struggles to survive and they learn to live with all. But they feel the constant pressure of performance at their school.

The 11th house stands for our gains, hopes and wishes and the work put in is for the benefit of the 2nd house which is for self-worth and self-earning capacity. Do not forget, the 11th house is 10th from the 2nd house. Whatever we do in a 10th house from any house, is always to our liking, whatever we want to display, whatever we do to get other's attention. Again, the Moon needs its friends placed in motivating houses like the 3rd house in this case.

Pisces

It is hard to believe but the Moon in water signs or in the 12th house causes a fear of water itself. These children have difficulty learning to swim or later play any water sport. This Moon loves isolation from all so much so that choose to live in a foreign country or live in a house that is usually far away from busy areas of town. Some like sea shore, banks of any river or a lake, or they live in a high-rise building. How is that near water? I did not understand well. Perhaps rain reaches there first? I think. How do these use their isolation? They love their hobbies; plants, horticulture, cooking, reading, writing books, writing poetry, writing romantic stories or even children's books are all very appealing. These people have an interest in anything that is silent, dumb, or shows a disability of some kind. The compassion is poured on these if these happen to be animals. They are often found pursuing music, any kind of healing art, the occult, magic, or subjects that have mystery attached but no one has yet solved those.

These people are very sensitive. They cannot take criticism well. That is one definite reason for seeking isolation thereby no one really knows what are they up to. Or else, comments will be received on social media! For the same reason they keep few friends so that they are never hurt. They are very intelligent and are capable of absorbing the subject very quickly. They can teach well, they do not put barriers or difficulties around their students testing them, are very easy going but give very little response if feedback is asked. Why? They do not want to hurt anyone.

There is secrecy around them too. These people put up with a lot of nonsense from others; too much respect for superiors and elders followed by a situation wherein they are afraid of getting close to anybody. The mother is usually seen as someone who is ready to serve anybody. The first lesson of showing sympathy starts here. These children see her working a lot alone and get abused too for certain reasons but the children will be saying, "Why does she have to do that"? These issues lead to isolation from the most people. They have a firm belief that people take favours whenever they want but promise nothing in return.

I have also seen different placement of the Moon in the chart of siblings. You might wonder how that could change the personality of just one woman? It does change from the eldest to the youngest child. The eldest gets a sterner side and the youngest gets the softer side. Sometimes the only son gets pampered between sisters. The smarter of the children gets a little extra attention. These differences change the outlook. There are these zodiacal signs that are always demanding attention and appreciation more than the other siblings. For example, Aries, Leo, Capricorn, Scorpio have a greater need to be identified as smarter or simply important. That struggle may be noticed in their charts.

The Pisces or the 12th house Moon is also interested in telescopes and in the space over us. It loves watching animated cartoons irrespective of its age. Music too is one of them. Whatever it takes interest into it goes to the depths and learns it. If you hear them sing or play any instrument you are definitely going to notice their emotional involvement in the fine art. The sign Pisces is not a perfectionist like its opposite sign Virgo. It can read volumes to know the truth without perfecting any. Then it gets stressed out and likes a little inebriation. I am still searching for a Piscean or a 12th house Moon without an addiction of something. But I know where they hang around mostly!

An Exercise

Let me give you an example and see if you can solve.

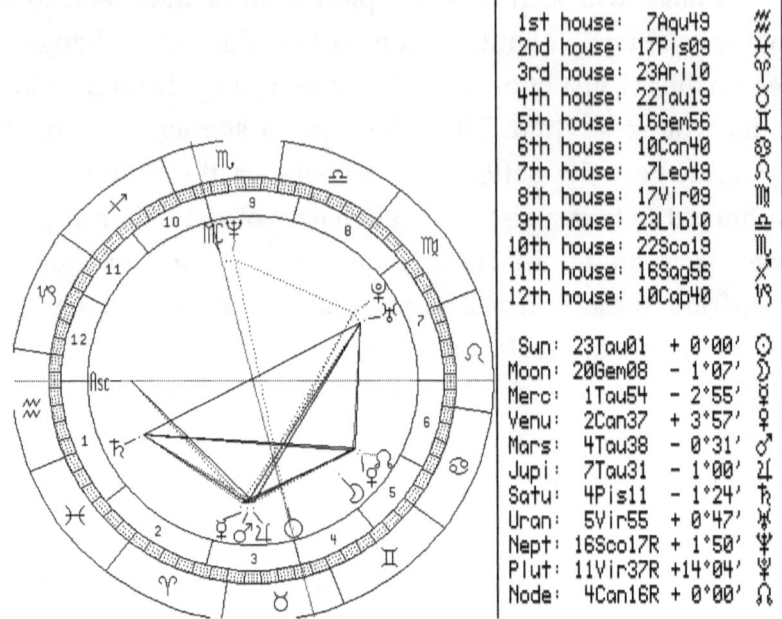

```
1st house:  7Aqu49
2nd house: 17Pis09
3rd house: 23Ari10
4th house: 22Tau19
5th house: 16Gem56
6th house: 10Can40
7th house:  7Leo49
8th house: 17Vir09
9th house: 23Lib10
10th house: 22Sco19
11th house: 16Sag56
12th house: 10Cap40

Sun:  23Tau01  + 0°00'
Moon: 20Gem08  - 1°07'
Merc:  1Tau54  - 2°55'
Venu:  2Can37  + 3°57'
Mars:  4Tau38  - 0°31'
Jupi:  7Tau31  - 1°00'
Satu:  4Pis11  - 1°24'
Uran:  5Vir55  + 0°47'
Nept: 16Sco17R + 1°50'
Plut: 11Vir37R +14°04'
Node:  4Can16R + 0°00'
```

In the above example, you will notice that the Moon has no aspects at all from any of the planets or the Sun. How will this Moon manifest its intent? You all know by now that the Moon can only create a desire and vision in our head. It also functions like planet Mercury. Planet Mercury is also a planet that works in our head and acts. Although, it is slightly better that it can cause our hands to function and let our tongue do the talking and the strength for these is supplied through the lungs. In a similar way the Moon too absorbs ideas and emotions and let these enter the heart and become part of the memory. But for most functions the Moon uses the planets in the motivation house or if possible, it causes the motivation in another that is exactly 120⁰ away.

Now try and answer, how does the Moon do any function if there are no aspects to it?

We must consider the natural ruler of the house, followed by the ruler of the house in the chart. Under the circumstances, planet Mercury and the Sun will help the Moon to fulfill its intent. Although the two planets are not connected, these two have aspects with other planets. Whenever the Sun, the planet Mercury and their aspected planets get activated by the transiting planets the Moon's agenda will be included among other functions. One needs to bear in mind that that the outer planets in the chart take long to activate due to a transit of any personal planet. So those may be ignored.

In the above chart, planet Mercury is conjunct planets Mars and Jupiter. Planet Mercury is sextile with both planets Saturn and Venus. The Sun is right on the 4th house cusp, which is ruled by the Moon. I have not considered the outer planets here at all. So that is sufficient for the Moon to remain happy. The Moon is in the 5th house where there are more chances of it being high handed, egocentric, vain, self-loving, pompous and full of pride. That makes this Moon a spender wastefully to show how financially well off it is. That is a danger and the opportunities could come frequently because of the number of connection that Moon has. The person has already experienced bankruptcy twice already in life. So, it is a good example to remember.

Chapter-VII

Mr. Dryden: "A man who tells lies, like me, merely hides the truth. But a man who tells half-lies has forgotten where he put it". (Meaning even the place where the truth was hidden has been forgotten) .... Claude Rains in "Lawrence of Arabia".

Planet Mercury

The Identity

Planet Mercury is very close to the Sun. It revolves around the Sun very quickly. It rotates around its own axis in about fifty-nine Earth days. It rotates three times around itself, while it revolves twice around the Sun (around eighty-nine Earth days); the orbit around the Sun is counterclockwise, like the Earth and planet Mars. This is general knowledge and has nothing to do with astrology. One needs to understand that there is a planetary speed and that has a lot to do with our psyche. That is when astrology comes into play. With the certain available information, the subject of astrology is able to extrapolate situations and events. This too, precedence after precedence astrologers documented some events through experience. Those become research material for future discoveries. Every score of years one finds a paradigm comes to prevail. Such should be our approach to the subject also. What has been experienced, tried, and noticed in a number of cases that we try to solve, must be documented and later produced for the upcoming enthusiasts who may be in their teens or early twenties.

Planet Mercury certainly has governance over our thinking ability. My question to you is, do we know about any of our functions that are voluntarily carried out without thinking? Virtually none. Although, absentmindedness cannot be ruled out that is mainly due to our own pre-occupation with something more important. Planet Mercury is still hatching our strategy for us during our preoccupied state. If such is the situation then we all must sit together and bring a consensus to decide on the function of the planet. In most places when you normally search the word 'communications', it is seen attributed freely to this planet. To my wonder I have seen and felt that planet Mercury communicates silently too; within oneself.

Any Listeners?

Let us begin with 'talking'; an easy modality of communication. How does 'talking' really matter to us? Please think and see if you can answer. I always felt that it was an urgency to feel comfortable with someone around us and stop wondering about what they are up to. As children, teenagers, and later into our twenties until then, we are not concerned about everyone around us. We express our needs and we somehow seek those from the 'doyen' of the family, friends, and other elders. Planet Mercury is not loaded with our concerns until adulthood in most cases. It is only after we begin to rely on our abilities to serve us better, that we find difficulties unless one is trained before. Most of our earlier habits of communication do not let us to get to the place or stage where we want to be. It is during this time of our life we all begin to overload planet Mercury in our charts. So that could be around the mid-twenties. How do we usually begin? Most of us with an ethnic background will want to improve 'diction' first. There are numerous ways to do that; an easier choice would be to develop conversation ability with someone who has better diction. This is where true 'talking' has its origins. We learn and we put to use what we learned. This is planet Mercury's primary function. The rest of what we do is just 'overload' planet Mercury.

Amidst Harangue

Do you have friends who just 'talk shop'? Do you know someone close who enjoys 'gossip'? Then you are already around your subject 'planet Mercury' in crisis! If planet Mercury is weak or has been weakened in our horoscopes the ability of that planet drops to below average. It has difficulty retaining what it learned through literature, media or experience. It uses it for reference only. It cannot advice anyone else with certainty. We use the term 'critical thinking' these days and I too have difficulty interpreting that many times. The idea of 'critical thinking' allows us to be critical about everything we see, we do, we advise, we solve and we adjust the original thought to make it workable. That's a lot of work if planet Mercury has to do it all by itself.

A Critical Thinker

If we can do a proper 'critical thinking' then is it possible to 'talk shop' or 'gossip'? It will appear a waste of time. Then planet Mercury is simply not interested in loading itself with supercilious judgements about others. It will definitely be interested in knowing about it, analyse it, and apply it on its own self to arrive at a conclusion. That conclusion is not for the public or anyone. It will be used where it is called upon to solve a situation and its efficacy will be felt by others. That is the power of planet Mercury at its highest capacity. So, a good placement of planet Mercury will produce good writers, good lawyers, doctors who can solve mysteries surrounding ailments, detectives, journalists, teachers, accountants, people who handle finances for large organizations, etc. What does

Mercury lack? It lacks the energy or a will to succeed. Planet Mercury must be well supported and pushed, made to feel miserable and then it starts to move. Tell me honestly. Are you one of those types?

An unaspected planet Mercury will have a big difficulty to operate as the world wants it to. In that case, planet Mercury needs to receive an aspect from others or an outsider to function as required. There is a function of the brain called 'emulate'. That is strive to excel or equal what has been given to notice as superior either consciously or sometimes subconsciously. That is a function of planet Mercury. There is another function of our brain called 'mirroring' carried out by the neurons sitting at the back of our head. In this, there is no trying to be better than any other. But trying to equal the other is definitely present. That mirroring is a function of our Moon. These are not found as characteristics in other planets. Not even Venus; it is our poets who felt that grace could be connected to our feelings. But we aren't poets!

The Learner

This phenomenon facilitates planet Mercury to do its job of 'learning' first and then 'reproduce' as demonstrated. Have we realized that we have this quality anytime? Please do. That is how we let ourselves be trained from our early childhood. When a child fails to pick up even after repeated demonstrations and gesticulations, a parent becomes disappointed and begins to fear a weakness in their child to identify as 'slow' or 'special' later on. Aren't we fortunate that we appeared 'smart' to our parents? Thank your planet Mercury for that and never let that be damaged.

The antics thrown in during childhood, recalcitrant behaviour in adolescence, taciturn during the early twenties, doting during mid-twenties, devoted during late twenties, to casual, indifferent, disagreeing, challenging, uncaring and the list stops at reminiscing in old age, (if the memory permits!) become the various stages of our planet Mercury in our life. It is all about what is convenient to planet Mercury that is shown here. There could be exceptions that stretch a particular stage given in the order of the list above but will not avoid completely. To cope with our weaknesses, we compensate through our friends. Have you heard, "Know thyself through your friends!"? Please do read, if possible, a paper published in Current Directions in Psychological Science, a journal of the Association for Psychological Science. The paper is written by Vazire and Doctoral student, Erika N. Carlson. You may find it on www.psychcentral.com. Socrates said, "True wisdom does know what you do not know". What Socrates did not know is that the planet Mercury sitting in our horoscopes knows all about what we do not know.

Friendships

One of the functions of planet Mercury is to make friends from different zones that we move about. From each zone it lets us pick up only those who are smarter than us than dull. Each one of them serves to help us in our distress times. It is planet Mercury that first thinks that we need not know everything through hard work or diligence tly. Find a via media and the world will be your oyster. So, start counting your friends and attribute that special quality to each one of them that you do not possess. Keep a count of those friends who depend on you for certain other reasons. That is how planet Mercury operates when it knows its limitations. The weaker the planet Mercury gets the greater your friend's circle will be. It is a case of mutual dependency and growth. This attribute is sometimes gifted to planet Venus under the banner of relationships! Do you realize how wrong we have been always? A weak planet Mercury may not look scholarly or show oratory but has a capacity to build friendships and relationships.

In business, usually an office is set up and alongside business, contacts are created single handedly, first. This weak planet Mercury has the ability to do all that. After the business is established, the jobs are deputed to others who are employed and the business continues. A weak planet Mercury could be poor in a particular language to converse or write letters to other business associates but is quite savvy in handling employees at all levels.

Your Company HR Manager better has a weak planet Mercury in their charts to help better rapport with everyone. When each friend is serving a necessary purpose in our life, we could have a party of friends in our domain, and if we have a habit to boast we might do that as well. But planet Mercury has limitations in giving time to each one of them as there is a chance of getting stressed too much. Planet Mercury lacks energy and needs other planetary support. So then look for such support in the chart of your fellow mates and relatives. You will know that yourself.

It becomes a bit of Bohemian culture here when planet Mercury deals with friends. A few do get discarded whenever planet Mercury is stressed or during its retrograde periods. Some old ones return too during these periods. All you need to understand is that the planet Mercury serves our need to appear intelligent to everyone either directly or indirectly. The corollary here is that a strong planet Mercury, has a lesser need for friends, a lesser need to set up an independent business and handle different classes of people, a lesser need to go out of the way to establish one's career, a lesser need to rely on others for help, it is self-reliant when it comes to gathering information, knowledge and do critical thinking. It is happy with almost any job that is relevant to its qualifications. It can talk only with a purpose and is very enthusiastic in passing knowledge to others as it has no fear of losing that. It flourishes when it becomes a consultant to others. It is hard to make close friendships when the planet Mercury is strong in the chart. Sometimes weaknesses have advantages too.

The Materialist

Let us talk about how weak Mercury becomes a victim of despair and despondency. Too much dependency on others may be for encouraging the self, seeking help, building contacts, remaining socially popular, being able to achieve higher scores while studying at a university or seeking empathy from others have a drawback. That drawback is to remember to return a favour with a favour. It is of no use presenting a gift on a birthday with a 'thank you' note when on a day you were suffering from pain or a disease your friend came to give you relief from misery. On that day the 'distance' did not matter only 'you' mattered. When planet Mercury returns that favour with a gift it usually thinks that an obligation has ended. It can only think in terms of 'material' when it comes to exchanging favours. That emotional binding, when needed, comes with a strong Moon from our chart. Sometimes the Moon is connected with planet Mercury in our charts. That helps to connect with friends better. This connection weakens the planet Mercury quite a bit. The same is the case when planet Mercury is connected to planet Venus in our charts. With the Moon, planet Mercury assures itself of 'unconditional' love from all. With planet Venus, it manages to display or exhibit itself to remain likeable. With planet Mars there is a touch of bravery, to be alert, show perspicacity, be carping, be witty and be a raconteur. So long as planet Mercury is strong it shows a great capacity to perform. But needs to be likeable on personal terms. So which kind did you like so far? Is your choice the weak version or the strong one?

With Friends Moon and Venus

When other planets aspect planet Mercury, they only help, to help themselves. Planet Mercury being so fond of friendship quickly obliges every planet to its own self-undoing. With the Moon (taking the effect of all aspects here) planet Mercury has to adopt a new set of vocabulary. The 4th house and the sign Cancer wherever these are located in a chart get additional support from planet Mercury. Moon likes to be present in planet Mercury's dealings, talking, buying, and selling, in seeking knowledge, its performing ability, and retaining memories. The Moon looks for 'unconditional love' and planet Mercury has to accommodate that. Businesses and dealings that build good relationships with clients flourish under this aspect.

The Moon loves to reminisce always of its good times and bad times. Its mood always fluctuates and carries us through a number of emotions on a daily basis. Planet Mercury is affected by that changeability in Moon's scenarios daily. If planet Mercury is placed in the sign of Cancer, the 4th house, or in an aspect with the Moon from anywhere, planet Mercury's focus has to change every two and a half days to accommodate the Moon; the Moon will change its sign every two and a quarter day. What a punishment!

If planet Mercury is allocated a place close to planet Venus or its aspects, placed in the 2nd or the 7th house, or placed in the signs Taurus or Libra, its subservience to planet Venus increases. Planet Venus could be well-groomed, has attended a Swiss finishing school, has educated itself well and has managed to earn a doctorate. All these new attributes will be over and above planet Venus's basic features; to be dressed well, to be able to attract attention and admiration, post selfies over social media, be in the constant company of wooers and display talents if any. It looks alright if planet Mercury is given a job of philanthropy but at a cost of losing certain other qualities. Planet Mercury's business handling capacity, managing finances, fighting court battles, diagnosing and investigative qualities, its concentrating ability reduce. One must warn the clients if they have high ambitions and expectations out of their career.

The Magician

While planet Mercury is in its weak state, an exaggerating aspect from any of the outer planets or from Jupiter or Mars causes 'craftiness' in planet Mercury. The greater the influence of any outer planet, planet Jupiter or planet Mars on a weak planet Mercury can cause a high degree of stress. Stress brings in anxiety. Anxiety is always, "What will happen next"? kind of a feeling So we develop a need to be with someone in whom we can confide or confess. Although that does not produce any great help, it can create a 'false' confidence.

The other thing that stress does is that it produces cortisol. Cortisol in the pre-frontal cortex region accelerates dopamine activation. On the other hand, the serotonin even though produced enough cannot reach the receptors because the cortisol has downregulated (making it less sensitive) the receptors. Now the person gets affected in two ways; lack of serotonin benefit and an increased need for dopamine. That damages the neurons at a faster rate. To remind the readers, dopamine is a pleasure producing hormone and is addictive. Serotonin is calming and produces sleep. Cortisol produced on account of stress does not allow serotonin to reach the receptors and we lose our sleep!! So, stress usually causes anxiety too if you all have some experience in that. Long term anxiety disables our capacity to face the future. With that, the person loses the ability to visualize the future from what one is doing today. It becomes just "Live for the moment". We then have a special name for such; a lizard like living.

When anxiety increases many other disorders start to find a home in us. It can start with a loss of hunger, dehydration, skin rash, a drop in working, sensible and short-term memory, at a later stage could rise to dementia and a loss for words during a conversation. The other functions that one can notice are, that most conversations become superficial, our focus is only on the main theme of any document that we take to read, details are missed, and we cannot remember where we spent our money during a day's transaction. Sometimes we forget what we have said to someone or promised something. For students studying subjects that are new, that becomes difficult. They feel a greater need for help from their teachers which could be difficult too. Adults at work begin to worry about what will happen to their future if they lose their job on account of non-performance. That I think is an elaborate list of what can happen due to anxiety.

Relievers

The anxiety stricken could seek medical help at the earliest but shame puts the biggest barrier to most. Then there are fears attached to the after effects of drugs too. The last one is that when planet Mercury is weak or stressed in the natal chart there is a reluctance to consult someone or take advice. The subject is more interested in finding someone who would describe the situation as 'all is normal and there is nothing wrong at all'.

These people are not professionals by any measure but suppliers of false assurance to gain an advantage over the victim. The sad part is the victim welcomes it too.

If one wants to seek a solution without medical help then, improving nutrition taken in needs attention. I have gathered my information from the internet and I have inculcated new habits in myself after gaining knowledge. Our brain is controlled by gut bacteria. The gut bacteria need to flourish in the intestines. These need fibre from our diet to proliferate. Our diet nowadays consists mainly of processed foods, fruit juices with their skin removed, trans fatty acids, and other high calorie preparations. The gut bacteria suffer on account of this and their control over the brain also diminishes. It is important that we eat the rind or the zest that is covering the fruit although might not taste palatable. It is no use crushing a couple of fruits in a fruit processor along with the rind because these are cut to smithereens. These smithereens are not retained in a net like a layer that is inside the intestines and these passes away into the large intestine and passed away as faecal matter. It is better to consider a diet that has more fibre than mere taste engendering food.

The second solution is to stop sugar entirely. The fructose in the sugar is bad for us and not glucose. Glucose is useful and is used by all the cells in the body. Fructose is sweet and is digested only by animals and cannot be by humans. Fructose damages our cells and increases triglycerides in the blood. Even our liver has no alternative but to convert this into fat and store as visceral fat. All these add up to cause a poor metabolism in the body. Dr. David Perlmutter (the Brain Grain fame) and Dr. Robert Lustig have both in their numerous podcasts and books illustrated these for the easy understanding of a common man.

These facts are now made popular on YouTube. I request all of you to pay attention and spend some time on these.

The other alternative is to consume a teaspoonful of castor oil daily. One may start consuming just half a teaspoonful followed by a spoon of plain yogurt. One must make this a habit so that relief is sought from anxiety.

In Romantic Pursuits

These anxiety-stricken individuals eventually turn to their friends to tell their tales. The tale is usually about their inability to surmount problems at work or their relationships with spouses. In most cases, the friends are of no help except one or two pay a heeding ear for a while in the expectation that a new development of a short-term affair could happen. All this becomes natural because of a co-dependency shown by the anxiety stricken. It leads to infatuation soon and a clandestine affair actually happens. Most other friends do not pay attention as they could be fed up with a moaning planet Mercury. It is worth taking notice here that planet Mercury becomes responsible for a relationship to happen without any help from either planet Venus or Mars. Most astrologers miss this point altogether.

When planet Mercury is strong enough these situations do not arise. In fact, even with the help of the planets Mars and Venus it becomes difficult to develop a relationship. Planet Mercury must become involved fully and engage in conversation, rehearse before going to meet that someone after return finds some way to communicate again then the foundation laying may be assumed. With planet Mercury in close proximity to the Moon or planet Venus or if aspected then planet Mercury does not take too long. If planet Mercury is strongly placed or independently sitting in a house with an aspect from the outer planets then it is very difficult to start and maintain a relationship.

The Addict

Talking frequently, for as long as thirty minutes or more due to an anxiety condition slowly leads to addiction. The addiction is not felt for long until one day a doctor's diagnosis reports that. I shall digress a little here in order to explain the events that happen in our brains.

Dopamine is a neurohormone that is released by the hypothalamus. This acts as a smart control co-ordinating center. Its function is to keep the body in a stable state called homeostasis. Neurohormone means a hormone produced by neurons. This is carried out in a two-step process. First, the amino acid tyrosine is converted into another amino acid, called L-dopa. Then L-dopa undergoes another change, as enzymes turn it into dopamine.

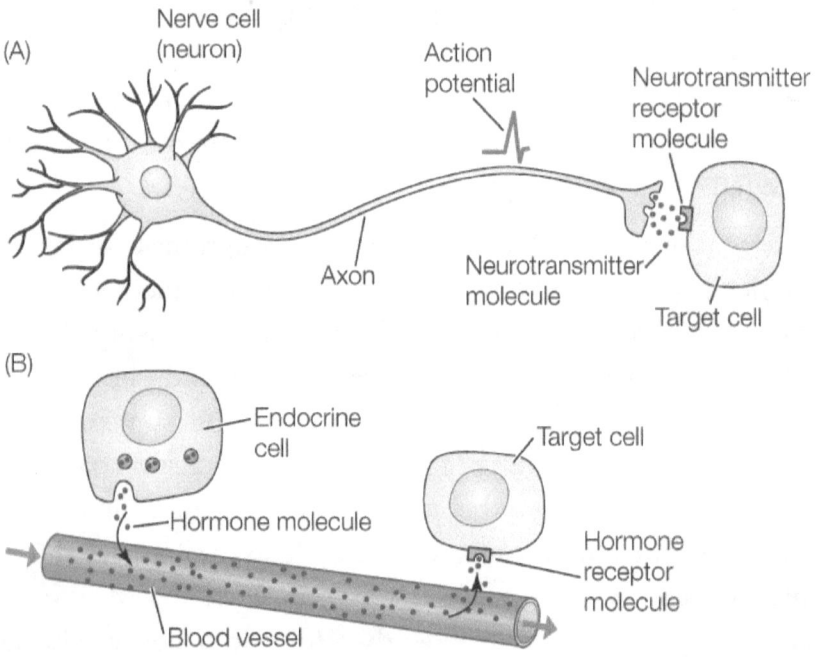

Neurons are transmitters in the brain that carry an electrical charge to transmit signals. Neurons in the region at the base of the brain (hypothalamus region) produce dopamine

Fundamentally, this hormone plays a role in motivating us to do many functions like learning and paying attention, controlling our mood, our physical motions like walking, running, playing any sport, and other internal involuntary body functions and sleep. (Although, sleep is more connected to the hormone called serotonin; a deficit of both dopamine and serotonin is linked to a condition called depression. In particular, people with depression often suffer from a lack of motivation and concentration. Lack of sleep affects these people directly).

Our feeling of pleasure then becomes a part of the brain's reward system. Activities like sex, shopping, seeking information, playing a sport, smelling anything sweet are all pleasure producers and this pleasure is short-lived; that is why we feel like repeating such activities. At times we get a "dopamine rush" too on seeing something, tasting something, watching a good comedy or television show and even if we happen to meet a person and talk to him for a while on most excitable issues. If there is a dearth of dopamine occurs, we feel a loss of mood or lack of enthusiasm.

This dopamine needs to act as a reinforcement substance once after a pleasure repeats itself a couple of times. The neurons that transmit dopamine to the reward centre of the brain downregulate (meaning are less sensitive to the usual dose of signals) themselves for their own survival. A higher electrical charge if conducted frequently damages these neurons. In order to feel pleasure again, a higher dose of any substance or activity is required to bring back our 'mood' or 'motivation'. In short, we need to increase our doses to get to the point of pleasure.

These higher doses increase the charge carried by the neurons and slowly damage them. Most brain disorders begin here. That repeat activity can be anything from alcoholism, drugs, playing cards, or any other habit-forming activity that may be increased as required to produce pleasure. Sex, seeking romance, talking frequently to a person to feel good or relieved, eating and other ADHD activities are some of the outlets we all find. These lead to addiction.

I Give Up

Highly stressed planet Mercury in a chart looks for outlets to seek relief from its inability to extricate itself from its involvements. Many times, the problems originate from within its position in a chart and sometimes due to planetary aspects that are transiting. I have written to great lengths about the retrograde planet Mercury in my first book titled 'Karma is hidden'. You may read that when you are ready for more. The planet Mercury during its retrograde is very weak to bear additional stresses. There is a tendency to give up on confidentiality. It finds comfort in betrayal. Either we turn into betrayers or become answerable due to others' betrayal. Need to watch out when aspected by the outer planets during planet Mercury's retrograde transit.

To know more about how the houses 3rd, 6th, 2nd, 7th, and the 1st suffer please read the chapter on 'The twelve Houses' along with their signs. Because these houses suffer, whenever planets Mercury, Venus and Mars become combust.

With the Good Sun

There are a number of ways that planet Mercury shakes hands with the Sun because it revolves very close to the Sun. if it ever goes even one sign ahead of the Sun it turns retrograde and reaches a point that is one sign behind the Sun's. It takes around twenty-six days usually. This shows that planet Mercury has just a few aspects to make with the Sun like, semi-sextile, semi-square, conjunction and becoming combust. Even with the planet Venus, except for the combust only the other three are possible.

Only in the case of planet Mercury, we may use these minor 'semi' aspects and these operate like reminders. Planet Mercury during its transit has governance over whatever we handle in our daily life. We use our thinking, communication skills, working skills, reading and writing skills, equipment handling skills, and even cooking, painting, etc. So long as planet Mercury is free of blemishes from other planets our daily chores also progress smoothly. This is one of the reasons we seek prior information from the weekly predictions given in periodicals. It is more of a confidence building act by keeping prior knowledge with us. That is not a bad idea at all.

The aspect semi-sextile with the Sun is to be seen as a miniature sextile aspect. If we have certain people to meet and negotiate terms then this helps. There are other possibilities like making a payment toward what has been purchased on credit, supplying or taking fresh orders, getting certain documents updated, sitting to take tests, etc. All of these have one thing in common. A date was set in advance and you were somehow reminded to seek a consultation or service from another. Always apply that.

The second is the semi-square. This creates a presentiment about a future event. You also know the difficulties that go with the event and become worried and start preparing a strategy. Mercury's affairs have to do with what one needs to do with others for closing a deal, closing a transaction, giving or taking promises, deciding on how to face a superior or a colleague, etc. So, think on these terms. The zodiacal sign during transit for planet Mercury will matter to a point. For example, if Mercury is transiting the sign Gemini (or the 3rd house), more time is wasted in talking than on the actual subject of business initially. When everything is clarified after some time, you realize that there is a need to re-do the job.

The conjunction is the most important and felt aspect of planet Mercury with the Sun. The effect starts at least 8^0 before the actual conjunction. This conjunction is called the 'combust'. All the personal planets like Mercury, Venus, and Mars become 'combust' during the conjunction aspect.

During this aspect the planets that become combust lose their power to the Sun. The Sun uses this power to its own benefit and seeks success. It has advantages and disadvantages too. The Sun, the sign Leo, and the 5th house, the planets within these houses, all benefit during a combust. Remember that this 'combust' aspect is applicable only during transits. If a transiting planet Mercury is conjunct over the natal Sun, it does not become combust. It benefits the Sun but it does not lose its power. A transit to any natal planet is like motivating the natal planet into an action. If the planet is too fast like how the personal planets are, too little can happen. If two transiting planets are acting together on any one of the natal personal planets, the Sun or the Moon there is a better chance of mooting a characteristic.

When planet Mercury becomes combust during its transit with a transiting Sun (otherwise it is never combust), its own houses 3rd and 6th houses, and the houses with the signs Gemini and Virgo lose their power. So, planets sitting in these houses of the natal chart become ineffective. You stop seeking benefit for that many days of 'combust'. The benefit of the planet Mercury goes to wherever the Sun is placed in the natal chart, the sign Leo and the planets therein, and the 5th house with the planets placed inside. The 5th house is an important house from a motivation point of view. We remain cheerful on such days when the 5th house is benefiting in some way. If the Sun receives aspects from planet Jupiter or any of the personal planets even then the 5th house gets the benefit. The 5th house becomes weak when the natal Sun or the transiting Sun receives an aspect from any of the outer planets, an aspect from a lunar eclipse or even if a new Moon or a full Moon makes a hard aspect to the Sun.

The 5th house stands for our good feelings toward everyone and our motives become more hopeful of good events coming our way. One may say that we all turn optimistic toward everything around us. That is the only danger when optimism enters into our nature; we begin to take risks. The 5th house stands to give us happiness from children, love affairs, education, getting trained to be educators, going on foreign trips, gambling, making purchases freely, etc. Most importantly, the activity that you have in mind excites you when you wake up in the morning on those days of an excited 5th house. Life seems to be revolving around you and you feel everything is working out for you.

The Sun has an interest in self usually. It means taking attention, admiration, appreciation, etc. on account of the dress worn, achievements, a promotion at work, the wealth generated, etc. When Mercury comes close to getting combust, the Sun finds more friends first. Later, the Sun starts to believe in its ability to talk, its bashfulness goes away, people identify its qualification, experience, an ability to analyze a situation, concentrating ability, etc. This excites the Sun further. The Sun develops a new quality in itself to tell lies to get more flattery. If any person has a combust planet Mercury in the natal chart, be assured that this person loves admiration for qualities that are not inherently present.

When the 3rd house and 6th house get weakened, the qualities of working hard toward a goal by convincing people with ideas, sincerity, and intelligence all diminish. 'Greed' also shown by the third house will be less. That is the only good loss. Otherwise, methodical work, attention to detail (6th house qualities), reservedness, attention to regular habits, and daily chores all suffer. In fact, on account of over exerting importance to the 5th house, indulgence could increase. Remember, Mercury is habit forming.

It is important to remember that a combust planet can only give so much depending on its strength in a particular house. For example, let us assume that planet Mercury is transiting and becomes combust in the 4th house and the sign is Sagittarius. In Sagittarius, planet Mercury is not as active as in Gemini (its own sign). So, we say it is in its fall. In Pisces, it is to its detriment. How much strength will the Sun gain? Planet Mercury may not be so agile in Sagittarius but is fond of subjects that are complex in nature. There could be some mystery attached to it. It enjoys finding ways where most people would not dare venture. Spelunking, archaeology, rock climbing, yachting, and equestrianism, are just a few to name. It is interested in learning as well as bringing the quality of a sport to its adventure. These the Sun assumes on itself to get some importance during a transit. If you find the aspect in a natal chart, then it will be always noticeable.

The 4th house properties are touched grazingly. One might expect the 4th house properties in the transiting Sun already because the Sun too is in the 4th house during combust. But changeability in the perception of the Sun happens depending on the houses that the Moon is passing through throughout this period. A similar situation needs to be expected if the Sun or any personal planet is passing through the sign Cancer. Every two and a quarter day the Moon will change its sign; so, will our state of mind.

With Warrior Mars……." Hey! Speed up".

When planet Mercury gets aspected by planet Mars, there is a special exchange that happens between the two planets. Planet Mercury becomes a sports commentator! Not an exaggeration by any means. Planet Mercury develops speed talking, speed reading, an athlete, and brilliancy in whatever planet Mercury is interested in. The drawback is that its expectation is the same from everyone else in response. It becomes too pushy and thinks that the people around are too lazy and tries to motivate and importune them frequently.

The other side is a disability to take defeat or a failure. This combination is a sure indicator for people who become depressed too soon, especially with a square or an opposition aspect. These people are so used to getting other's admiration that they start expecting success everywhere. The elders around too ignore to prepare them for such situations of crisis. This aspect has very impressive qualities to notice if seen in isolation. In a group of people, you will notice that there is someone who is in a hurry to finish something. If you notice them in an examination hall these are the ones who finish their paper at least thirty minutes before time. Have you noticed someone regularly at a library or during morning walks or jogs? Perhaps you have seen them with their sports kit rushing toward the nearest gymkhana.

I shall now produce three cases to notice these aspects that we have finished discussing. I have the confidence that you would have fully understood these at the end of this chapter regarding Mercury.

Case 1

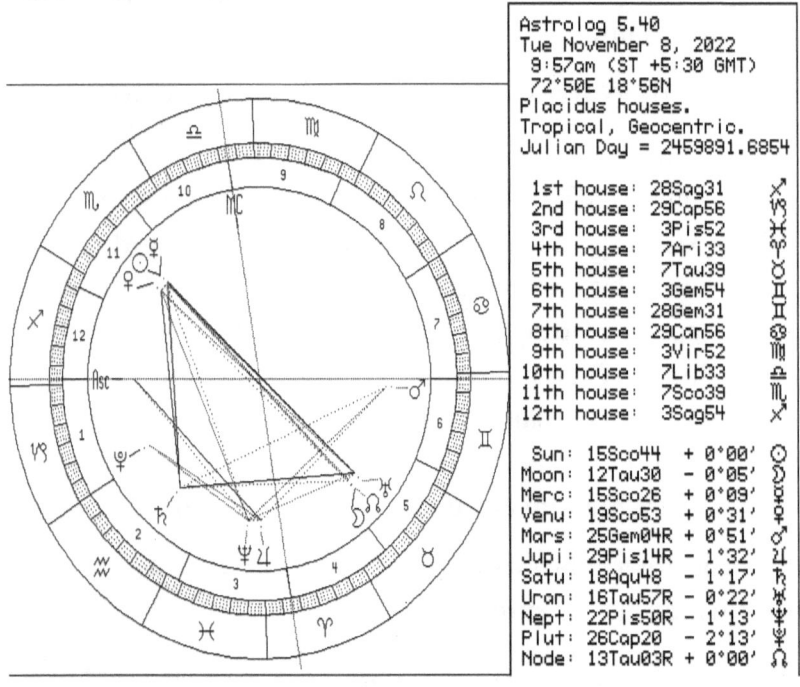

PLEASE NOTICE: Both planets Venus and Mercury are combust in the sign Scorpio, 11th house.

Venus is weak in Scorpio. The sign Scorpio stands to seek power everywhere. It is very conscious of how it can influence others. This influencing means by hook or crook one must be able to use the advantages that others possess. So, the Sun will inherit these qualities along with a strong will. Has tenacity and is ready to take the hardship to earn wealth. Very sensitive to situations and emotional too. It is ready to take responsibility at all times. It is possessive of its mate.

Planet Venus in this sign has more awareness about who is paying attention to it and with what in mind. Planet Venus wants to directly seek power through its attractive looks. It can dress, it can talk, it can perform and it can make sure the attention drawn is never lost. It believes that without power its appearance has no value. With regard to talents the signs Taurus and Libra, the 2nd and the 7th house are par excellence.

Planet Venus is also interested in gossip. But has few friends as it fears that its own secrets are such so, they better not become public knowledge. It has ideas so clever that no one around will even suspect what it is up to each day. Towards superior it shows absolute obedience. It will never allow any confidential matter to leak on account of its own folly. So, all these qualities will be passed to the Sun during the 'combust' period. Besides this, the regular qualities of planet Venus will also be passed on too like, looking for a companion everywhere, wearing dresses that are expensive, finding ways to earn wealth through one's ability, developing talents that will earn admiration from others, etc.

Since the sign Scorpio is bang opposite the sign Taurus the five senses are not fully developed to show good taste in selecting certain materials or items. There could be shabbiness present in the way the planet chooses to live can be noticed. The most feared thought for planet Venus is that societal 'taboos must not get it into trouble. That is why it takes a lot of care regarding secrecy, in the sign of Scorpio.

If the above chart is a natal chart, then these qualities will be permanently passed on to the Sun and due to that, the qualities become identifiable to others. The houses 2nd and 7th will be weaker along with the signs Taurus (5th house in the chart) and Libra (10th house). That makes the thought of 'self-worth', 'self-earned' income, and welfare of its family, a permanent concern. The 10th house with the sign Libra could make use of planet Venus's talents to the public and let it earn both money and admiration. The Sun in the 11th house brings a large network of friends and fans to this individual. This too is a motivating house. But the desire is toward others more than the self. The 5th house has all to do with one's own self. In the 11th there is a humanitarian concern. People with a strong 11th house will be seen more as politically motivated or simply as samaritans. So that is how one should do a preliminary analysis.

Planets if weak due to any reason, causes them to develop a special sense or an ability for survival. For example, the crippled learn to use the crutch, the deaf and the blind learn a new language for their own benefit, the person with a prosthetic arm or a leg has to learn adaptation, a person with an organ transplant has to take special care for survival. These planets too develop a new skill to face their environment.

A weak planet Mercury, works hard to study its environment for weaknesses outside of it so that it appears smarter in comparison and finds a way to survive. It learns those survival tricks quicker than those that are expected of it. A weak planet Venus understands the limitations of others (others of the same sex) by observing them closely and develops certain qualities that will outsmart all its competitors. I know a woman client who has planet Venus in the 12th house, in the sign of Virgo. She owns three tenements in a large city. Not bad at all. What she does not value is the primary purpose of the planet Venus. A weak Venus does not value togetherness or marriage for too long. It turns toward compassion and service to people. The companion or companion's choices become secondary. It continues to do whatever it wants diligently without much disappointment. A weak Mars becomes a trickster. The brutal strength, it realizes is of less use. It begins to win its battles with wiles.

The danger is in the aftermath. Once the planet Mars regains its strength, it continues to use this trickery forcefully and gets into trouble with the law. So, each time planet Mars, planet Venus, and planet Mercury go retrograde and turn direct, or an eclipse aspect and goes, or an outer planet aspect and moves away, and a New Moon or a Full Moon occurs quite close to these planets and proceed, we all would have improvised on our weaknesses because we would have gone through an exercise of survival.

I digressed a little because it was relevant here; let us look at combust Mercury in the sign Scorpio. Planet Mercury is not weak here. It is constantly cautioned by the sign Scorpio to be conscious of the power it holds. In the water signs, planet Mercury is never in a hurry to achieve anything. It is always circumspect, patient, and waits for its turn. It respects power only. If there is anything standing second, it is money. Besides these, the usual interests and activities of planet Mercury remain efficient. Care needs to be taken to see that planet Mercury is not stressed due to any other reason.

In the above horoscope, for example, assuming it will belong to someone, both planet Venus and planet Mercury have aspects that are quite stressful. Both Saturn and Uranus along with North Node and the Moon make a square aspect with both. Planet Neptune is in trine with both planets Mercury and

Venus. The outer planets along with North Node have the capacity to bulldoze the two planets. It is a Full Moon Day eclipse; a lunar eclipse under the North Node. The opposition aspect from the Moon to both Mercury and Venus including the Sun is quite strong.

The Full Moon gets everything it wants from other planets if it has aspects with them. The strain is on the planet. The Full Moon wants to end a past chapter always. That does not mean that it cannot give a benefit. The North Node could pass on a new opportunity that we desire unethically sometimes. Sometimes hard work to be put into some project or plan comes to an end and results show up. The South Node can close anything permanently when it causes a lunar eclipse.

In the chapter 'Sun, Moon and Eclipses' you will read a lot more and understand. Remember, the personal planets are life giving and life taking. If they are stressed too much then the person cannot survive for long. In the above case, even the Sun is stressed.

Returning back to our topic, the planet Mercury, in an as is where its condition passes its power to the Sun everything. The Sun becomes the sole owner of these two planets for a while. The Sun with its new abilities appears graceful due to planet Venus and appears very clever due to planet Mercury. A problem that you will also notice later on with planet Mercury is that when under duress (due to certain conditions as noticed above), the planet turns into a betrayer because of its inability to remain a confidante for someone. Sometimes friends are lost, enmity toward siblings develops, fraudulent acts take place, or mental depression can occur. The finer qualities of planet Mercury will be found missing if Mercury is weak. Only the most superficial or obvious qualities would be passed if 'combust' when weak.

It does not mean that if a planet is weak due to some reason means a failure. Please never give such life sentences to any of your clients. Discuss the likely weaknesses and then suggest. This will be of help.

Case 2

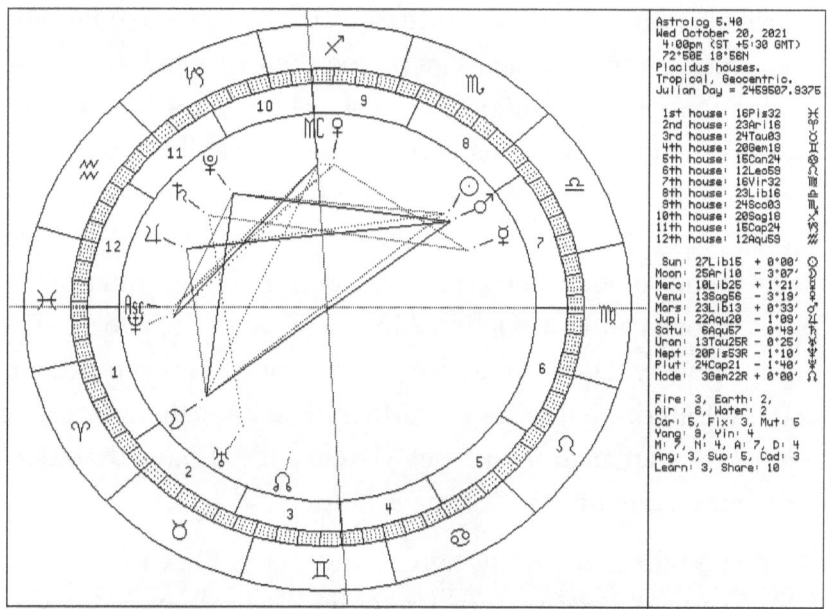

PLEASE NOTICE: Planet Mars is combust in the sign Libra. It is a Full Moon in Aries, 2nd house. Planet Pluto is square to both Sun and the Moon. Planet Jupiter is trine planet Mars and the Sun. the ascendant is the sign Pisces and its ruler planet Neptune is right on top of the ascendant. This is a very strong position. Planet Neptune squares planet Venus in Sagittarius.

Planet Mars is in the sign of Libra. It is a sign of its fall. If you take due care to notice, the planet Mars is on the cusp of the 8th house, but falls in the 7th house because it fell short by just

$0°2'$. When we are in such an indecisive state, it is better to ignore the previous house and take planet Mars as on the threshold of the 8th house. The Sun is definitely in the 8th house and all the qualities of planet Mars are bestowed on the Sun. The Sun will act with more courage. The Sun will absorb the qualities of a weak Mars. Remember a weak Mars is always crafty. What is important to understand here is that not all of us turn crafty whenever planet Mars turns retrograde during its transit every two years. If we are expected to achieve something even during a retrograde Mars period then we need to become 'crafty' than march straight to face a challenge to show we are brave. When planet Venus is retrograde our abilities to charm goes to seek a 'time out'. Start giving true value to what one is capable of or try to put some time into past failures. We might have failed in our performances, presentations, interviews, projects, or even in a relationship, all of those need to be dug out for review. During that pursuit, Mr. or Miss Serendipity is usually found. That takes us further once after the retrograde ends. It is similar to the planet Mercury too. I have described that in my earlier book, 'Karma is hidden'.

The Sun is naturally honest and never likes to put on a false façade of a crafty Mars. Under the circumstances, the sign Libra where the Sun is in detriment and planet Mars is in its fall comes to help. With a weak Sun, it is easier to accept the qualities of a weak Mars. A very noticeable feature here is that the Sun will ask for its usual attention, admiration, and importance from all as usual. Add to that the quality of courage on account of planet Mars. But people can tell this after noticing that the Sun is simply showing off false courage and shows conceit. That results in a lot of dissatisfaction.

I wanted to raise a situation deliberately so that you too would be helped in situations such as this one. The Sun in Libra cannot survive without seeking encouragement from others because it has low self-esteem (detriment). Under the circumstances, the Sun is burdened to carry poor self-esteem from the planet Mars too.

Please notice the other aspects and I shall explain those after you have read the relevant chapters in this book.

Case 3

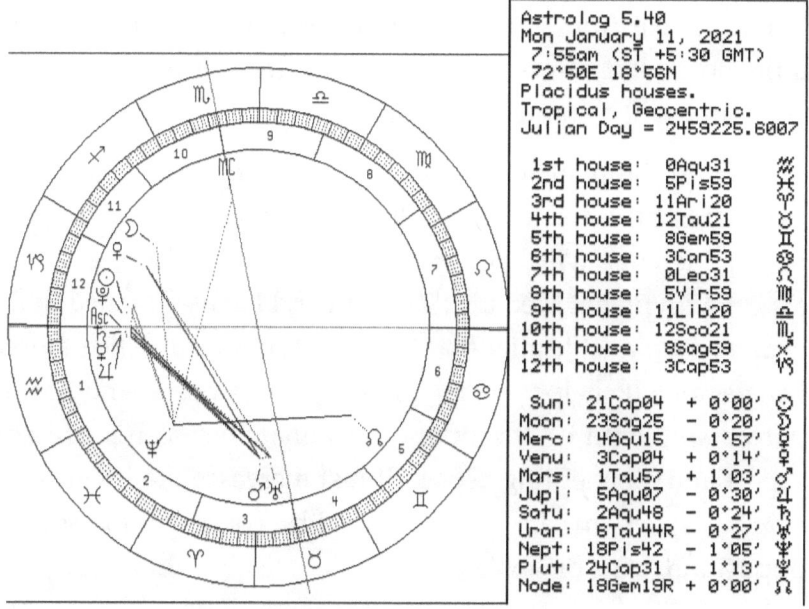

PLEASE NOTICE: Study the state of planet Mercury in the above chart.

Such instances do come from time to time. Even though these periods pass in about eight days, the planetary aspects cause enough permanent damage to planet Mercury.

i. The Sun is conjunct planet Pluto and sextiled by planet Neptune.

ii. Planet Mercury is conjunct planet Jupiter.

iii. Planet Mercury is squared by three planets Mars, Saturn, and Uranus.

The square (a 90^0 aspect) has an underlying compulsion attached to it, "I will and I must somehow". The desire is to achieve a task at all costs. The cost is in a currency called 'stress'. We usually suffer sleeplessness, loss of hunger, feel dehydrated, and a constant thumping of the heart is felt. In simple words, a doctor may say, "You are suffering from anxiety". The problem is not visible from the outside because our exterior appears quite normal! If someone observes our dress or our hair or our skin, they will comment on that.

Here the planet Mercury is stressed by two major outer planets; Saturn and Uranus. Planet Jupiter which is conjunct planet Mercury will help the two planets that have a square aspect with planet Mercury. Remember, I have explained in the chapter on planet Jupiter that this planet is an altruistic natured benefactor. It helps every planet that aspects another in partnership with it. It cannot discriminate between a stressful aspect and a benefiting aspect. It just increases the intensity of every aspect in its presence with conjunction, square, opposition, trine or sextile.

In the above case, planet Mercury is under stress but planet Jupiter does not save it from any distress. That means the square effect of the two planets; Saturn and Uranus increases by two or three times as much. Under such circumstances planet Mercury gives up its fortitude and sways with the prevailing conditions. It prefers to straggle off instead but never will it beseech for help. It intoxicates frequently through various means. Mercury's outlets are friends, self-medication, sleeping pills, and going on short trips somewhere in order to forget. It even spends on frivolous items to seek a temporary pleasure so that some solace is obtained. In some cases, prefers to talk to relieve anxiety.

In the case above, the conjunctions are happening in the 1st house of 'self', the squares have come from the 4th house of 'seeking unconditional love'. It becomes a matter of emotional loss that has caused planet Mercury to suffer. The presence of Saturn so close restricts planet Mercury to feel guilty in its dealings. The sign Aquarius is a relief because it is not such an emotionally excitable sign. Planet Saturn too encourages 'discarding' something that is not of much use. So, not much to regret here. The double disturbance from the 4th house is a tempest.

The aspects of the Sun are short-lived; one conjunct and one sextile from two different outer planets. Planet Neptune causes Sun to imagine different scenarios of crisis. Planet Pluto nudges the Sun to seek a 'lost' power as quickly as it can.

A last question about this chapter arises about 'Who will betray then?'

In any chart, think of the working houses first.

1st, 2nd, 3rd, 6th, 7th, 8th, 10th, and 11th are the working houses. If you want to assign the zodiacal signs to them, then Aries, all the earth signs, all the air signs, and only Scorpio from the water signs will work. Sign Scorpio is a power seeker or a money seeker. If these two advantages are not available then it will not work so hard to betray someone. Only sometimes, a 'revenge' might get motivated. Sign Leo is not too far off when it comes to avenging. If this sign does not fall in the list of houses that I have mentioned then it cannot betray.

The remaining signs and the houses do not betray anyone but will reflect or feel the hurt for long. They will always be the receivers of such 'stabbing'. But not to ignore the fact that they are the 'doers' of something very annoying; it is the secrecy that provokes others. Imagine if a person has a Scorpio ascendant, and the planet Mercury is stressed in the 4th house. What can happen? Will this person betray? Not unless there are enough ulterior motives. But will do it unabashedly. People with 'out of Bound' planets will do it even without much reason. One must be careful of these 'out of Bounds' persons. In general, during eclipse times, we must be careful of everyone; because we do not know if the eclipse is doing anything to their planet Mercury in the natal chart.

The chart laid out was for a day last year. If you want to know what must have happened to you on such a day, then simply transfer the planetary positions of that day to your natal chart and compare if any natal aspects also happened. That will further substantiate the results of what has been given above. The periodicals that give certain predictions use the method that I have just expounded.

I presume that explanation was good enough. We can go further and add a few more points about what could have happened as precedence. But we will leave that for the time being.

==

NB: https://www.heysigmund.com/subtle-signs-of-anxiety/

The link given above will lead you to an article that will elaborate on my point on anxiety even further. Perhaps not you but a friend might need some help. After all, what are friends for?

Chapter-VIII

(To his generals observing the English Channel)

Field Marshall Erwin Rommel: *"Just look at it, gentlemen. How calm and peaceful it is. A strip of water between England and the continent.... between the Allies and us. But beyond that peaceful horizon... a monster wait. A coiled spring of men, ships, and planes.... straining to be released against us. But gentlemen not a single Allied soldier shall reach the shore. Whenever and wherever this invasion may come, gentlemen... I shall destroy the enemy there, at the water's edge. Believe me, gentlemen, the first 24 hours of the invasion will be decisive. For the Allies as well as the German, it will be the longest day."* Werner Hinz; from the movie *"The Longest day"*.

Planets Jupiter and Mars

I have considered the two planets together because both of these planets have similar characteristics if observed closely. Planet Jupiter magnifies everything it influences or aspects. For example, if transiting planet Saturn has aspected a natal planet Venus in a chart and is in a square with it, planet Jupiter could be in any aspect with Venus, just a contact is sufficient, then whatever results the first square aspect is likely to produce (from Saturn in this case), that is increased by a couple of times. In place of Jupiter if planet Mars was present, it will accelerate a situation (two days before the exact aspect) and will also bring a dynamic quality to it (disturbance using talk, physically moving to another place by travel etc.).

A normal aspect between transiting Saturn square to the natal planet Venus will cause a test of strength in the relationships of planet Venus. It will be appraised for its use, its value, its sincerity and its likelihood of forming a stable relationship even in the future. There is plenty of stress, sadness, and anxiety around it. With planet Jupiter also aspecting planet Venus under the circumstances will increase the sadness and could spread to the household. People living with that person will also feel sadness. If planet Mars has an aspect with planet Venus (instead of Jupioter), there can be a little arguing, fighting for one's rights, or respect perhaps. A little depends on the signs from which aspects are happening. If planet Mars is aggressive in these signs, then definitely a fight will ensue. One has to analyze a chart beginning from the most serious aspect to the more frivolous side of the aspect. You must not start the assessment with the aspect of planet Mars or planet Jupiter. Both are 'effect' producers. The 'pain' of the aspect is from the planet Venus on account of Saturn.

As 'optimism' is Jupiter's greatest gift to all of us, let us study one by one each house and what we will be made aware of with optimism in mind. The following are the likely thoughts we get with optimism in mind during the transit of planet Jupiter.

1st House: Optimism regarding self. We will all feel that we shall be successful in any test, interview or any selection to be a team member in some capacity. That our health, personality is very good and we will appear impressive wherever we go. None of the above need is true. There is nothing wrong with being an optimist but the decision is taken by an outsider about us. Such optimism will not be of any use. Let us look at the 'self' again. This time let it be introspective. Assuming that we have been performing badly at school, at work or at any sport, we can resolve regarding an improvement in 'self' and start working towards it then that will turn out to be successful. Some need to go through surgery on their face, head, or some delicate part, and this optimism is required. At such times the optimism shown or assumed will help. Even if planet Jupiter is in sextile or trine or even a square or opposition or conjunction with the ascendant the optimism gained will help.

2nd House: We all have to assess our self-worth, self-earning capacity, our family welfare, our problems with the respiratory organs including the throat, and our talents if any from this house. Once again starting with whether we need to improve in our abilities to face up to any situation will bring about an improvement, improving conditions or careers of family members, etc., should become our concerns. If we show optimism in our plans to overcome our shortcomings in any way, that will work during the transit of Jupiter through this house. Usually, planet Jupiter leaves a 'gift' of some kind or gets some family member to seek a career or help to get them married. It is the self-confidence building house.

3rd House: In this house, the relations with siblings and neighbours improve. They will be seen as useful and dependents. The optimism shown toward one's ability to convince people, perform in front of people like on television or in front of a camera, improve voice, perform as a sales and marketing person must be backed by a special effort or training then it will work. The house also stands for educating the self in way of sports, competition, or anywhere one wants to appear superior in intelligence then showing optimism helps.

4th House: Remember, this house stands for seeking unconditional love from all. There are plenty to seek in the form of materials too, but these are for the home and its beautification. The entire activity is to build a secure home by conducting ceremonies, driving spirits away, holding important events like weddings, etc. The desire for money too is unconventional and that is by seeking gifts or bribes. Under these influences, you may decide in which way you would like to be optimistic! Again, what is in your ability you must strive to achieve? When you leave the rest on others it becomes 'optimism' then; but not without you putting in your first effort.

5th House: Here, it is like a playground and many activities are taking place. All motivate you. You want to participate in all of them. You don't mind learning some and teaching some. You enjoy taking a risk or two and see if your luck favours you. You also run into like-minded people who are searching for someone to be with them and give hope to achieve together. This is where romance begins. The children are everywhere, there is a readymade audience, readymade stage, and visions appear in which you see yourself as a hero. Please rewind, and do a retrospection if you have put in any work from your within into any of these activities. Only those get a good response. Be optimistic about it. One might want to turn into a fashion model suddenly. Why? It is so easy! Without thinking or even finding what it takes to be one if one delves, there are only new lessons coming your way at a cost of a price. Beware, planet Jupiter becomes a teacher here and we all end up becoming one in about thirteen months.

6th House: This house demands a lot from everyone to put certain efforts to bring about an improvement in the habits and chores. There is no dependency except for our friends a few unreliable ones too. Help is sought from law and order and the institutions of health. Staying optimistic will not harm in any way. Our efforts turning sedulous day by day become a cause for the decaying of our health. So, the attention goes into our habits and diet quite naturally. The optimism that we hold brings forth the kind of people we require to help us like they were God sent. It is a good transit to have to experience how to live well. In employment planet Jupiter brings more freedom. So, entrepreneurship is possible. Self-reliance stands next.

7th House: This house primarily represents our partners and friends who are both business associates and part of our life. Friends generated here are close friends and include spouses who also need to be treated as friends. The house has shades of Saturn to it and causes work situations to come naturally. Planet Jupiter brings a certain sense of freedom in order to expand our outlook and pay less attention to bonded living. Our optimism now needs more trust than usual because we are trying to achieve by remaining all alone. Help is scarce. Even the charms of planet Venus let us down. We need to be optimistic by all means.

8th House: I wanted to leave it completely blank under this heading. Scorpio and secrets! How can I reveal and betray? The trouble may arrive from Mr. Jupiter himself; you see! Then I decided that I must oblige. But you will not know all their secrets. It is the hardest thing to do. Even then one can remain positive if it comes to all the clean deals. If you hope and build secrecy around your activities then planet Jupiter will not allow that for too long. Jupiter here brings a number of hopefuls who have their own benefit in mind for investing their savings with you. On one hand, you might begin to think that life has turned around to help you in your business of investments and money lending. Even the stock market is lucrative with planet Jupiter here. But optimism must not go too far. Love affairs are sure to leak and there will be few alternatives afterward.

9th House: A place to go on an adventure, looking into a foreign culture, hobnobbing with people in high positions, even your boss will invite you for dinner with the hostess showing an extra interest in your care during the transit of planet Jupiter through this house. One might even think of making new deals with foreigners in order to benefit a business or simply learn about their culture. But risk and adventure get a different definition. Your optimism sees no bounds. Even students who want to seek higher education find their way easily. If you have court battles to fight, even these go well. The law and higher authorities become familiar with your work and shall not cause any problems. Does it mean you can lead a carefree life for thirteen months? If you have created wealth in some manner, you may live off it. This house cannot bring much earnings to reach home. That is why your optimism will help and nothing else.

10th House: The house of work and showing off lets you think all is well at the workplace. This is a house of Saturn and anything offered to you will look lucrative only on paper. The moment you decide on committing yourself that optimism will end. From that day on you will be optimistic about everything else other than your commitment to the offer you saw on paper. Jupiter will show you a number of solutions to the problems you face but that is just a small part. Your comforts will be taken care of but your job will leave a sore leg.

11th House: You will be optimistic about your plans for the community, political party, friends' network, plans made for research, any designs made, any paintings made, etc. and all get a nod from approvers and you make big progress. Your optimism about success on a future date will bring good results. Please do not forget about the work to put in. this is a lazy house. Planet Jupiter will make you lazier. Work put in here yields money from the 2nd house. Otherwise, this house can only yield the result of hard work put in from the previous 10th house.

12th House: You are now into space; just empty space. How will optimism help you? Perhaps expecting that you will run into an alien! Only an alien who is much superior to you could show you the way out of that empty space. After all the word 'optimism' relies on an expectation of getting help even when efforts were not put in. The meaning of the word changes in this house to 'trust' and not 'being helped'. It is important for all of us to believe there is a supernatural force that is looking after us irrespective of whether we pray, think about it, or show gratitude. It is best to see what comes our way in its purest form and beckons our acceptance. While planet Jupiter transits this house we are confronted with abstract ideas, philosophies, occult, research into subjects that are simply not understood easily, travelling to far-away lands in search of or solving mysteries, etc. and we get lost in those. We in fact enjoy this more than simply getting intoxicated with alcohol. By the way, Mr. Alcohol and Mr. Drugs also visit us during this period. Please say, "Thanks, but no, thanks!" The best thing that happens is that we learn to relax and even our friends take us with them to places where we enjoy relaxing. There is no material gain here during this period. But planet Jupiter prepares you for that 'Day after Tomorrow'. On that day, it is possible that Jupiter would have moved on to your 1st house again. You could be busy packing your bags. In one of your pockets, you will find this paper; a letter that you forgot to post on arrival. You open and see and read it all. You had reminisced so much about your life and then you had written, "I just want peace and nothing else"! You pick up your phone and write off a quick message, "Shall be seeing you tomorrow, Bye" and shut your bag and leave your room.

Planet Mars is known so much for the drive, passion, conflict, and discipline that plays a variety of roles while transiting through various houses. The qualities are conspicuous if seen in a natal chart but nevertheless, you will certainly glimpse the crack. I want you to read about that too.

1st House: Planet Mars is now in its own home. That does not mean it will misbehave. This is the house or the 10th we all want to wear some kind of uniform and feel patriotic. If not, we will be found fighting for some dogma or a self-righteous thought that we want everyone to follow. Perhaps that is the reason why we have been ostracized from our community. If planet Mars is found in the 1st house, unless weakened due to the signs like Cancer or Libra, causes us individuals to stand out like a 'Maverick'. It wants to protect all but the ways chosen are inadmissible to the people. Its bravery brings trouble and it faces the situation to be deported to some other planet. It is childlike, playful, could have some cut marks on its head or its face but all in good spirit. This planet will never snitch against anyone if found in the 1st or the 10th house. It suffers alone, and that suffering is understood by all of us years later. That is followed by a lot of crying and sobbing afterward. We realise that we could not accommodate a person so serviceable to us but went away ignoring it searching for our own way. That is the level of generosity shown by planet Mars in the 1st house. It is born to help and protect. In this house, it obeys superiors but might do a little bit of its own quietly. It will come back with humour and the friends love it. It's efficient, clever, and strong in this house. While transiting its attention could be more on self-improvement but that is for just those forty-odd days. Did you dislike planet Mars? I wish all my friends had planet Mars in the 1st house of their natal chart. It has a tendency to take burden, blame, and responsibility and lead the way. No wonder planet Mars owns a house where the Sun seeks maximum pleasure. Planet Saturn accommodates planet Mars as its special guest in the sign Capricorn or the 10th house.

2nd house: Our speech quality **is seen** through this house. With planet Mars here it appears like a one-way street. First comes a mild suggestion and later followed by a rapid fire of expletives for not obeying the orders. The children and other family members are quite used to this type of insensitive behaviour from planet Mars. They all have that 'special potion' that Mr. Invisible man used. They just vanish and return when they hear guffaws from the kitchen. It is the father cooking today they will shout and give him help in every possible way. That yesterday's episode has been long forgotten. It is important to know that planets absorb the qualities of the sign they are transiting through. In the natal chart, the planets must be at least 5^0 into the sign otherwise, they would not be able to show so much. The same thing happens toward the end of the house. The quality of the house and sometimes the quality of the sign too begin to diminish. In the 2nd house planet Mars loves to work like a bull in the house, has talents of planet Venus inculcated in it, and it turns into a gourmet chef. If planet Mars has aspects from Venus, the talents are shown ardently. The self-worth comes from many sources here. Planet Mars proves its worth through a good earning capacity and a strong libido. In order to look good, planet Mars could become a gym-freak, reinforce with different protein powders, and will experiment with every herbal drug to improve its manhood. Isn't that fascinating? Planet Mars is good at sports too. But stay away when it is about to lose its temper. You would go deaf in a few minutes!

3rd House: Ever seen in your neighbourhood a guy or a woman talking to most people and always having an urge to say something? Did you ever take a chance talking to him or her anytime? You will realize they are into neighbourhood cleaning. They have suggestions or possible solutions to any problem put across to them. Their planet Mars is into cleaning the neighbourhood this time through their 3rd house. They take an opportunity on all national days to either attend or throw a public speech and put across some very valid suggestions and muster support from all for their upcoming campaign. Then suddenly you might even see them on television interviewing a politician or reading the news. Then they would be away for a couple of days and your eyes could be searching for them during your morning or evening walks. After a few days, you begin to miss them too. Then you get to know from someone that they have gone to help their siblings as they had their house broken due to bad weather. Planet Mars if found in the sales and marketing career then they are the most aggressive. That doesn't mean they shout and scream to get a "Yes, Ok sir, we agree to the terms" from customers. The variety thrown in, the information provided, offers made, and even facilitating a credit is such the customer would rather prefer to die than refuse this planet Mars of the 3rd house. Planet Mars learned all that from planet Mercury here. The clever trickster? No, the witty entertainer of the sign Gemini. The price Mr. Mars paid to Mr. Mercury in exchange was a promise that he shall not pick up a fight with anyone but on a sports field while playing football.

4th House: It is unfortunate that the Christmas tree which had been so painstakingly decorated had very few gifts left in the precinct. It was just that the overtures of generosity shown to all friends, extended families, and children were forgotten. The few that came remembered this planet Mars and were grateful. Such becomes the state of planet Mars towards the end that all its life went in search of 'unconditional love' and went on offering generous gifts to win friends and relatives. What was the mistake? The trade perhaps. When Mars is helpless in signs Cancer and Libra or the 4th or the 7th house, it turns into a trader very efficiently. Here the fight does not come into the picture. It becomes cleverness and looking to the needs of the people to win them through an offer of help. Planet Mars is certainly deprived of its share of love from its parents, especially the mother. Due to that, it tries to get a little from everyone. In return, it does give away many gifts and favours but it is a short-lived memory that everyone suffers from. Planet Mars is still courageous in these four houses of weaknesses, what it does not get to achieve is a platform that stands solid underneath. In water signs planet Mars is contemplative. It is like seeing the leadership spread out over a large territory. It is quite a similar story in the other two water signs too. Planet Mars takes satisfaction that it managed to shower affection on all and helped them grow. The children remain grateful forever. From its parents, this planet Mars separates very early in search of new pastures. The home is not such a happy place for this position. Yet when it moves into its own house, it loves to work from home, deal in real estate, or work from a shop, and because of its large circle of friends it manages some business.

5th House: Planet Mars adapts to the nature of the Sun in this house. A desire to prove to the world its unique quality is very high and is achieved through being well dressed, showing good manners, and seeking ambitious people as friends. If the Sun has an ambition it works at it in its own unique way. But planet Mars uses everything at its disposal to achieve. The danger is in its risk-taking tendency. Be it on a stage as an actor or cinema, sports, entertainment, or as a teacher of risky sports or adventures. It must remain active as much as possible. Even if it is mentally sharp here it cannot accept the idea of relaxation.

That is one danger to develop mental anxiety. The overactive 5th house or highly dominating planets present here like the outer planets are unhealthy. The tendency to gamble is also high. One of the sports enjoyed is playing cards.

6th House: The Virgo house is a sculptor, surgeon, goldsmith, painter, or lawyer's domain. Planet Mars here can painstakingly operate on a patient, or finish any job with precision. It has an interest in language learning and vocabulary building; be it in any language. Many are writers. Although the 3rd house also produces writers, the 6th house produces writers with a large vocabulary. The work is usually well acclaimed and is nominated for Pulitzer or the Nobel prize for literature. Planet Mars should not be weak here; the only condition. Like the Taurus Mars, here too planet Mars is regular with house chores and other health-improving habits. It keeps itself busy planning, thinking, and executing. Likes to make new friends, likes to chat if time permitting, and keeps the house spick and span.

7th House: This house primarily represents our partners and friends who are both business associates and part of our life. Friends generated here are close friends and include spouses who also need to be treated as friends. The house has shades of Saturn to it and causes work situations to come naturally. Planet Jupiter brings a certain sense of freedom in order to expand our outlook and pay less attention to bonded living. Our optimism now needs more trust than usual because we are trying to achieve by remaining all alone. Help is scarce. Even the charms of planet Venus let us down. We need to be optimistic by all means. Being in its fall, planet Mars is clingy toward the partner and then as the relationship turns a little sour start to show indifference. It is struggling to maintain a balance here throughout its life. Planet Mars is thrifty here.

Even on profession planet Mars is cooperative with colleagues and tries to cheer up everyone if there is a conflict. Planet Mars here has a fault-finding habit. It thinks it is cleaning up the mess in everyone's life. But it cannot understand the difference between interfering and counselling. So, we leave that to planet Mars to sort out.

8th House: The eighth house causes disturbance to planet Mars because it cannot adapt to a new role that is so opposite to its own nature. Planet Mars cannot become a secret operator or a conspirator. It is always open, honest and has only the intent of winning every battle. The sign Scorpio has a need to survive at all costs. It does not believe in openly challenging someone for a battle. It believes in ambush. Many astrologers attribute planet Mars to be a ruling planet for the sign Scorpio alongside planet Pluto. The qualities shown by Pluto are far too different compared to the planet Mars. In this house, planet Mars learns other skills besides street fighting ones. There is an interest in horror stories and mystery novels. Planet Mars can learn the art of making guns and other ammunition. It could also deal in arms. Since the house stands for passive income, commissions, etc., it benefits through investment deals.

9th House: Planet Mars has an interest in foreign cultures and is hungry to know all about many foreign countries. Both in the 3rd and the 9th planets Mars travels with passion. It does not like to be a traveler in luxury yachts. If it really likes it will take a boat and do it all alone. It is very much into adventure sports, rock climbing, mountaineering, etc. Horse riding too interests planet Mars. Besides these, archery, rifle shooting, and physically rough sports are its favourites. Karate and Judo are their hobbies. If it takes higher studies anywhere then it will be in a subject that is generally not studied because of its complexity. Bravery remains the unique quality of planet Mars in this house. Unfortunately, planet Mars suffers in the hands of its spouse. Planet Mars lacks feelings that are required for intimacy. Most men and women prefer activities that are independent of each other. The children benefit a lot. So, extramarital affairs are common.

10th House: Sometimes the strictest teacher happens to like us despite not doing the homework properly, despite our school uniforms looking unkempt, despite we getting caught too talking in class, despite we skiving school to play a game against the neighbouring school's team. Any reason for that? Perhaps the teacher has memories of your performance when the school had visitors like the school inspector! Could it be that your field sports performance impressed everyone? It is possible that the teacher met your parents during the last three months or so and was very impressed by your father's position in his Company. See the effect of a lasting impression that is so unpredictable. Planet Mars makes you feel like that in the 10th house; owned by none other than planet Saturn. The 10th house could have a ruling planet depending on the sign it carries in your natal chart. But the natural ruler is planet Saturn.

Planet Saturn is a materialistic person and loves societal status. It can forgive every blunder, sin, anarchy, misbehavior or you may add a few more so long as your ultimate goal is to produce money and not waste it away. It punishes everyone the moment people turn sentimental. The punishments are severe. It brings despair and despondency. Thereby we try to get ourselves together and redeem ourselves. Planet Mars has been through all that. In the 10th house, it is ready to serve everyone (Saturn's interest is serving and being of service). Diligence may be learned from planet Mars here. There is a small problem. Planet Mars expects the same from others and causes harm to itself. The 10th house Mars cannot reach the position of authority. Even if it reaches it cannot stay there for long. It's that traffic policeman you get caught by frequently. You can't bribe him and he won't forgive and let you go. You wish he is transferred from there soon. No one really likes a 10th house planet Mars.

11th House: Planet Mars in the sign Aquarius or any of the air signs turns into a talkative, disseminating knowledge, training, teaching, and reforming a community kind of a person. It is just that in the sign Libra, it turns into a free advisor to all. In the sign Gemini it wants to tell everyone the books it read or the books it wants to write. Even in the 9th, it is fond of publishing books about history, ancient excavations, archaeology, etc. In the 11th house (same as in sign Aquarius), it has great hopes and wishes to improve the community, country, any of the departments in the government that has a primary job of rebuilding or restructuring, etc. this Mars is very good when it has authority and power. Until then it is mostly giving speeches and building hopes. That does not make matters easy. It collects a large clique of friends. Very few would be close ones there. But its satisfaction comes from building that number. It is that number that gives its hopes and wishes a lifeline. Have you seen anyone volunteering to do any work in their spare time? Ask them what do they gain from it? They will most likely tell you a lie. They carry planet Mars in their 11th house and soon they want to be a candidate in the Municipal election.

12th House: Have you heard the story of the renegade? That renegade lived in disguise in a mountain cave not too far from a city. He was quite scared of the government. But because he was in the Military, he had skills that were quite useful to the community and other traders in the city. He would never take initiative or leadership in doing any job. He did not mind working from behind the scenes. He could teach a trick or two to the needy, but his lifestyle was that of a parasite. Planet Mars is as useful as he has been everywhere in a chart. But here it loves a hideout to operate. Is Mars scared then? It is scared of the law for that one blunder it did. It now fears prison but does not mind living in a prison of its own. Planet Mars is weak in the sign Pisces and 12th house. Because the 12th house is 12th from the 1st house. So, Pisces becomes the 12th house from Aries. All planets suffer like that. They give up their fundamental characteristic and survive. The weak planet Mars becomes 'crafty' or simply put a 'crook'. It loves to operate at night or anywhere dark. It finds itself very comfortable there. It will work at its best in such environments. Are you thinking just the same as I am? Planet Mars 'the spy'! Probably true. It could be a medicine man who has tried a number of herbal medicines and now he has discovered a solution for cancer patients. There are a number of such possibilities. It manages to build trust in everyone first and then embarks on its own private venture. No one ever suspects. Haven't you heard of extramarital affairs that go on for years but do not break their marriage? Next time try your best to get access to such a person's horoscope.

Now tell me the answer to the question. What will happen if planet Mars is in the 11th house, with the sign Pisces there?

Planet Mars will can play a dissembler, as a sympathizer, community service worker, a samaritan, a hospital nurse, a doctor who works for charity, a philanthropist and you name it and it is working. . But it is in fact 'the devil incarnate' in its little private life. Public attention is never likely to notice or even believe if told about it. Do you like a 12th house Mars in your chart? Please let me know, I have some work for you!

Chapter-IX

"There is a way out of every box, a solution to every puzzle; it's just a matter of finding it."-Captain Jean-Luc Picard, from the "Star trek".

The Two Systems

The Precession of Planet Earth on the Ecliptic

The topic that we are going to discuss and learn about an astronomical phenomenon like a few we have already learned. These phenomena may be understood and astrology may be allowed to progress with a new perspective. That there exist two schools of thought on the subject of astrology is what it leads to. The first phenomenon that needs to be understood is the precession of the planet earth while orbiting on the ecliptic. Let us again recollect from our memory certain terminology so that we can negotiate our way through the space and identify any changes that we notice.

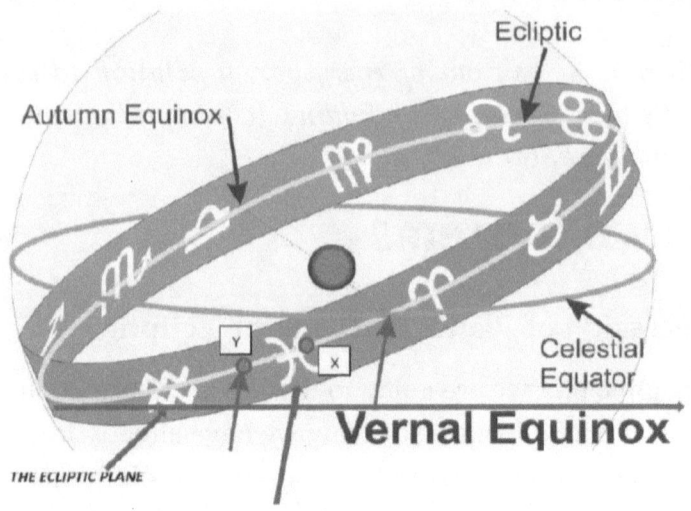

THE ECLIPTIC AND THE ZODIACAL BELT AS SEEN ON THE CELESTIAL SPHERE.

THE VERNAL EQUINOX IS ALSO SHOWN. WHEN THE CELESTIAL ECLIPTIC CUTS THE CELESTIAL EQUATOR THAT POINT IS VERNAL EQUINOX. ITS OPPOSITE POINT IS CALLED THE AUTUMNAL EQUINOX. MARCH 21ST IS TAKEN TO BE THE DAY THE SUN ENTERS THE SIGN ARIES. IT IS ALSO THE SAME DAY ON WHICH THE EARTH CROSSES THE CELESTIAL EQUATOR. IT IS JUST A FRAME OF REFERENCE THAT MATTERS. IN THE SKETCH ABOVE, THE SUN IS AT THE CENTRE AND THE EARTH IS ORBITING ALONG THE ECLIPTIC. DUE TO PREESSION, THE VERNAL EQUINOX IS 23°47' INTO THE SIGN OF PISCES. POINT 'X' IN THE SKETCH ABOVE SHOWS WHERE IT IS TODAY. IN THE FUTURE IT WILL BE AT POINT 'Y'.

The tropical system does not consider the precession. But that is not by any means a reason to say that, 'it is wrong or incorrect' in any way.

Our planet besides its two motions of rotation about its axis and revolution around the Sun along its ecliptic wobbles too as shown below, in an undulating fashion. This wave-like motion can be delineated on a circular path, traced by the earth's tilted axis, above the poles. The sketch below is as viewed above the North Pole of the earth.

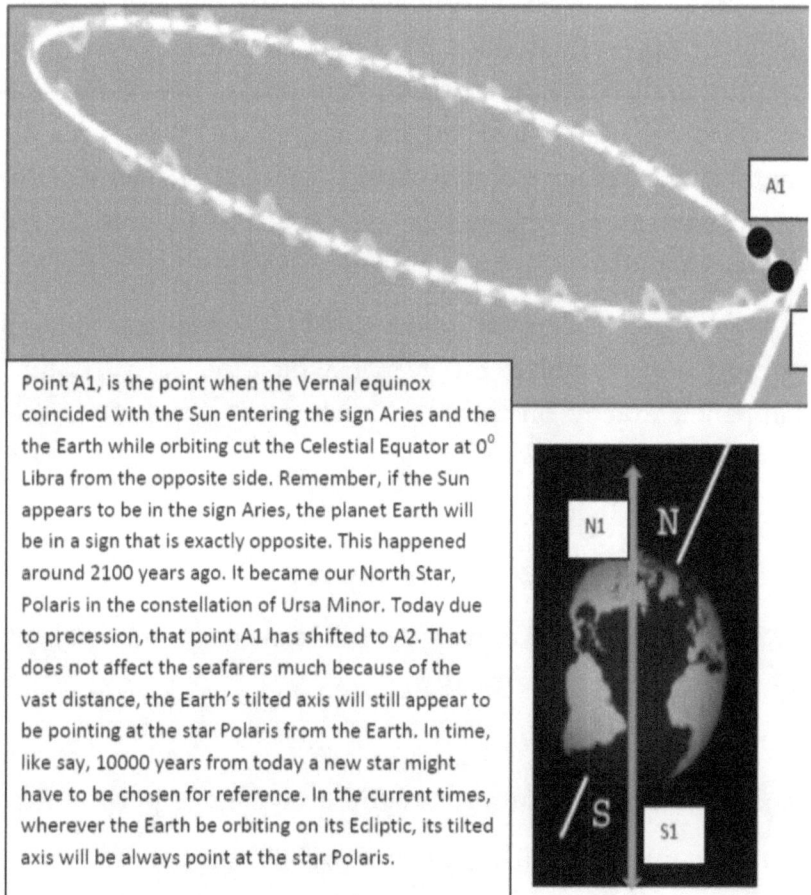

Point A1, is the point when the Vernal equinox coincided with the Sun entering the sign Aries and the the Earth while orbiting cut the Celestial Equator at $0°$ Libra from the opposite side. Remember, if the Sun appears to be in the sign Aries, the planet Earth will be in a sign that is exactly opposite. This happened around 2100 years ago. It became our North Star, Polaris in the constellation of Ursa Minor. Today due to precession, that point A1 has shifted to A2. That does not affect the seafarers much because of the vast distance, the Earth's tilted axis will still appear to be pointing at the star Polaris from the Earth. In time, like say, 10000 years from today a new star might have to be chosen for reference. In the current times, wherever the Earth be orbiting on its Ecliptic, its tilted axis will be always point at the star Polaris.

The Earth's shape is considered to be that of an Ellipsoid. The Earth is wider than it is tall. It bulges at the equator. It is flattened at the poles. These factors permit other bodies like the Sun and the Moon to cause a differential around the earth with their gravitational pull. That causes wobble.

The wobbling causes the Earth to reach its point of start, somewhere in the sign Pisces, around the dates April 14th or 15th of each year, late by 50.29 seconds. That is why in the last 2100 years the Earth has managed to go back by $23°47'$ on the ecliptic. Today, the Vernal Equinox is not at $0°$ Aries but at $23°47'$ in the sign of Pisces. This is real; as one will see any event or as planets and stars appear in the sky. It is called the Sidereal system. It is another branch of astrology that relies on 'as is where is' kind of astrology. Isn't that interesting? Please remember this method of astrology has a lot of calculations to deal with. It does not consider only the nature displayed by planets. It goes deeper than that.

The precession of the Earth by 50.3 seconds annually permits us to calculate the year in which the Vernal Equinox happened exactly on the 21st March, at 0^0 Aries. Today, the precession angle is $23^047'$.

Let us calculate.

The precession is by 50.3 secs every year.

50.3 secs means 0.838 mins. (50.3÷60 converts to minutes).

47 mins will take 47 ÷ 0.838 = 56.09 years or 56 years and 10 months and 24 days……………………………..1

0.838 minutes per year means 0.838 ÷ 60 degrees per year.

For 23^0 it takes, 23 ÷ 0.014 years = 1642.85 years or

1642 years 10 months and 6 days………………..2

Adding 1 and 2 we get 1713 years and 9 months.

Subtracting this number from 2022 years and 5 months, we reach the year 308 AD September. This is still an approximate calculation to arrive at a figure because we have not gone into very accurate figures. The idea was to show you a method to calculate a year when the Vernal Equinox was exactly whatever it was known to be.

The difference in the two systems; the sidereal and the tropical

It takes 72 years to the Vernal Equinox to regress by 1^0. That difference is too small to be noticed. One will realize a difference after at least 5^0 of regression. The Vedic or the Sidereal system always followed an equal house system. Perhaps this was alright then because most of the Vedic system followers were settled in the tropics or near about. Only in the last fifty years or so, the Vedic followers also have changed a little and they construct the horoscope according to the latitude of the birth place or follow the Placidus system of constructing the horoscope. The Vedic system or the sidereal system has other 'complex' methods to make matters simpler for the assessment of the horoscope. Those interested might try and see whether they can handle that but what I felt is that there are very few who can confidently claim that they can manage a correct horoscope analysis. Many become experts in different aspects of 'life' as a whole. Someone could be very good at predicting earnings, someone could be at predicting marriages and it goes on.

The tropical Astrologers differ to consider the precession. To them, the outer structure and the paraphernalia remain unchanged. It is quite possible that the planet Earth is suffering a delay in completing its revolution around the Sun on account of the wobble. This factor is ignored and the rest is considered as it is. In doing so, the planets of the tropical system appear ahead of the planets in the sidereal system. The difference in the angle for all planets and the nodes is a constant of the angle of precession for that moment. It is easy to convert a horoscope from the sidereal or the Vedic system to a tropical system by adding the angle of precession to every measure. Just add the precession angle for the day to all the planetary angles and the angles given for each house of the horoscope prepared using the sidereal system. Your tropical horoscope is ready. There are free software available on the net to prepare a tropical or Western method of making a horoscope. I use, 'astrolog 5.4' for making the horoscopes and this may be downloaded from the net.

The tropical system attributes certain qualities to the planets, the nodes, and the sensitive points. This is used in the analysis of the horoscope. This cannot be used in the sidereal system. The astrologers who use it will be wrong because the planets have been taken to be trailing the planets as considered in the tropical system. Whatever is calculated using other methods to arrive at some conclusion could be correct. But to use the qualities or characteristics of the planets that have also been attributed with houses or the zodiacal signs (in the background) in mind would cause an error. So please do not get prejudiced when you read somewhere that is stating something contradictory.

I guess that you have understood why there is a difference between two systems.

Chapter-X

Twins: Two to kiss and two to hug, and two to love.

The Nodes
Part Two

The Nodes are imaginary points caused by the Moon's orbit around the Earth. This orbit of the Moon, the so called 'path' traced is at an angle of 5^0 to the Ecliptic which is the 'path' traced by the planet Earth around the Sun. The Moon is orbiting around the Earth and the Earth is orbiting around the Sun. Both the Earth and the Moon have different speeds to do this. The Moon takes around 27.3 days to complete one revolution around the Earth and the Earth takes 365.25 days to complete one revolution around the Sun. if all was well organized, like there are 360^0 in a circle, and if the Earth moves 1^0 a day on this circle while revolving around the Sun, the Earth would have come to the same point at the end of where it started the previous year. Of course, the year would have been of just 360 days. It was found and proven by astronomers who by using the frame of reference of the stars that lie further to the Sun, that this phenomenon is not true. They proved that the Earth takes longer and the path taken was assumed as an ellipse instead of a circle and all facts fell into their proper place.

Even then there was an error creeping now and then. The calculation had something missing, what is called 'precession'. The planet Earth was taking 50.3 secs extra each year as if it was getting late due to 'traffic' on its way! The reason was attributed to a phenomenon called 'wobbling' due to which the Earth was losing its speed, although diminutive to think even. But that set things right. Today, we firmly believe that the first point of

Aries, when the Earth crosses the plane of the Ecliptic (or cuts the Celestial Equator) creating an imaginary point called the Vernal Equinox, has moved into the sign of Pisces by as much as $23^0 47'$. That makes the period of daylight and night equal on a different day. Some 23 days after the usual date of March 21st. Today it is around April 14th or the 15th. This fact is considered 'ipso facto' and 'ad verbatim' by the followers of the Vedic or the Sidereal system of astrology. That does not mean the tropical or the Western method followed by some is wrong. The rules to be applied are entirely made of different precepts. The methods adopted by the tropical way if tried upon in the Vedic way one become wrong. Both the methods have the capacity to reveal and predict events depending on how far a person has devoted to studying any system. Their usage is dependent on what one was exposed to from the very beginning due to which an expertise was developed. It is just like every medical doctor has some very good fundamental knowledge about health and uses that while curing someone. But there are times when expert knowledge is required and a specialist is referred to. In the same way, astrologers must not attempt to play too much in the 'unknown' but stop where their knowledge does not permit them to solve a situation.

Having understood the situation mentioned above let us get back to how Nodes are formed. There are 360^0 in a circle, if the Moon has to cover the twelve zodiacal signs in one month while it is in an orbit around the Earth, then after every 2.5 days, it would have covered the 30^0 allocated to each sign and return to the same point 'A' after transiting through all the twelve signs, as shown in the sketch below.

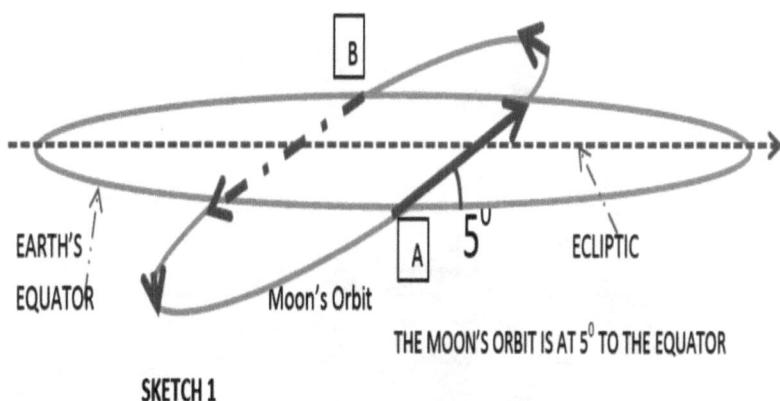

THE MOON'S ORBIT IS AT 5⁰ TO THE EQUATOR

SKETCH 1

The reality is different. The Moon moves about 12^0 to 14^0 per day (longitudinal measure), in a sign, throughout a month. Even if we take an average of 13^0 per day as the Moon's speed, the Moon will require less than 30 days to complete a single revolution around the Earth. At the end of 27.3 days, after the Moon has crossed the point of cutting the line of the Equator, the Moon will arrive earlier when this point 'A' is to its right as shown below. If the Moon had taken exactly 30 days to complete one revolution around the Earth, it would have crossed the point 'A' again. Point 'A' is on the Ecliptic; although in the picture it appears to be on the Equator.

The gap between is shown to be a large one for convenience and understanding purpose only. The difference between the points 'A' and 'C' is around $1^0 25'$ usually.

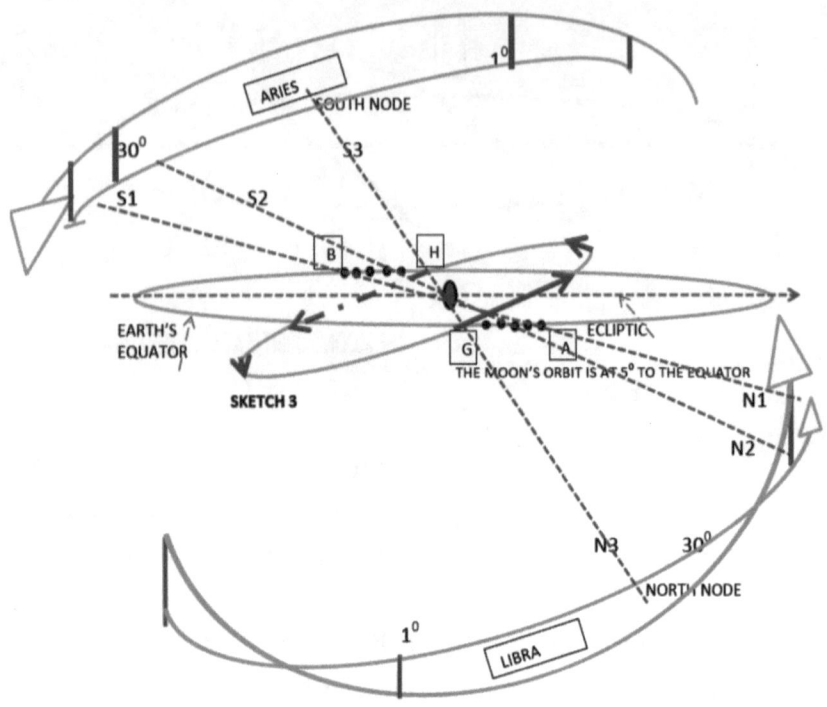

In the above sketch, the point 'A' has further moved to the right and new points are being formed as the Moon crosses the Ecliptic each month. These new points are all moving to the left. For reference, I have shown the two zodiacal signs and drawn a line joining the two points formed by the Moon on opposite ends; once while going from the southern side to the northern and the second point, starting from point 'B' while going back to the southern side. These points when projected onto the zodiacal sign, will see them moving from a higher degree to a lower degree. These points are called the Nodes; N1, N2, and N3 as marked are North Nodes formed each month. On the other side, S1, S2, and S3 are South Nodes. The Earth is shown in the centre.

What do the Nodes do?

The Nodes perform a special task in our life. The North Node has taken up the 'fulfillment of desires' task. The South Node does the job of proving to us that the desires we went after were fulfilled no doubt, but the pleasure was short-lived; would have been better if we had devoted ourselves to a task of serving the people, led an upright, morally correct, and ethically exemplar lifestyle. In the bargain all one does is to chase gratification and then regret. The regret is brought about toward the exit when the North Node is about to leave the house it is in; usually the last 4^0 of the house that come three months before the North Node enters the next house. That is the period when the South Node takes the opportunity to prove the right from the wrong. The North Node takes about eighteen months to complete the entire house and these months we do our best to achieve whatever has been kept hidden as unethical or considered immoderate or intemperate in our heart. It just happens that when the North Node comes to transit a certain house, situations change and make it convenient for us to assume that the opportunities that are seen coming were the very ones we had been waiting desperately. We forget our touch with reality and accept the situations to be real and forever. In fact, the North Node is only there transiting for eighteen months and after that once it moves to the next house everything about the last house it was in will be forgotten. Everyone needs to experience these so called 'halcyon months' that just come and go. After a couple of years the experience repeats itself too. The North Node returns to the same house after 18.6 years. Only after such repeated experience of initially winning and followed by a loss that we learn it is no use becoming fools as soon as we see an opportunity to gratify our secret inner desires. It is said that the North Node awakens the desires that did not see their end in our previous lives.

The North Node is just an imaginary point and so is the South Node. Since the Nodes do not have any mass, no planet can influence them. But the Nodes can and their influence can cause the planets to act to co-operate. The Nodes are usually happy to influence the inner personal planets and the bodies like the Sun and the Moon. These are not only fast but are provocative too. Our attention, focus, and intent are all driven by the inner personal planets. The outer planets are slow. If they hold any of our personal planets or bodies then their influence is usually very strong. The outer planets transit during both their motions of direct and retrograde a couple of times and not just once like sometimes the planet Saturn does not get to transit thrice over any single point.

The Nodes transit slowly and transit over every point just once. Their transit usually lasts for about a month over a single point since their transit speed is about $1^0\ 25'$ per month on an average. If we choose an orb of even 1^0, which means a degree before reaching a particular point and a degree after transiting a particular point, the entire period lasts for at least two months. The North Node while getting into the act of aggrandizement of a desire in any person needs to isolate the person first. For that certain events need to happen and those become the paving stones to walk on to reach a particular goal.

Most hidden desires are usually combined with fears of a loss of respect in society. There is a 'taboo' attached to them. The person knows this well. The moment a person embarks on a venture to seek certain desires, clandestine nature takes over and thereafter the person trusts very few, becomes secretive, operates after everyone goes to sleep, and seeks advice from no one. It is this particular nature that lets the person proceed faster on this newly adopted path and becomes happy with whatever little is attained. It increases from a little to a maximum in about six months. Thereafter, it becomes a habit and turns into an everyday affair. It is when one becomes careless and overconfident which takes another six months or so, the South Node usually acts to abort all the activities through scandal, crime, offence and attracts the attention of the law. The law does not mean the Police force here. It means what is normally considered proper by the society in which we live takes notice of the surreptitiously done acts. The person is now forced to give up their activities one way or another. The lesson of the house in which the North Node was transiting, thus ends. The North Node has another situation ready for you in its next house. Usually, we all get tired after one big-time activity that is carried on for a year and a half. Not every house is full of clandestine activities either. So, a short respite comes every once in a while.

The houses, 5th, 7th, 4th, 2nd, 10th, and the 8th houses are where the North Node can tempt us to take up our hidden and objectionable desires. Look at the houses, 5th and 4th, 8th and 7th are consecutive houses. They do have certain thoughts that may be carried forward from one house to another. If the 5th house is a starter for love affairs during fun and entertainment it does not have any emotional involvement. The 4th house demands it (unconditional love) by hook or crook. The 8th house too brings people together while doing business but secrecy to their activity builds up eventually. Intimacy is kept a secret. In the 7th, a legal contract is demanded. It is after all Saturn's house of exaltation. The Libra sign is always looking for a partner for life. Here, a love affair will not last for long if the North Node is not pushing a person into a legal binding. It will break as soon as the South Node gets into its act in the last four degrees of the transit. Let us see what Nodes do when transiting through houses and also when noticed in natal charts.

Before you start trying to analyze you must know the current desires or needs of a person. These need to be fulfilled and that is possible in two ways. One way is if the personal planets or planet Jupiter is favouring in some way. The second is to see if the North Node is transiting an appropriate house for that matter. For example, a person comes with a query about whether there is any possibility to find a new job. You find that the North Node is transiting the 12th house and the personal planets are all between the 3rd and the 5th houses. Planet Jupiter is transiting through the 9th house. Do you think it is possible? Planet Saturn is transiting through the 1st house. Is there a possibility now? Planet Saturn alone is in a house that will probably give a start to this person in an entirely new way. It will be a fresh start and planet Saturn should not be retrograde. Next, look for a possible New Moon occurring in any friendly houses if not in the 1st house. Lastly, check the position of the ruling planet for the 1st house for its strength. Check the natural ruler, planet Mars in a similar way. The North Node is definitely not in a position to help until it moves into the 11th house. The other personal planets are transiting in the house between the 3rd and the 5th houses. These houses are for getting trained, seeking education, furthering past skills, etc. The 3rd house might help in courageously putting forward one's abilities and ideas in front of others. This house also indicates possibilities of building new friends and associations to seek new opportunities. When handling the North Node it is important to know one's immediate desires first.

The Nodes through the Houses

1st house: Ever heard of narcissism? The North Node will make you a narcissist first if seen in the 1st house of a natal chart. There are plenty of podcasts, and articles written on narcissism. I can suggest a name or two; Dr. Ramani is one of them and the other is Mrs. Lisa Romano. The North Node has every intent to bring the right things to appear like Superman. Most of us want to look better than before when the North Node transits the 1st house. One might want to improve health from within, someone might change the kind of shoes or clothes they wear and many would go for a special diet. After doing all that you need an attention giver. That is when the North Node arrives in your life. North Node is direct contact with someone who becomes the provider of the need we have. It could come as a coach, a guide or as a teacher. After all, self-improvement is always on our minds; whenever any personal planet or North Node transits our 1st house. We also end up spending a lot more when such planets do their transit. So, it is self-love in excess.

The South Node is transiting the 7th house during this time. It develops complete discard toward anyone who is trying to cultivate us. Could be anyone who is trying to build a matrimonial alliance, someone who is trying to employ us in an important position in his/her company, or anyone who is trying to befriend us. Even the wife is ignored and isolation from all is sought.

The North Node naturally adopts the qualities of Mars in the 1st house and tries to be assertive on all issues, tries to drive us to lead and take up additional work or simply pick up a fight with someone. But the South Node rejects Venusian qualities to the extent that earning well is not a desire anymore. The care shown by Venus in Libra is totally missing. One has to think of this as a weak Sun with no ambition. Toward the end of the transit, whatever was excessively present or developed is driven away. In a North Node to the South Node relationship, the pull and push are both presents. The South Node is active toward the end.

Unlike the North Node, the South Node's character will not be played by any human face that is living. You could notice an advice given by one of the characters played by someone. Someone might notice a character in a novel or a television series saying something wise. These are appreciated well but never followed because of the influence of the North Node which is beckoning us to come and enjoy the offerings made to us. The South Node does not bring any unwanted advice but what is appropriate to its transiting position in the chart.

For example, if the South Node is transiting the 7th house, the advice that emerges out of unknown sources or strange sources will be usually about the futility of staying committed to one person or expecting happiness from just one. It asks us to remove a dependency that is inherently present in a relationship. It even asks us, not to rely on law or justice. But simply avoid a situation that might get us involved into one. The very thought that one must seek a companion in order to feel complete is removed. Likewise in other houses different advice will be received. Everyone will appreciate but no one ever follows that advice.

2nd House: When we are facing difficulties like, someone is ill in the family and the illness does not seem to go, the earnings have been hurt and no immediate relief seems to be coming, children have grown up their educational expense, someone is going to get married in the family and the list goes on but the funds are just not enough, our talents brought in a lot of additional income earlier but lately nothing seems to be working, even personal health is suffering and there is self-doubt, self-worth question haunting the mind always. Was that the longest sentence was ever written? The 2nd house has plenty of talents and a determination to save the house from cracking up. No planet except planet Jupiter might bring in big hopes to survive any calamity but the North Node is much more. The only difference is that the North Node advices us to keep ethics and morals on the side. As soon as the transit starts one begins to see the horizon clearing and opportunities appear. One by one our problems begin to get solved.

The only danger is when we begin to like one of the activities far too much than the others while going through the problem-solving phase. This activity is usually an addiction that becomes part of us when we 205ausing205 that good days are back again. So, the North Node gets us hooked on a habit and we lose track of our earlier goals. Abundance and excesses are the bane now. The confidence is high but there is 205 ausindge of how long would this period be. Just eighteen months to see through and the Roman Empire appears to be falling. So, the North Node with all its good intentions will still turn out a delinquent out of a sedulous individual. Once again the deception angle gets proven. In the house of planet Venus (naturally ruled) abundance followed by relief from financial issues, causes a tendency to earn friends through catering and imbibing. It has a lot to do with precedence of 'financial and social' anxiety in the life of a person. With financial success one usually attracts a variety of people. This is then followed by a thought that these people should not abandon me tomorrow for lack of resources. In the end, one loses the battle in keeping up with the Jones and Joneses. The warning should be based on the transit period which is just eighteen months and not forever.

If planets Jupiter or Venus bring in opportunities to improve earnings, there is a difference. They bring in a couple of new friends or contacts that raise a person's status without any compromise. In the case of North Node, one is poached after temptations or the new association becomes such that nothing seems as wrong and modesty appears silly. The opportunities that come are different in everyone's case. Even the compromises made are subject to how courageous a person is. Lastly, if the planet Saturn is transiting the 2nd house, the opportunities to get trained further are more. There is hope for improvement in financial status in the future. But during the transition one usually struggles with lack. It becomes important for someone who is counseling to give encouragement to the attempts that are made and let 'hope' take over.

The South Node in the 8th house develops curiosity about human nature and psychology. Sometimes occult interests are also possible. There is a lack of interest in generating cash through business, joint income, using a credit or taking loans or from any other sources of income that are considered additional or 'unearned' or 'passive' income. The 8th house represents our secrets that we want to hide. But the South Node does not let that happen. It is self-revealing in this house. That means the activities that we do somehow betray us to admit to the misdeeds.

3rd House: There are a couple of houses in our chart where the North Node might encourage us to excesses yet it turns out to favour us. The dual signs and the houses 3rd, 6th, 9th, and 12th are safer. Although the 12th house will appear tentative, the situation here is that the personal planets if placed here are usually helpless. So, the North Node cannot use these for leverage. If the North Node aspects any planet elsewhere, then it will be for a short period only; maybe for two months or so.

If financial crisis was a cause to improve upon self, in this house one feels that he/she is too good to seek a job elsewhere than where he/she is present. The 3rd house has a lot of mental and communicative abilities. There is greed present also. What works in our favour is competitiveness. There is the courage to go and seek a person irrespective of one's own position or status. One has great faith in the self to convince someone else. This house is ideal for people in the field of sales and marketing. The North Node can only tempt and increase the 'greed' factor but the house demands much more. Only if the planets situated in the house are weak, if the ruling planet of the house is weak, or if planet Mercury is stressed in the natal chart there are good chances that during the North Node's transit through this house there is greater anxiety.

If the other planets are of adequate strength, our ability to improve ourselves becomes our focus. Language learning, travel for fun, reading and writing are all the traits seen here that also increase during a North Node's transit. The media has a great appeal to these people. These people seek jobs like radio jockeys, voiceovers, sports commentators, etc. The person shows great interest in using and repairing electronic gadgets, motor cars, etc. If the person is a trained engineer there are chances that working in locomotive factories, car manufacturing companies, aircraft industry are possible. Interest to become a pilot or a seafarer is always present. If the other planets give good support, then these are all realized. The North Node has a lot to do to support these interests.

The South Node from the 9th house likes to be with religious monks, priests and others who in the name of a religion, sect or caste try to reform the community. The person might take a trip to pilgrimages, distant places in search of some religious artefact or a temple, or a person to seek more knowledge. The social ladder is not appealing to the South Node.

4th House: The 4th house is naturally ruled by the Moon and there could be a ruling planet of the 4th in the chart. Both of these are important from their strength point of view. The North Node brings the interest of the two planets together and increases their needs especially the unfulfilled ones. The 4th house looks after the 'unconditional love' seeking side of our life. The greater crisis comes in this matter.

For some reason or the other, this position resembles that of transiting Saturn in the 5th house. The difference is that one gets nothing out of any relationship and the time is wasted on building one rather desperately while the planet Saturn is transiting the 5th house. In the 4th house, the North Node brings choices to seek that 'unconditional love'. Now, the second part of the North Node's stay here is similar to the planet Jupiter transiting the 5th house. Strange people come into our life and we seek 'love' from them. In every department of the Moon's choices what is very dear to us becomes distant and is replaced with something else. For a short period, this makeshift arrangement is gratifying. But, not for too long. There are plenty of emotional losses to bear here. These remove our interest from all the temporary gap-filling arrangements. The South Node from the 10th house sees to it that nothing gains momentum in the activities of the 4th house due to the North Node.

The South Node causes job losses, and scandals from the 10th house so that one will not have the courage to face society. The 4th house North Node's efforts become waste in about a year or so. I have sought estrangements in the family, illness to my mother, selling the house to which one had great attachment and move into another smaller house because of a financial crisis, etc. there is a constant disturbance in the head about future security. So, I always warn my clients with the North Node leaving the 5th and entering the 4th that do not think your last relationship will continue but the one happening next might ruin your home and family. In the 5th house, the 'love affair' does not have an emotional value or involvement in it. It is mostly, playful and flirting. Neither of the two has any firm commitment to the relationship. Both of them remain carefree. Then it ends in a strange way as soon as the North Node leaves the 5th house.

In the 4th house, there are events occurring that sadden us a lot as soon as the North Node enters. Someone has to leave town on account of the job but the family cannot accompany on account of other commitments. One of the parents dies. It is possible that one of the parents is suffering an illness badly and the whole household is stressed on account of that. There are many issues that cause us to seek sympathy from others during this period of the North Node transit. These issues that cause crisis attract characters into our life and we become emotionally dependent on them. All the three water houses and the signs begin to face an emotionally cut-off type of experience from their most loved beings. Sometimes children leave home for education and stay far away for a couple of years and causing similar grief. I have seen the death of the spouse and estrangement in a couple of cases when the North Node entered the 4th house. The strength of the ruling planet of the 4th house and the Moon sometimes save the day for us. The North Node in spite of trying its best will not be able to do much damage. When we say a planet is strong, we mean that the planet does not let us act in an undignified manner. We show temperance and conduct ourselves in a moderate fashion. Loose characterized women or a philanderer cannot tempt us into their charm. The moment the North Node sees opportunity in the 5th, 4th, 12th, 8th and the 7th houses on account of a weak ruling planet or the natural ruler of the house there is every chance that we will burn our fingers and learn a big lesson.

The North Node will always help us to improve our health in every house it transits. It is the South Node that brings illnesses in order to stop us from responding to the calls of the North Node. It is a deterring act from the South Node. Once again I reiterate, do not go for excess enjoyment, entertainment, or carefree attitude for too long. Remind yourself that it is the North Node that is pressing upon you to act this way. Then return to sobriety and moderation.

5th House: This house is where the Sun shines the brightest throwing all optimism into the house. A word of caution here is that the Sun in the chart must not be weak or stressed. Then there will be strange tendencies and outcomes. The Sun is never happy with outer planets beginning with planet Saturn and ending with the planet Pluto. It is just that the Sun cannot take orders from anyone. The outer planets have a habit of arm twisting to get the personal planets and the bodies like the Sun and the Moon to work for them. That is when we see different and odd results coming out of the 5th house. We get to see the results in the form of children that are born, a personal attitude toward integrity, their demeanor when in love, their craving to get fun and entertainment, their desire to educate themselves and others, and their ambition to perform before the public. When the Sun is under stress all of these results mentioned turn haywire. We are dismayed to see people stabbing behind our back or simply put, letting us down. In such a house the North Node rides on the optimism offered by the Sun and takes us further to reach peaks desire and leave us disillusioned. It is not that the entire period of stay of eighteen months is filled with disappointments. On the contrary, we do enjoy the passage of this entire transit of the North Node but remain unfulfilled even at the end. Who damaged our happiness?

It is the South Node of the 11th house; the house stands for gains, our hopes and our wishes. None of these get any success despite the North Node taking full charge of the 5th house. The emptiness caused by the South Node leads us to take more and more risks and we begin to gamble in order to reach that ultimate in happiness. The South Node disallows that. It permits community service, reform, service to the needy and the poor. That is the success from the South Node side. Do not forget that the 11th is the 10th house from the 2nd house. Whatever we work hard on will yield an income from the 2nd house. The 5th house is 10th from the 8th house. The excesses carried out will let us lose our passive income, joint income, trade income and 'unearned income'. That is how these houses are connected and produce results.

6th house: The North Node is in a house for health, meticulous work, seeking perfection in everything that is required to be done, getting to know the nitty-gritty of law and enforcement rules, working with hands to do manual work, and never satisfied with the details provided about everything. In this list of characteristics, the family is also included. It loves to serve the family in every possible way. The sign Virgo has plenty of friends too and few hidden enemies. The enemies happened when the Virgo person was trying to enforce some law and enforcement on someone or finding fault with their work rather too much. This sign loves to use the written word in both fight and love. It also uses symbols to display love and affection. Flowers will be sent on time, letters of love will have a regular periodicity and finally, every word from the book

'Etiquette's and manners' by Mrs. Emily Post has been practiced, still one finds that the Virgo sign lacks a romantic vision. There is no room for surprises, spur of the moment humour or a change in agenda, and experience the thrill of it. With this in the background, the North Node has not much to sway a person to do something for titivation or titillation. The planet Mercury which is the ruler might ask for some relief from the anxiety that is carried by this house. It does it through women and intoxication. If the Virgo person has lower moral values then these are to be expected. The North Node might be successful in getting things to move.

Having said all that, the North Node also brings lawyers, doctors, and educated people as friends to our aid if we show a need. Someone might be ill and trying to find a doctor who can solve that problem, someone might be having problems in their accounts; salaries, returns filing, etc., will then find a suitable Chartered Accountant. Someone might be trying to get their pets healthier they will find a good veterinarian, and in some instances a good lawyer to advice and bring the court matters to closure. In matters of business, trade and selling the 6th house, being a servicing house, will do well if you are in a service industry or maybe manufacturing items that are of great use to the public. The North Node will find a person to do the needful and find better outlets to sell your products. In every aspect of need, the North Node will come and provide help. But do not shut your backdoor during this transit of the North Node. It normally enters from where the exit is usually. Just a reminder.

The South Node is busy doing philanthropic work now from the 12th house. We all become interested in plants and herbal medicines for a while. We might want to go to far off lands in search of peace and tranquility. Certain secrets of our life are revealed to us. We might want to diarise or even write a paper or a thesis. Students do well with zero distraction allowed, and manage to earn a Ph.D. from somewhere far. That work is considered unique after a while. The South Node is never visible as a person. It is visible in all inanimate, cinema, stories, articles, or perhaps in lectures given by the enlightened personalities. It is hard to keep up but it certainly helps to unburden ourselves from many unsuitable activities. The South Node can expose to people who practice with strange concoctions and medicines sitting in far-away places. So be ready you shall see a hermit soon; but do not mistake him for the South Node. Only the force is with him, that the South Node passed temporarily.

Chapter-XI

When twins get separated, their spirits fly away to look for the other.

The Nodes
Part Three

7th House: The nature of Venus is to seek a companion in everyone. Besides that, the planet Venus shows plenty of talents to show us some ways to earn friends as well as an income. But to hold on to a steadfast nature and wait for the final outcome the planet Venus needs to remain unflappable for long periods. It cannot distract itself and assume it is still progressing. The North Node knows that if planet Venus sets its priorities well, it can arrive with baggage that is befitting the requirement.

Planet Venus has a habit of doing a tight rope walk in this sign. It loves to hold on and take support from both sides; knowing well it vacillates frequently. The North Node knows this too. Planet Venus loves a materialistic lifestyle in this sign and is not easily attached to anyone emotionally too soon. But seeing an opportunity it is ever ready to throw away its talent-pursuing role and take an easy path any time it wants to. These are some of the weaknesses that I have listed so that one can expect the North Node's direction of arrival. It is also quite easy to tempt and subvert planet Venus when it is weak in the natal chart or during its transit. In the 7th house, the North Node misleads the planet Venus to provide a short term of fulfilling its desires. The sign of Libra is where the planet Saturn exalts. So, on a good day, planet Venus will be seen to behave well. Even planet Saturn is generous to let loose a yard or two of thick Marlene rope. Planet Saturn does not restrict until it realizes that the freedom given is not being used well. In this interim period of a year and a half, the planet Venus escapes the bondage with planet Saturn's tenets and elopes with the North Node ideology.

That is enough to break any heart, isn't it? That's how it ends too.

The South Node from the 1st house is seen to carelessly lead a life of self-abandonment. One becomes a victim of self-medication or a seeker of wrong advice. The wrong advice is usually in the form of admiration or approving whatever one does to the self. It is a kind of validation seeking but not realizing that it is false or there is a lack of knowledge that is supposed to lead you well. The South Node seeks false confidence from others here and wrecks the health. The crisis of the 7th house caused by the North Node is such that one is ashamed of seeing a doctor. The North Node of the 7th house causes mental disorders during its transit through the 7th house. Mostly mental anxiety followed by depression. The South Node on the other hand looks for solutions but in the wrong places. In the end, the person who is going through all this suffers self-destruction. The South Node produces a feeling or a thought of 'abandon all' and being a seeker of peace, throughout this transit.

8th House: This is the house through which people earn without putting too much hard work. It has a touch of Midas to it. Most people who are in the movie business, theatre business, the lobbyists, the estate agents, the bankers, the money lenders and launderers, the people in the occult business, the people who deal in arms selling to countries, the people in liquor business, the people in drugs business, the people who operate using women as a business commodity, people who play with stock market fluctuations are all blessed by the 8th house profits. Just make sure that planet Mars and planet Saturn are away from it. Planet Mars has plans to spend on a luxury yacht. Planet Saturn is a Police himself. Of course, planet Saturn will not stop anything earned legitimately. But planet Mars has no scruples left while passing through this house. Planet Venus waits to be adopted here. When planet Venus is in the sign Scorpio or the 8th house, it wants to seek a companion with power because it has experienced a number of bruises from abuse in this world from a very young age. The thought of marriage which takes birth in the 7th house dies here in the 8th. Planet Venus hates the wedlock. It goes around telling its sad story only to attract someone who promises protection but not marriage. Again, there may be exceptions to the rule always. But planet Venus here does not believe that its husband is everything it has got. The Moon too likes attachment to power but has a lot of secrets to hide. It gathers power through legacies and money given or deposited for safe-keeping. There is a peculiar message it carries that was passed on by its mother. She maintained a secret lifestyle herself that caused enough anxiety to the children. That mother was both influential and wealthy. But the children dreaded that kind of living dangerously or perhaps shamelessly. So, the Moon is left with fear and is afraid of attachment. It repeats and learns (is it practicing) through various acts or activities the art of getting something and losing it. Here, the Moon suffers from mental agony. As astrologers, you will see these kinds of horoscopes frequently. The North Node comes on the stage amidst all this background. Now, what does it give?

The North Node will come as a character to fill all the gaps left by the other planets. The best of all is the one who says, "I will show you how to make money. But do not tell anyone".

Then a new relationship begins here, laden with money. A lot of many things happen too before one gets a taste of bankruptcy. Again, not all of us fall into that trap but those who show greed and dependency do. Many begin an interest in the occult and learn. But most will have a single common story to tell and that will be of how they managed a fraud.

With the South Node transiting the 2nd house, the major issues of the family emerge and become too important but there is a lackadaisical attitude created in us toward these. We let the issues hang around, we might not spend so much on the family but the little that we do creates dissatisfaction in the family members. As there are no efforts put into the family, earnings, or proving self-worth, the 5th house suffers because the 2nd house is 10th from the 5th. The children do not perform well due to the lack of interest shown in them. The 10th house suffers too as the 2nd house cannot motivate much. All this is the effort of the South Node in order to dissuade the North Node from letting a person do anything in excess. This is on the assumption that the failing domestic and work front will cause some awareness to come to the person. The South Node does not interfere with religious activities that go on in the family. If the person is not distracted by the North Node, then the South Node does not even bother. So, there are ways to handle the North Node by not being greedy, controlling others, trying to prove oneself as the best, or showing a need to be needed by others. The moment we show an excessive desire like many people have towards money, luxuries, food, clothes, shoes, jewelry, alcoholic drinks, etc., the North Node immediately awakens to come to our aid. It does not have any conscience. It is coming to fulfil our desires that were perhaps deeply rooted in us but remained unfulfilled.

9th House: You may be surprised to know that the 9th house represents people like our bosses at work, people who are higher than us in status, the people who have an authority in executing law and enforcement. See the connection here, when any misdeed or misconduct is taking place due to planetary movement in the 9th house, this house is 10th house from the 12th house, the 12th house suffers; the 12th house is also known as the house of isolation or prison. The Sagittarius nature too can be seen on the same basis. The sign works hard to seek freedom from all commitments only to seek isolation. The 4th house motivates the 12th house to get back to home again. When the North Node does anything illegal in this house, usually a person faces the authorities of law and order. It is a good house for publishers of books either as authors or as a publishing company. The North Node encourages us in every way if we are desirous to seek the company of the elite or people who are placed above us in society. It can be religious authorities also. The 9th house has its own firm beliefs to follow like Henry the VIII. He created the Protestant Church in England and broke away from Roman Catholicism and the Pope. The 9th house has radical ideas and could hesitate to display them. The North Node eases this all and causes the person to accept someone from another culture or religion or a citizen of an entirely different nation.

As I have said before, the North Node actually comes into our life as a person to inspire, lead, bait, deceive, build trust even when we know we are at risk, and then leave us gasping for breath. In some houses, it comes as a suave, well educated, superior looking, someone who has travelled the world and has superior knowledge. It does not come to teach us anything but to cause our weakness to accept it as our mentor. We emulate the North Node and its practices, work and wait to receive its admiration. In the 9th house which is an improvement over the 8th house of illnesses (both mental and body), we see a very good doctor coming our way and treat. The 9th house causes mental impressions to go too far. Even in the 6th house a similar situation can arise. In the 6th house the North Node sets new habits and new practices in our life. Diet is one of them. In the 9th, we happen to understand our illnesses better. The North Node causes us to read more about it. Some go for higher studies to other countries during the North Node's transit.

The South Node goes to prove that seeking people in order to make them understand our ideas, principles, and our viewpoint is just not necessary. One should live for oneself no matter what. The South Node does not interfere with travel plans in the 3rd house. It interferes with 'modernism' which is a passion of the 3rd house. One loses interest in all kinds of gadgetry. The travels that happen are usually full of purpose. It is just like the planet Saturn transiting the 3rd house. The greed goes away because we suffer losses in our life. We begin to think of a use for everything we do. The 3rd house is a trend setter so we start a new trend in our life. It is always something that keeps us sober and modest. Our reading habit continues. But the shallowness that was present earlier turns into in depth information seeking. If there is anyone who suffers it will be our siblings. We seem to take them less seriously during this transit.

10th house: The 10th house is naturally ruled by planet Saturn. An actual ruler for the 10th house may also exist in the chart. You will wonder whose influence is greater.

The nature or attitude toward work has to be to the liking of the planet Saturn. What modality has been decided will be according to the ruling planet. For example, someone with a Taurus ascendant will have the sign Aquarius on the 10th house cusp. The attitude that needs to be shown (according to planet Saturn) must be sincerity in purpose, regular, leaving all distractions, focusing on the goal, keeping the amount of money earned through work on our conscious side, always seeking the help of superiors, standing up to please the superiors with abilities than simply fawning at their feet, fulfilling responsibilities to the best of ability and to realize that hard work is not merely meeting office hours or spending long hours at the place of work but to find a way in improvising one's methods and dependencies on co-workers. Such a long list fits only for planet Saturn!

The responsibility of planet Uranus is to whether one wants to be a courier person, a computer operator, a doctor, an engineer, a lawyer, or a chartered accountant. The modality is not under any stress of any kind but its presence that makes the 10th house shine has a lot of anxiety attached to it. The 2nd house will always prove to be a motivating factor; the self-worth, self-earned income, etc. Whatever happens in the 10th house is a motivating factor to the 6th house of regular, methodical, attention to details, a command over written word, and knowledge of the legal system automatically fall in place. That is how human performance is connected. Lastly, the 7th house is the 10th house of work for the actual 10th house in the chart. In the example that I mentioned, the sign Scorpio falls in the 7th. Its natural ruler is planet Venus, and planet Pluto is the ruler of Scorpio, both their position decides on how much are we ready to cooperate (7th house Libra nature) with anyone. There must be no distinction when we choose to decide on a team, or work with, or try to make a deal with. Do not ever look at planet Venus as a habitual voyeur or a womanizer in the case of gents and a charming seductress in the case of women. I have to say this because the articles, and periodical predictions focus mainly on these aspects. Planet Venus is as powerful as the planet Mars in most activities. You will mislead yourself by simply thinking that this represents a very goody goody person. Observe a couple of Libran women and a few Libran men. Include the sign Taurus too. These people rarely die in poverty.

Planet Saturn does not value anything that people are emotionally attached to; like children, spouse, parents, friends, and even inanimate objects like a car, clothes, perfumes, etc. Aren't we faced with a huge situation here? Yes, we are because we all get carried away by the attire worn by the high achievers and never really get to see what work went into before they wore one. These high achievers rarely think twice about their dress, their class during travel, the hotel in which they stay although it could be a 5-star hotel, the place where a meeting is held with them, and the people who are either their associates or subordinates to help. At least now are you able to see differences that exist between an ordinary person who also thinks that he/she is involved with hard work and the high-end achievers? You must have already made a mental list of all the weaknesses that most people have and the large space that the North Node can come and occupy during its transit through the 10th house.

The North Node's nature is all very well understood by now, and has a major job of making life easier for us despite insincerity. It comes as a godfather or as a very sweet likable boss, or a lobbyist at a workplace to make things move for us. We still need to remember the validity period; eighteen months. Most think they have been blessed for life. They waste so much of their time that they do not realize the gates closing behind their backs at the end of the term.

The South Node transiting the 4th house builds a loss of hope in ever getting that 'unconditional love', the attachment building bonds, the items that symbolize security, the secrets that we held close to our chest in fear of ridicule and lastly the mother is now a burden and one is only wondering how soon the end would arrive. There are other issues like the home and their members quitting under some excuse or the other. The biggest of them all is struggling to see who do we belong to? Is it the emotional ties that we valued or is there something outside of the house that one needs to go and seek?

11th house: The 11th house is a house for gains, hopes and wishes for the future. Such a minimal weightage is given to this house that many times one does not know what to say if the planets present in the house are conjunct or square or in opposition to some other planets in other houses. Yet, astrologers are concerned. They do make their observations based on planets situated here. What must they be looking at assuming is our question to solve before we take on Mr. North Node here? Any planet situated here will try to do something in order to produce wealth in the 2nd house. This house is a motivation house for the 7th house and gets motivated by the 3rd house. In short, all houses do not operate independently but in unison with other houses. It produces a result of the future if anything extraordinary is done today. Doing alone is important and one needs to remain enthusiastic about the results attained because in the present nothing is visible. Imagine there is a planet here like say, planet Jupiter. The planet Jupiter is known for its "I can't care less about religion or norms of the society' kind of attitude. It is also sitting here to motivate the 7th house. Does that mean this person is enamored by persons of other cultures and religions? Planet Jupiter carries the 9th house message wherever it goes. It has no fixed way of giving opportunities in order that we grow using those opportunities. Many times we miss those and this now becomes a challenge to identify the opportunity from merely a piece of information. The person consulting must know this; the placement of planet Jupiter in the 11th means that a person will work in many different ways in order to produce wealth from the 2nd house. The North Node too shows us plenty of ways to gain in the future. But nothing of what the North Node does now is visible to anyone. So, it is quite safe.

The North Node brings a hoard of people as friends to let us pursue whatever we want. The 11th house also takes advantage of the 10th house by using the efforts put in that house. All 2nd houses use their previous houses this way. If the 8th house is vitiated (damaged), indirectly it means that the 7th house is struggling and is now fighting to survive.

Have you heard of conducting certain devotional activities or prayers in order to get children or for the good of the children so that they do well in their careers? Both the 4th and the 5th houses seek satisfaction in conducting ceremonies including the wedding ceremony of their family members while this South Node is transiting the 4th and the 5th houses. The South Node may be dead against the excesses that we all indulge in or fall prey to. But it encourages all activities that are praiseworthy, done for the upliftment of society, for the good of the home, family and children or any activity which brings the person to show he or she is humble enough to admit in front of the almighty.

The South Node has no interest in the 5th house affairs like, entertainment that has become an addiction, casual love affairs, children that have been pampered and neglected; are now misusing their freedom, and gambling, etc. But it can promote new learning because this house stands for some impersonal activities like learning more to help the less virtuous and take up teaching.

12th house: The 12th house is naturally like the South Node in many ways and perhaps it is the best place for the South Node to be in. The 12th house has a natural quality to give a feeling to us even before experiencing something that most activities that the material world is fond of have been already done. So, there is a rejection toward anything that is suggested in order to spruce it up. This leads to constant failures where competitiveness is required. Unless there are other planets in the chart that encourage an active lifestyle and compensate their lifestyle remains more or less a dreamy kind.

Failures do not matter to them. They like people who are easygoing and spend time chatting, skive, spend time watching movies, escaping serious talk or responsibilities, wandering about etc. These habits do not let them take charge of the family later on but live off what might be received as legacy or will. Although there are plenty who have applied themselves to a great extent and built a good life for themselves, their later years are spent in service to a religion or religious bodies, activities that bring them closer to a place of worship than any kind of social revelry. Except for planet Venus and planet Neptune, there are no planets that work to the benefit of any individual in a chart. Planet Venus brings compassion and planet Neptune creates dreams to fulfill in the future. There could be a mental worry, quick exhaustion of the faculties, easily misled, and therefore they develop a self-pitying condition. Even the friends do not stay close for long seeing their indifference to certain practiced norms of society. That causes these 12th house dominated individuals to look for escapism through drugs or similar addictions. Religious bodies might help here because these individuals have faith in the almighty.

With the 12th house providing such amenities, the North Node has a tough job. It manages to carry the person far off in its tenure of eighteen months and exposes to superior people who have abilities to bring the lost 'vigour', 'enthusiasm', 'cheerfulness' and 'love toward self' back to the individual again. The North Node always uses its time to bring the person to a threshold from where it can bring in new ideas to chase for the remaining period of its stay in any house. Here it is engaged fully in first getting the person to have desires. The attempts are made from all directions like letting the person travel to far off countries, bringing opportunities to study, teach the healing art, read ancient books and bring mysteries to the fore, archaeological work, search for artefacts in ruins, dive down into the ocean and study creatures of the underwater, and get the person to seek adventure. The North Node performs well in this house except for the person who is depressed on account of mental exhaustion. It is a South Node territory and we realize that the Machiavellian is now a rehabilitator.

I guess that this introduction to the Nodes is sufficient for a beginner to get a hold of the concept. As you read further and practice alongside by reading horoscopes of your friends and family members you will gain more knowledge.

Chapter-XII

Professor Henry Higgins, "Why can't a woman be more like a man?" from the movie, "My Fair Lady".

Planet Venus

I have covered the planet Venus in my previous book, 'Karma is hidden' in a very lukewarm fashion because I wrote the book for readers who are experienced and I thought I would waste their time. This time I shall try and get to the basics. As beginners in the study of astrology, you must remember that any planet has little power if left alone in a natal chart without any aspects from other planets. You might read in several articles or watch podcasts that might ascribe a great many qualities to the planet Venus, planet Mars, planet Mercury, the Sun, and the Moon in a chart. Look for aspects first if there are any and start on an assumption that there is a certain ability in the planet to bring results.

If the planet has no aspects or it has been excited by planet Jupiter alone, then an outsider's planet can have a big influence. That is when we see an association of two people that appears to be very strongly connected. Whether for good or bad is not such a concern but that is a likely vulnerable situation. The inner personal planets are sensitive, excitable, irritable, and prone to get angry and emotional. Spur of the moment decision become imperative than contemplating over an impulse. There is deep satisfaction sought from these personal planets and a desire to repeat certain habits, acts, events and interactions. Although, the outcome has a short life the person wants certain experiences to come his/her way just for the fun and excitement. The contrary to this can also be true.

In Fire Signs

With all that has been said above in perspective let us try to identify the planet Venus in our life. Like planet Mars, planet Venus is also influential. Planet Venus too uses power, vigour, appearance, and a drive to possess something or someone. Writers and poets connected the planet Venus to feminine behavior and nature for convenience and we all still live with those old analogies. I request you all to start thinking that planet Venus is as powerful as Mars. Planet Venus can also fight, argue, possess, snatch, steal, show talents, be a sportsperson, be dominant, cheat if it has to, and abandon people when it wants to. There is a small difference that planet Mars is more belligerent and desirous of success than planet Venus. Planet Venus is likely to go for bigger battles and prizes for permanent keeping than planet Mars. Neither is capable of long-term emotional involvement. Their emotions are short-lived and they prefer forgetting than lament someone's absence. Both enjoy attracting opportunities and prefer the opposite sex for company and conversation. It is a question of 'how many' and 'how long' as that depends on the strength of the planets. Sometimes these planets are under the influence of outer planets like, planets Saturn, Uranus, Neptune, and Pluto. Then their independence is lost. Sometimes these become weak due to placement in a particular sign or a house in a chart. Venus is weak in, houses 1st, 6th, 8th and signs Aries, Scorpio, and Virgo. Planet Mars is weak in houses 7th, 4th and signs Libra and Cancer. There are periods of retrogrades once in eighteen months for planet Venus. There are New Moons and Full Moons that come and go. These lunations can aspect any planet and cause then to start something new or close something that is already happening in our life. At such times, if planet Venus is aspected then it is subverted to act in accordance with the wishes of the Moon's placement during a lunation. Lastly, there are eclipses occurring twice each year which are more powerful than a Full or a New Moon. We need to notice these and other aspects in order to assess if a planet is strong enough to implement its own wish or if it is obliging some other.

Planet Venus is less sensitive and more impulsive in fire signs (Aries, Leo, and Sagittarius). That means there are more body reactions, gesticulations, and action using physical movement, and there is usually, 'I can do whatever anyone else can do' kind of attitude. This masculine demeanor is received well when involved in a certain type of activity. For example, some friends have arranged a day out in the country side and they are looking for volunteers among their friends. There is going to be a big event somewhere and they too are looking for people who can participate as well as help. A Company has a new project involving travel, making arrangements for people, planning their stay, subsistence, etc. The fire sign Venus is always ready to participate and show active enthusiasm and never shows signs of tiredness. It is another matter if someone happened to casually flirt but found planet Venus did not show much interest except for a couple of minutes of conversation. Planet Venus of the fire signs enjoys a large gathering of friends than just a few or even a one-to-one intimate conversation. There is a lot of desire to have and show that it has a large circle of friends than merely having a few good and close friends. Whether at work or at home one will notice that planet Venus is not touched by the troubles of others. It is another issue totally if the planet Venus is found in the 4th house or is in the sign Cancer or is aspected by the Moon in someone's chart. You may include planet Mercury in the same way too. If planet Venus is found in the 3rd or the 6th houses, in the signs Gemini or Virgo, or aspected by planet Mercury, there is a chance that causes some associations or chance meetings with people, bring planet Mercury into the picture. Our meetings and conversations are well heard and remembered by planet Venus with the help of planet Mercury. If planet Mercury enjoys that brief period then there is a desire for more. Planet Mercury has a habit of reminiscing and deliberate planning for future meetings. It begins to plot a way to get into the conversation again. In that way, planet Venus becomes successful in seeking a mate, which is its all-time wish.

With Moon too it is similar. Moon does not plot anything but brings the association closer by giving it a special place in the heart. So, each meeting will cause expressions of desire to come out of planet Venus. So, even in fire signs, there are good chances that planet Venus will find a mate.

In the sign Aries, the planet Venus is devoid of its normal grace and emotion (the exception has been explained above). One does not get to see more variety than a normal Venus is able to provide. Even if there is no sarcasm in its retorts, a shade of irritation or dislike may be noticed. Seeing a mild form of brusque behavior will usually keep friends and relatives at bay. Planet Venus may be good at sports and outdoor activities and will always be an entertainer if there is an audience sufficient enough. When planet Venus is in its fall, do not look too much for those affectionate tones in whispers. There is a lot to be heard loud and clear. Especially the truths!

In the sign of Leo, Venus is programmed to be an actor. Even if the screen audition is far away or just may be at a dream level, one can see drama on a daily basis. Venus thrives on attention and it serves well to give it confidence. The trouble is we all get fed up with this 'pantomime' frequently. Then there are plenty of tantrums thrown in to get their way everywhere.

Like the sign Taurus, Leo is stubborn too. But with generosity like the Taurean, there is always a gain for the friends if they stick around. These people dream big and put effort too. But will always appear easygoing, unlike the Taureans. You will probably feel jealous of their dress sense and make-up. I am sure one thing you will not fail to notice is even on a playground or at sports meet there will be that someone who is dressed and decorated immaculately.

The planet Venus in Sagittarius is talented and intelligent. All the fire sign Venuses are good at studies, extra-curricular activities, including drama, music, and sports. With planet Venus here one sees a voracious reader. They would have read all types of books by the time they reach years twelve or fourteen. Their parents find it difficult to select a future career or a branch to study. Most end up studying weird subjects at far-off universities abroad and remain jobless for long. Usually, these end up as lecturers and professors at the universities. Research, archaeology, excavation, space, working in distant lands in search of some fact that these people want to establish and win a medal is their all-time ambition. Their wit is interesting; it is never to hurt anyone. In fact, their generosity is taken advantage of by many. Out of the three fire signs, Venus in Sagittarius cries the most. Sometimes even while watching cartoons!

In Air Signs

Planet Venus in the air signs is full of talents, especially in Libra, and even in Gemini and Aquarius, it is sufficiently loaded with curiosity and intelligence. The hunger is for appreciation and seeking security from its associations and friends. If one finds anyone with their planet Venus in any of the air signs, the first thing to notice is their innumerable activities and interests.

In fact, one benefits a lot from their association. The sad part is that planet Venus must gain the right attention; until then it struggles. The air signs are particularly unclear about the ways to make money. They experiment a lot before they get hold of a way. Unlike the fire signs or water signs, the air signs do not show passion very much unless there are aspects from outer planets or planet Mars. They are slow to show their feelings toward someone. They can talk a lot.

The sign Gemini and Aquarius have a penchant to venture. In that, they see more opportunities. The sign Libra is less adventurous. It seeks a surefooted way to earn wealth. Planet Saturn is exalted in the sign Libra and that shows there is a greater degree of practicality in this sign. But to remain steadfast to seek something is lacking usually. The Libran Venus is easygoing. The Gemini Venus is happy if it is surrounded by friends while it is busy talking about its achievements. The Aquarian Venus is busy researching and experimenting. It is happy too when it earns its doctorate. So, who is better? That's a very hard choice. But you want a good wage earner? Then wager on Libra Venus.

While looking at the transits of planet Venus one must see if there are aspects formed or not. Without an aspect forming between transiting planets, it is very difficult to elicit a result even if the planet is passing through a favorable house. The aspects made by the transiting Venus to a natal plant take long to show results because the planets in the natal chart are dormant and by the time, they charge up to give any result this planet would have moved on. This is true with all personal planets, the Moon and the Sun. only the outer planets have the strength to pull and push the planets sitting in our chart. The other planets (the personal planets) join hands sometimes to give results.

Let us take an example, if the planet Venus is transiting through the 3rd house or the sign Gemini, the attention goes to a competitive thought. Also, multiple tasks come into our hands for solving. We reach a stage where without any help from others we just cannot go ahead. We start looking for help. Then we ask and then we seek a solution and solve our own problem. Because planet Venus is amiable, serving our interest, bringing good behavior in us, especially in Air sign houses, Earth sign houses, and Water sign houses, we end up completing our tasks somewhat easily. When the planet Venus is in Fire sign houses, be careful of an urge to use expletives at any person because the chances of getting irritated are high. Planet Venus has no patience in Fire. A primary task is not to be forgotten. That is assessing planet Mercury's position during transit while planet Venus is transiting Mercury's signs or houses. This practice must become your second nature.

With planet Venus in Libra, the talents require some application and sincerity. The person usually uses that in his/her profession. If the position of Venus in Libra is strong on account of aspects from the Sun, Jupiter, or Mars then academic performances also improve. If the planet Saturn aspects Venus in the natal chart it is usually unfortunate because the planet Venus needs to perform against its own will on account of economic pressure or parental pressure. Planet Venus will still do well but it yearns to escape from the hardship. Planet Venus cannot take stress for long. A stressed planet Venus goes to seek inebriation quickly; might seek any bad company to relieve its pressure, and might even neglect its primary duties. The only good thing is planet Venus does not take anything to its head and suffers. Planet Mercury has that tendency and the Moon is well known for mental disorders if stressed in the natal chart. Planet Mars too does not take stress to its head. It turns into a trickster; from a jockey riding a thoroughbred to a chess player in a matter of days. Don't go by the macho image that is portrayed in the periodicals that we all read with great expectations. In my previous book for seniors "Karma is Hidden" I explained this in detail. I shall explain how to treat a transiting Venus at the end of this chapter so that you too can start applying.

In Water Signs

The planet Venus is quite comfortable in water signs and the Earth signs. Since planet Venus has to express in multitudinous ways it finds the liquid state suitable. In the sign Pisces, it is exalted. It means the planet has a tendency to be generous in its qualities without much hindrance coming in its way. It is in the form of compassion that it shows its generosity. It is very happy serving a community, serving persons who are handicapped and ill. Fundamentally the helpless people attract its attention. These people with the planet Venus in Pisces or the 12th house usually work as caretakers, in hotels, in hospitals as both nurses and doctors. Because they love this job, they do it with sincerity and they are liked by all. But planet Venus has difficulty in choosing its mate. It does fool itself by choosing to marry someone handicapped too and ends up serving all its life. Some seek satisfaction by serving hundreds of people in a charity trust, airlines, hospitals, and hospitality industry. Their love toward people who are friends is also from a compassionate point of view. The real lover who is supposed to be given more attention usually suffers. These 'lover boys' keep wondering if this Venus will ever decide or continue distributing her love and affection among her suitors? It is a loss to the planet Venus under the circumstances and it does go through a number of heartbreaks as in the case of the sign Sagittarius. Planet Venus is unable to decide in the dual signs;

no wonder it goes through two weddings in these. In the water signs planet Venus is blessed with money by hook or crook. I am saying this because, in the sign of Scorpio, the crooks come to serve the needs of planet Venus. Planet Venus still cannot discriminate. It is equally skilled to handle them. But it goes through a lot of abuse and exploitation in the sign of Scorpio or when in the 8th house. It does not mind remaining a spinster but it wants a 'crook' to guard her. Even the trust in the Police or the legal system can't assure security to this Venus.

In the sign Cancer or in the 4th house, planet Venus is paired with attachment, insecurity, and public image. These water signs produce charismatic people who have the power to capture people's attention through grace. Most movie actresses have this position or at least planet Venus, in water signs with a location in the 1st house. Attractive looking gents have a Scorpio ascendant with Venus placed in there. Sometimes aspects of Pluto make them hypnotic. You must have realized with certain actors possess a universal appeal. Not just good lookers. Their mere sight causes our hearts to beat faster. It is as if they possessed their power, their looks and attraction from someplace that we do not know at all. Some said if the parents have good features the children too become good looking. Is that true? Parents might be capable of passing on genes and skin color. Nothing more than that; charisma is special.

In Earth Signs

In the earth signs, you will be lucky if you noticed planet Venus in its usual state which is striving for attention, dressed to impress, or even letting you think that it has enough time in hands to subject of its choice. You will only get to hear, "Loads of work to do", "I will be late tomorrow", "I need to cook and then maybe", "I will miss my bus", etc., etc., interesting, isn't it?

In my life, I learned my lesson once, my burnt fingers healed well and I use gloves for all my jobs. But the thing is, I was told it was all a mask! The planet Venus here has plans to overcome its insecurity on its own. It relies on no one. Very early in life this planet Venus of the earth signs was thrust with responsibilities, taking care of siblings, to start earning for the family, and complete its own education and becoming a career woman or a career guy. It never had any chance to even think of romance, entertainment, fun, holidaying, etc., on account of poverty.

Planet Venus in the earth signs, be it even the sign Taurus where planet Venus is better off, its face-off with poverty is unavoidable. The talent side will still blossom at its own pace and it will show a much better class than in the sign Libra. The planet Venus being more in touch with reality does not have superficial relationships. It is faithful and trustworthy. There is a tendency to put on weight if, in the sign of Taurus, there is a tendency to pay too much attention to perfection and skill if placed in the sign Virgo, there is a tendency to earn and gain power if in the sign of Capricorn.

The earth sign Venus is fundamentally a working woman with loads of work at home; whether married or not does not matter. Until and unless it sees material security for real it is not impressed by anyone much. This Venus compares itself to others too much and makes life hell for itself; for either sex this is true.

Let us take an example and see through the transit of planet Venus. My attempt is to make you feel that it is easy and anyone can do an analysis for their day-to-day use. Assume the chart to be a natal chart of someone born today. I am going to discuss only planet Venus during its transit through this horoscope. So, let us start.

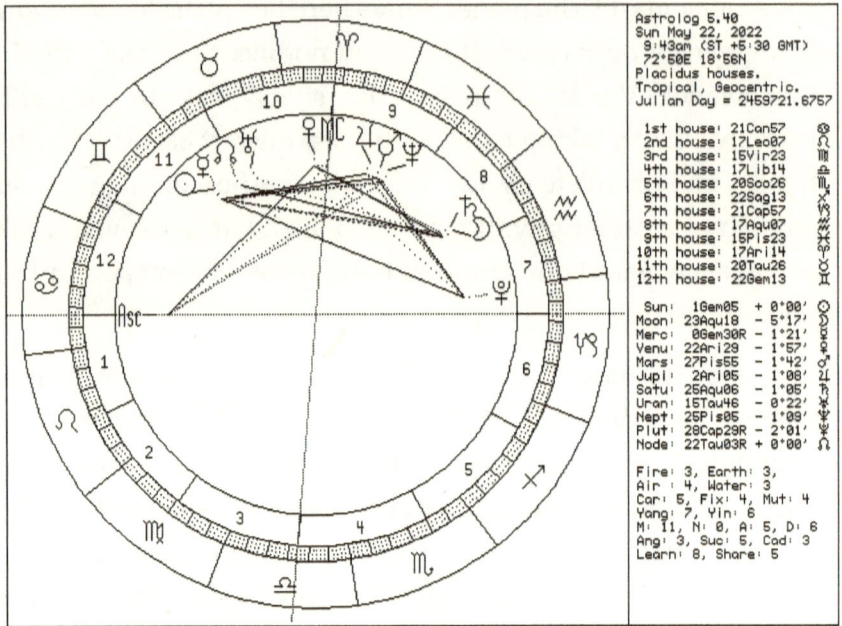

I use Astrolog 5.4 for making all my horoscopes. It is free software available on the net and there are upgraded versions too. There are other softwares available for use on the net. It is a question of what you like.

A Walk in the Park: For Beginners -Tropical or Western Astrology ☆

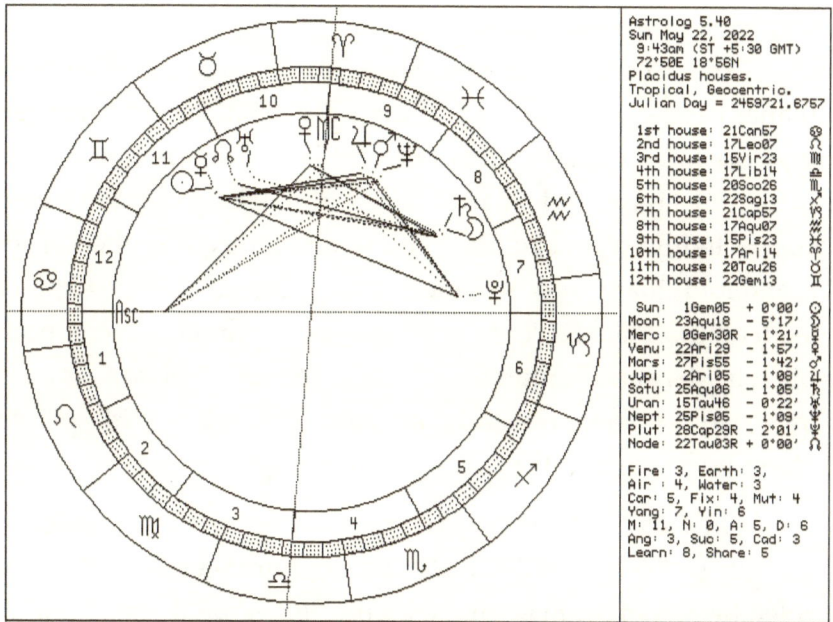

The chart has the sign Cancer on the Ascendant, its ruler is with the planet Saturn in the 8th house, and the sign on its cusp is Aquarius (you must begin this way).

Aspects with the Moon: The Moon is trine to the Sun and planet Mercury.

It is square to the North Node and planet Uranus.

It is sextile to the planet Venus.

Planet Pluto is sextile to the conjunction of planets Jupiter, Neptune, and Mars in the 9th house.

Planet Venus is in the 10th, ruler for its natural houses 2nd (sign Leo), 7th (sign Capricorn). Ruler of its own houses 11th (Taurus), 4th (Libra). Here planet Venus directly indicates what the person will want to portray about self from the 10th house. That portrayal will be used for popularity, earning, and showing off talents, to attract the attention of the people in its ambiance. The sign is a fire sign, Aries. Its ruler is in the 9th, amidst Neptune and Jupiter. Is Mars strong? Good enough. It trines the ascendant Cancer. So is planet Neptune. The only planet Jupiter is a little out of the orb of 5^0. Planet Venus can now operate in the way it wants to. Planet Mars is courageous in the 9th house and guards our health. The position is well supported by planet Jupiter who will magnify this effect from Mars to initiate and self-motivated. This is a true sign of leadership. Planet Neptune helps us to dream. Here both planets Mars and Jupiter will not take impulsive action because they would have mentally envisioned a plan with planet Neptune's help and they will act accordingly.

Only planet Mercury is combust. Its power is usurped by the Sun. so the houses 5th and 2nd become stronger. The 5th house ruled by planet Pluto is trine with the Sun. so all the more value to the 5th house. Planet Venus benefits in the 2nd house of earned income, self-worth, family matters, etc. also some talents of Taurus can be highlighted. But when it comes to money earning this horoscope takes the cake. The 5th house is a life-giving force, motivating house for the first one. Despite the Moon being so close to Saturn, there is less moodiness. Most mental tensions get over on their own. Education, confidence, and health will be good. Because planet Mercury is combust, it loses its personal power. But the Sun is healthy and not vitiated and lots of Mercury's intentions get fulfilled. The 3rd house will suffer but the 2nd and 5th benefit. This will help higher education. The 9th house is strong and associated with people richer, well placed in society, and influential will come forward to help. The 9th house motivates the 5th and the 1st house will motivate the 9th.

The Moon in 8th, is to its detriment. In association with planet Saturn causes stress. Planet Saturn is rigid, observes law and order, legal systems are important to Saturn, and the Moon will be unable to hide its secrets and the problems it has with the mother. The mother suffers here with a bad repute. She cannot stand up to the children and be an exemplar. There will be difficulties in sexual matters, finance, cash in hand, risk-taking. Planet Saturn can provide locked assets here in the 8th but not lose cash. This person can advise others better on financial matters or any other but for the self needs a guide. There will be a deeper interest in occult like astrology, palmistry, and Tarot cards.

That is the foundation I have laid. Now let us see the transit of Venus through the horoscope.

Planet Venus must either support or not give enough support to everything that we have analyzed above during its transit. The planet will do plenty of good and cause movement in the houses which have strength in them on account of natal positions of other planets or maybe planet Venus itself.

The main chart is of a child born today. There will be no self-realization for at least a couple of years; maybe for another twenty years or so. So, we shall consider one such year for the planet Venus' transit through all the houses.

Planet Venus takes a year to go around the entire horoscope and return to where it started from. It is always close to the Sun and within two signs of it. Its period of retrograde comes every eighteen months.

Planet Mars takes two years to complete its transit around the entire zodiac. Planet Mercury too takes about a year to complete one full round of the zodiac. This planet is also very close to the Sun even then manages to go ahead of the Sun and retrograde every three months. Planet Jupiter takes thirteen months to complete one entire round of the zodiac and cause a Jupiter return. Planet Saturn takes twenty-seven and a half years (approx.) to complete one complete round. The remaining planets take very long.

1. As planet Venus starts its transit through the 11th house, we must check its strength if other planets are supporting its purpose first. Since we are only looking at planet Venus, we may ignore it for the time being. The 11th house is 10th from the 2nd house of self-earned income, self-worth and family matters. If planet Venus causes enough excitation in other planets and takes their help, then the 11th house which is for gains, hopes, and wishes begins to take shape. If the 11th house works properly with the help of planet Venus in serving its purpose of serving the community, society, bringing in reforms, selfless and devoted service toward friends, a big purpose, helping people to progress and make one popular among masses then the 2nd house will produce more money. The bigger the purpose taken the greater the achievement. In this case, the Sun is already strong here with the help of planet Mercury. The Sun is known for encouraging others, putting their own example first, bringing influence from higher ups, and seeking popularity. Political benefit is always possible from this house. The only danger is of a weak planet Mercury that might cause the Sun to be loose with its promises or tell lies about the progress made. Planet Venus can change that to sincerity and bring more help for progress. The 2nd house will produce money during this transit.

2. When planet Venus enters the 12th house, it starts to work in the background and not face anyone. It turns compassionate toward all, and in the sign of Gemini has a desire to be curious and become a problem solver. There are temptations to take too much on the head and repeat every task (dual sign Gemini). Will accomplish little but because

of its interest, it manages to study and find out certain information which otherwise lay hidden. Even if planet Venus stays in this house for just thirty days or so, there will be opportunities to serve someone who is handicapped, hospitalized or simply do some counseling for help. This house is very much for recovery of the self or someone related. Going on a short holiday is also quite likely.

3. When planet Venus comes to the 1st house, our own self-improvement gets prioritized. There is a chance to get a nice haircut done, purchase some good clothes, see a doctor, coach, or mentor for advice, become optimistic about one's attempts, and feel self-confident. I have noticed in my own self that I focused on health, exercise and reading something new, and increasing my knowledge. Not that it was planned and done. It just happened and situations came and I performed. There can be indulgence too here and that depends on certain signs that are already indicated in the natal chart. Mostly, everything happens for our good.

    An important matter to remember is that if any New Moon, Full Moon happens and eclipses occur during the transit of planet Venus through any of the houses then planet Venus, the ruler of the house all get the special impetus to start something new or for closures too. Closures could mean that all the hard work period is about to end and a result may be expected that is satisfying. There are a few occasions when pre-closures happen also. The eclipses have a lot of potential in activating a planet and its houses that are well influenced by the planet. For planet Venus of this chart, I have mentioned a few houses that gain strength on account of planet Venus. For this chart planet Venus is good and will bring satisfaction to all activities.

Only planet Mercury is weak, but if the Sun handles the extra power well, when it is not stressed then that too can bring success from gaining recognition point of view. Planet Venus for this chart is a motivator.

4. In the 2nd house, it is not only a good earning time but also an auspicious time for family functions, celebrations, weddings, and parties. There is a self-worth question and planet Venus will improve through certain deeds that build confidence and will. There is a tendency to glutton in some cases but 2nd house is 10th house (the house of work) for the 5th house. 5th house is enjoyment, entertainment, risk, children, etc. the hard work put in in the 2nd house by way of speech, certain talents like singing or playing instruments, etc., happiness goes up.

5. The 3rd house is again ruled by Mercury and in this case, the house has sign Virgo on its cusp. Weak Mercury brings doubts in the mind here. Confidence to meet people, negotiate terms, do a sales job, speak in front of public, write a good CV and ask for a job, curiosity to know about the environment one is in and do things to improve suitably, write and get people's attention, etc., are difficult. The other houses for planet Mercury if strong might improve the condition of the 3rd house. From the point of view of education and intelligence, the 5th, 6th, and the 9th houses are strong. The 3rd house quality of speech and handwriting alone suffers here. One could be poor at languages. Slow learner perhaps. But these improve with age. The early days of learning are difficult. With planet Venus transiting this house a brief spell of improved qualities of the 3rd house may result. In about twenty years, planet Venus would do the improvement twenty times and that is essential to this horoscope for the redemption of

planet Mercury's qualities. All the weaknesses mentioned above will see improvement.

6. When planet Venus transits the 4th house, the position of the Moon in transit through various houses needs to be observed, and accordingly planet Venus will give results here. The changes are frequent because the Moon changes its sign every two and a half days and planet Venus too will adapt itself. The essential thing to note is this house demands unconditional love from all. In order to seek that the planets transiting here will oblige the Moon generously. Planet Venus brings items that are needed by the Moon (attachment articles). Even with parents and other people relations are cordial. Guests increase at home and there is a lot of satisfaction attained from the gathering. Like in the 2nd house many occasions are remembered and celebrated. Ceremonies and religious activities take place. Sometimes a nice comfortable holiday to some place is planned. Pleasure through vehicles is possible too. The 4th house is 10th from the 7th house. The efforts put in through the 4th house helps us to get a companion to marry. Entertaining such persons or inviting friends over are common activities. The 7th also stands for business partners and friends too. There is a connection to justice-seeking in the 7th house. All these are worked out from the 4th house. Solving a legal situation through arbitrators is a possibility.

7. In the 5th house, in this horoscope, planet Venus is comfortable since it is strong. One side is to get educated, seek scholarship and even go for higher education and the other is to remain active motivated through the 9th house and in turn motivate the 1st house. The person is sensible enough not to gamble away the hard-earned money but will be keen to entertain the children, spouse, and all others

who are nearby. The 5th house when happy and active, the 1st house builds itself, repairs itself and comes fit to work anywhere. It has no qualms to show. The 9th house too plays a strong role in health matters and the person enjoys a long life. Planet Venus might even encourage love affairs when transiting through the 5th house. But usually, the time is too short. It can instead do an introduction and move on and let other planets take over.

8. When planet Venus transits the 6th house for a month, the place of work is a pleasure to go. The daily work does not tire us at all. We seem to be enthusiastic about everything that is going on. In this short period, a small introduction is made to a domestic pet. A decision follows later on whether to permanently keep a dog or a cat but the first impression comes during this transit. Servants and maids working for domestic needs tend to be cordial and regular. There is comfort on the work front.

9. When planet Venus transits the 7th house, all its qualities and desires get full opportunity to express and seek results. This 7th house is strong on account of the Sun too with planet Mercury's support. There is always an opportunity to give a public performance, to meet people who are eminent in their field because of the position of the Sun in the chart. Planet Venus feels powerful overnight. But because this house is partly Saturn's (Saturn is exalted in the 7th house or the sign Libra) there is uncertainty in the mind of planet Venus and it is hesitant. It goes to scrutinize the situation with lots of queries and delays an outcome. It is better if Venus is advised by someone to be diplomatic and continue its pursuit of a companion. It is rare for planet Venus to agree and tie a knot while transiting the 7th house. There is justice sought during this time. Old friends return

to say, "Hi". It is a good time to be in the company of a variety of people.

10. When planet Venus is transiting the 8th, it happens to notice an opportunity in carrying out a secret deal with someone. Usually, a benefit is sought from an old investment. There are chances of seeking a legacy in the future if Venus plans to serve someone well. The 8th house is the 10th for the house number eleven of gains, future hopes, and wishes. Such opportunities come and go. Planet Venus needs to be mature enough to realize what is beneficial to it.

11. In the 9th house, planet Venus has dreams to seek freedom and move out of the bindings of society, wedlock, community, religion, etc. But thirty days are too short for that. The thoughts do come and go. Some discussion about that does take place. The 9th house gives the opportunity to hobnob with people who are above us in status. Our boss in the office is sitting here in this house. Your relations improve during this period with him/her. Travel plans may come up, going for higher studies could come up, and religious understanding and dogma become part of our life. In thirty days, our mind travels farther than it had any time before. To explore the world becomes a sudden desire and it materializes in the near future if certain transits collaborate.

I have covered the 10th house at the beginning itself but I have to write something in support of combust planets. When planets like Mercury, Venus, or Mars combust, the Sun takes their power to produce results that are suited to its owned house (the sign Leo) and the 5th house (natural ruler). The elders of the family like, the father, the elder brother, or any senior person who is directly in charge of you get benefited too. One always feels submissive toward anyone who appears superior in some way; even falsely one may portray as very able or rich. That is sufficient for showing respect toward such people. The Sun in order to accommodate the interest of the other planet loses some of its own individuality or self-respect. It shows a tendency to fawn in order to take favors. When planet Mercury is combust, the sign Leo and the 5th house benefit through intellectual achievements, speech, the skill shown through hands, writing habits, language skills, competitiveness, building friends and contacts, knowledge and interest in legal matters, health and medicine, literature, etc., are common. But the Sun is more interested in putting these to use and is in a great hurry to promote through boasting, putting on pretense, and seeking self-importance wherever there is an opportunity. Planet Mercury is actually at the mercy of the Sun because Mercury needs time to prove its merits and then come before public attention. It is better that planet Mercury takes up such activities that do not come to the attention of the Sun. the Sun wants to seek popularity fast and will use anything and everything at its disposal. Planet Mercury must on its own develop habits consciously to grow into someone who has thorough knowledge and personality traits that are useful in the corporate world. Lack of confidence, forgetfulness, fear of the unknown, fear of underperformance, fear of not being able to achieve perfection, a consciousness of self, worried about criticism is common problems that planet Mercury has to face when combust. These need to be looked into and through practice planet Mercury will be able to overcome such weaknesses. Most mental disorders emerge from combust Mercury or stressed Mercury which is also weak.

A similar situation also exists for planet Venus if combust. The topmost qualities in Venus that are not seen on any other planet are grace, beauty, talent and money. Even the Moon has two possessions; one is its attachments or possessions, second is unconditional love that is both received and given. Planet Mars shows courage and a desire to win always, health and vigour are available only with planet Mars. If we all have a desire to secure a certain 'thing' and possess a certain unique way to seek it, it is our planet Mars planning for us. All such qualities go to the Sun and the planet that is combust waits for the Sun to perform and brings the 'combust planet' qualities to the fore. That usually happens with a 'chance' factor. So once a person knows that a certain planet is combust then consciously one will have to develop until it is mastered so that premature display due to the Sun does not take place.

That completes our attempt at understanding planet Venus.

Chapter-XIII

"The pessimist complains about the wind; the optimist expects it to change; the realist adjusts the sails."

-William Arthur Ward

The Outer Planets

We have two sets of planets to consider always. The inner personal planet; like Mercury, Venus, Mars, and the two bodies, the Sun and the Moon. Followed by, the set of outer planets; like Saturn, Uranus, Neptune, and Pluto. Planet Jupiter has distinguished qualities. It helps both sets of planets. It plays the role of countries Switzerland and Austria during World War two. Planet Jupiter is neutral and succours all.

The personal planets have an immediate purpose to create opportunities and fulfill any of our desires that have been formed, accumulated, waiting to be realized, etc. These planets being fast-moving planets appear to be waiting to fulfill their purpose. They do it quickly and our human nature is slow to react and take action. These planets probably think that we are still in the pre-historic days when even human beings acted on instinct to produce a result. The present humans delay in contemplating about results. That contemplation has advantages too but those desirous of fulfilling their primal desires feel frustrated. 'Jealousy' for example is a primal desire. Making 'physical love' is also a primal desire. To 'hit' or 'beat up' someone is definitely a primal desire. Like that there are so many and we do not act according to such passing fancies. The animals do even now. Perhaps the personal planets are happier helping them!

Our need for help comes from a thought of helplessness. Sometimes our parents, siblings, friends, and other elders are in no position to help except for advice on certain matters. It is during this phase the personal planets come and play a role for us. Again, not in every difficulty but I have always felt, that the help allowed me to solve a series of issues that allowed me to rise to the surface once again. So, it is a need-based help. It is important for us as consultant astrologers to find what is troubling the client in a chronic manner. The personal planets will be seen to be working toward that. You all must have already felt how to use the information that has been described under the heading of each house for so many planets. Am I right or wrong? So, decide today itself that after an initial perusal of the chart presented by a client ask the first question, "What is troubling you? What are you anxious about? Are you facing any crisis?" That should lead you the way. Sometimes the answers are not visible. Please do not force yourself to answer or find a solution. Stay clean always.

Pluto

The outer planets have an independent agenda. If someone is looking for the destiny of a person then these outer planets hold the answer. Their speed to move through the zodiacal signs is very less; time and again these outer planets have to seek the help of the transiting personal planets in order to achieve their intent. Once the personal planets move away, as their speeds are much higher than the outer planets, the matter remains in abeyance until the next opportunity. Meanwhile, the outer planets are moving slowly toward some natal personal planet in the horoscope. As they transit the natal personal planet, usually three times at least, there is a greater opportunity for these outer planets to manifest through that personal planet. The outer planets come as if with a vengeance always. They appear to be in unison with the natal personal planet at first because that personal planet could be a strong planet in a horoscope. There is co-operation at first and slowly the outer planet unfolds its agenda and turns the tide.

In anyone's chart, the outer planets will tell much in advance about the lessons to be learned on account of their placement. In each house, there are certain 'excesses' possible. These excesses are due to our own created desires. Perhaps we were deprived initially of many pleasures, possessions, and aspirations. We try to manifest them with the help of personal planets. We then feel remorse for keeping such desires on a 'wait' to be fulfilled one day. There are a few who never wait at all and they never show such high desires. They treat everything casually. I get very annoyed at such people because they are quite comfortable and never troubled by any situation. They do not put conditions for acceptance of any kind into their life. Most of us do and we isolate ourselves from many.

The outer planets initially let us seek whatever we desire so that we are fully consumed by our greed. Then they snatch that away from us. For example, if planet Pluto is seen in the 5th of a chart the desire is to feel and show power through all the 5th house activities. There are good and bad attributes to the 5th house but planet Pluto chooses those that are specifically connected to personal power. A thought and a feeling of you alone possess something covetous and others do not. This can be through fun and entertainment, travel, children, gambling, risk-taking, and love affairs. There is a lesson to be learned so you are allowed freedom with opportunity into these activities that specifically take you there from where you would not wish to return to lead a normal ordinary life. After you reach that state, you are like a ripened mango that needs to be plucked out of a tree. Planet Pluto will remove that greatest pleasure from your life in order to suffer its loss. That lesson can only come from the planet Pluto. Not any other outer planet. That is why you might have read that planet Pluto is a planet for transformation. A change brought about to completely give up certain pursuits in order to lead a normal and comfortable lifestyle. The excesses will not be wished for again. The excesses came from where planet Pluto was placed in the natal chart, 5th house in this case. The lessons come when planet Pluto is transiting over any of the personal planets.

So how does planet Pluto do it? If planet Pluto is transiting over planet Mars, a situation that resembles an unsurmountable challenge is brought on. Because of a powerful will inside us, we want to overcome the challenge and win to show how powerful we are. This will be slowly built with the help of the personal planet Mars in this case. It can also happen that a few months before the actual transit, planet Pluto might have aspected the planet Mars to initiate a desire. All these need to be noticed. Many times, the challenge has well triumphed. The aftermath is when we get the lesson that it was not worth fighting so much. The natal placement of planet Pluto is in the 5th house, as said before. The results will also take us back to 5th house outcomes. We must have achieved something in order to satisfy a need that has origins in the 5th house. That achievement crumbles. But not the lesson learnt.

It is similar when planet Pluto transits the natal Venus (a love affair or a money-making venture), natal Mercury (a business venture or higher studies), the Moon (an attempt to seek something very dear or try to save one), the Sun (an attempt to survive a crisis or yield to a predicament while trying hard) are the likely results. So always notice the natal position for lessons to be learned. Situations are dragged to the house qualities from wherever the transit of planet Pluto is occurring.

The signs do not matter much in the case of the outer planets while leading us to lessons.

Neptune

Planet Neptune is known to build dreams inside us. If planet Pluto made us power conscious through various means and showed the advantages of power, planet Neptune allows us to see, visualize and then temper our thoughts day after day to seek that dream somehow. What does the planet achieve by doing so? Planet Neptune has a desire to create a beautiful world around us. It does not use force. It uses reality first and says, "Look! Isn't this beautiful?", "Worth possessing or keeping?", "Come I will show you more!" Again, all depends on whether we are ready for the dream or may not. So, a repetitive occurrence in the real world happens before us so that a foundation is laid before us. Then we finally form a dream and improvise on it.

The quality of the dream or its type depends on the natal position of planet Neptune. Planet Neptune will show the dreams that magnify the qualities of the natal house that Neptune is in. There is no danger in dreaming something and feeling assured that it is achievable then set afoot in fulfilling it. This is possible if planet Neptune has certain aspects with the natal personal planets. That natal personal planet is capable of handling the dream well because the dream is well contemplated in the years that pass. Sometimes there are two or three personal planets that are aspected by planet Neptune in the natal chart. It will help that much more in fully realizing the dream.

The danger lies when the planet Neptune aspects a transiting personal planet for a few days or few weeks. This time is too short and whatever we dream is misleading and deceptive. In a storm of temptation, a small boat of desire is thrown around to the will of the tide. We end up as losers or cheated. When planet Neptune transits a natal personal planet it takes nearly a year to completely move away and remove its influence over the natal personal planet. This period is long and good enough to sow a seed of a dream in us. When planet Neptune aspects planet Saturn by a square, conjunction or opposition, planet Saturn's hold on our possessions, home, elders in the family, children, money, wealth, company, business, and jewelry becomes weak. There is a strong desire to fulfill what we want through the liquidation of assets. That is the biggest danger. The outer planet leads us to where we want to go but at the expense of our resources. This, all outer planets do with their aspects to the personal planets, the Sun and the Moon. They have a power or a charm to entice and release them from what they hold tightly from losing in our life. The Sun loses its dignity first, planet Venus loses discrimination, planet Mercury loses its integrity, the Moon loses faith, and planet Mars loses sense of purpose; planet Mars only wants a 'win' but does not know the consequences. By making us realize the dreams planet Neptune closes a chapter by showing that it is fatuous and not really worth it. One aspires to a different kind of dream after that. The travel bug that was biting is taken away instead pilgrimage may take its place.

Uranus

In the case of planet Uranus, we are confronted with new ideas and knowledge because we do not fully realize their use. Once again that 'primal' instinct takes over us. We try to solve our regular problems or very common problems with an unwanted, want to be original, using a great many plans and gadgetry sometimes. In the end, we get called different names on account of that; 'a fool' is one of them! The purpose of planet

Uranus is to make us independent enough so that we progress in life in a superior manner. Superior means, according to planet Uranus, doing anything and everything without any superior's permission or intervention. Does that mean recalcitrance? You are right. Whenever planet Uranus comes close to an aspect of our personal planets, the Sun or the Moon, we wish to be recalcitrant. We have the least respect for the law or the legal system. We enjoy breaking the rules with audacity. Reckless behaviour is common.

Especially, when the planet Uranus aspects planet Venus, misbehavior is very common in one. Planet Uranus makes one of the two pursuers (the one in whose horoscope is very active for that period) assume that the other is equally involved in the pursuit of gratification. That causes irritation and anger in both soon. It is very difficult to find two people to have a similar aspect in their charts. One may be mildly pursuing and the other could be aggressive. Planet Uranus might be able to cause one person to take liberties with the 'spirit' provided and let hell break loose. There is no emotional involvement here but mostly ravishing sexual rage.

Is that the purpose here of planet Uranus? No, do not forget we are the ones who use the 'knowledge' (intuitively) and the 'excitement' resulting from it in a 'primal capturing' manner. Most of the knowledge provided is usually not handled well by all the personal planets. They get into a mental trip and then feel remorse. The crisis arises on account of the speed with which planet Uranus fills us with the spirit of freedom, a spirit of action, and a spirit of urgency; all in quick succession. That is why most astrologers have called planet Uranus as a suddenly manifesting, disastrously precipitating planet. It is handled well if there are some natal aspects in the chart between planet Uranus and the personal planets. The person is quite used to planet Uranus' force in demanding a result.

With planet Mars planet Uranus causes irritability and anger. The rage results in a mini-war of words or fists. With planet Mercury, it is to try and conquer something with knowledge and research. It is usually something that causes others to accept defeat seeing a prowess. The person seeking this would have too great lengths in order to seek it; sacrificing many comforts like home and family. The common denominator is that we become devoid of emotions in trying to achieve under planet Uranus' influence. With the Moon, planet Uranus leaves the home to feel free. Most people leave home tearing their relationships with everyone in the family.

With the Sun, the person begins to hate the work place, position, rank and superiors. Planet Uranus has enough power to cultivate an interest in creative arts. Many pursue fine arts by leaving their normal jobs. There is a sense of being consumed by a certain idea during transit from planet Uranus. A person acts as if he just cannot resist an idea to bring that to practice. Many leave their spouse because they are pretty much taken by a new lifestyle and their old one does not seem fulfilling. This strange behaviour from very ordinary people otherwise makes it difficult to accept and forgive. The purpose of Uranus is to tell with his knowledge that one must seek the pleasures of life independently and not through leading a life of a parasite.

As before, planet Uranus' natal position tells us in which domain of our life that we are likely to use the knowledge passed to us by planet Uranus. If planet Uranus is in the 4th house of a natal chart, all aspects in the future from planet Uranus to the personal planets will drag the issue of 'unconditional love' seeking. That becomes like a challenge and the person just leaves the house trying to find it somewhere. There is no way of seeing cordial relations with the parents or family. The mother is the challenge here. Home is uncomfortable always. In the 5th it becomes children, love affairs, risks, education, and entertainment to become unseekable although they are the most desired. Getting grounded is what is feared and therefore all the flighty ways are followed. These people cannot see that are simpler ways to seek whatever they want. But they just neither see those nor have faith in them.

Saturn

In the case of the planet Saturn the name of the game changes. Although the planets create enough hurdles in our path we need to understand earlier on if we are driving our vehicle in the wrong direction on a one-way street. Again, its natal position decides in which aspect of our life we are restricted. Each time its aspects any of our personal planets, that one place where the planet Saturn is sitting in our natal charts, that part gets highlighted and the restriction is felt again. Let us assume that planet Saturn is located in the 9th house. This is the house of planet Jupiter which naturally supports an independent 'belief system' according to our wish. It allows us to keep an entirely independent view of religion, castes, cultures, countries, prejudices, adventure, higher learning, foreign travel, health, mingling with people, etc. if planet Saturn is present here, we have problems and restrictions felt if we try to express as planet Jupiter would wish us to. It is a different matter if the planet Saturn is weak or becomes weak due to passing transits of outer planets, due to New Moons or Full Moons aspecting or eclipses aspecting and during Saturn's return (once in 27 years). The restrictions are felt because planet Saturn is not interested in us wasting time on trivial issues. It is interested in producing wealth using all the attributes shown for the 9th house. You may use every quality mentioned above to earn money this planet Saturn will co-operate but not otherwise. Moreover, planet Saturn has been vested with powers and responsibilities like the law and enforcement, the legal system, the political power, etc. planet Saturn might look the other way during the period when it is weak. But when it becomes normal after a couple of months it regains what it has lost with a vengeance. It is dangerous to fool Saturn during its weak period. People pay double the price during the time they regret. It is best to understand the issues that one faces repetitively and is usually solved through hard work and not through petty amends. The repetitive issues emerge from that natal house planet Saturn is occupying.

Let us take the above example of planet Saturn located in the 9th house of a natal chart. Each time planet Saturn transits the four sensitive points (the cusps of the 1st, 4th, 7th, and 10th houses), each time planet Saturn aspects our personal planets the 9th house issues will cause some kind of trouble or the other. In the early days, it becomes learnings issues, later on, it changes to associate with different types of people at school or college or at the university. The authorities who are above us are also part of the 9th house. So, the hostel warden and departmental heads will cause strictures and issue warnings. Later in jobs, the boss causes problems. After marriage the in-laws cause problems. At each stage of our life, we feel that we are learning lessons. That is the trouble we face and constantly dread the planet Saturn. There is no solution or a remedy to this. Planet Saturn does not stop any good result from happening or snatch a precious item from our possession unless we stand adamant and disobey or turn into chronic offenders of the law.

Planet Saturn's guidance is a lot comparable to Hobson's choice sometimes. But the choice has to be made.

Lastly, I want to draw your attention to why are we lured toward a particular object, person, or situation that exceeds rationale. There is a concept of interestingness or interestedness that further is simplified to salience. I am quoting from a podcast that I watched on YouTube that described the point I wanted to make succinctly. It is called," What it is like to have schizophrenia". Each one of us perceives certain information with varying degrees of importance. If changing the weather is of consequence to someone then changing the stock market is of consequence to somebody else. If we randomly placed only the titles of this, the so-called vital information, then no one would perhaps be interested. On the other hand, if I gave sufficient information then certainly some of us would choose to give importance to certain titles like sports, weather, stock market, or politics. Salience comes when we start giving importance depending on how we perceive information. When something becomes important on account of information received our brain perceives that as a reward. When information is perceived as salient the brain releases a neurotransmitter called dopamine. A rush of dopamine causes us to pay more attention because dopamine produces pleasure and we like to feel that more. It also motivates us to continue doing the act of receiving information over and over again. That cultivates a habit; with each onrush of dopamine, we think that a lot has been gained. When habits cultivated in this way become a compulsion, the release of dopamine becomes erratic. What one needs to understand here is that the dopamine release is more in anticipation than when one actually gets what is anticipated. The salience that gets attached to anything producing excitable information causes addiction. All addictions have just one common factor which is dopamine release. Then we begin to attach salience to falsehood or unreal situations simply to feel the excitement. That is when we fall prey to the guiles of the outer planets. The initiation of activity is carried out by the personal planets. That is when the salience is attached. As we involve ourselves more the outer planets reach to complete the 'getting us involved act'. Later they defuse the situation in order to break the dependency. After all the outer planets have a lesson in wait for us all. They have no interest in bringing us a gift. In short, if we stop giving salience to certain issues, we never grow a habit of seeking an increased supply of dopamine. When we let ourselves be roped into circumstances that do not deserve so much importance then the outer planets cannot trouble us at all.

Chapter-XIV

"The path of least resistance is the path of the loser."

-H.G. Wells

The Disorders

Under the chapter of Mercury, I wrote that several mental disorders happen if planet Mercury is either weak or stressed in the natal chart due to outer planetary aspects, hard aspects from planet Mars or planet Jupiter or the Nodes, if Mercury is combust, if planet Mercury is aspected by a New Moon or a Full Moon or an eclipse, if planet Mercury is retrograde in the natal chart. Stressful periods during Mercury transits to come and go; their period is short and planet Mercury is fast moving. Planet Mercury represents friends and siblings. If the relations with these are maintained well most of the disorders can be avoided. A proper understanding needs to be developed between the individual and others only then relief is offered by the association. When that is missing like in the case where the person is the only child or friendships do not form easily and the child grows up and continues to be a loner, or for some reason or the other the child changes its school frequently are some of the reasons certain relationships do not form. These become vulnerable individuals if they possess a weak or stressed planet Mercury in their chart. Although I have listed a few symptoms for certain disorders, it is meant to be a guide for you to use.

It is difficult to generalize a particular weakness in a chart as seen by us and link it with the symptoms listed below. You might be able to notice a pattern later as your experience gathers momentum with time. I began to notice only in the last twelve years or so. Until then I had no idea what happens to a person with stressed planets like Mercury, Venus, and Mars. Even the Moon and Sun could be stressed and a person may be suffering silently. So let your observations play a dominant role and not so much of what I have shown as symptoms for certain disorders. I have in fact collected my information from the internet, their links are also mentioned, the sites are particularly meant for students who are about to embark on a deeper study of the subject of psychiatry.

When planet Mercury is combust, the Sun takes the power off planet Mercury and uses it to its own benefit. Under such circumstances, the Sun should not be stressed by aspects from the Nodes, or the outer planets. If so, both the Sun and planet Mercury will suffer. The Sun is our personality which means that we want to show ourselves as someone worth noticing, respecting, show value, and consider as a person who is liked and wanted by everyone. It is because of our own drawbacks or weaknesses that we succeed sometimes and fail sometimes. That does not deter us. If we have a physical deformation, disproportionate features or a harsh voice and poor diction or say, bad habits then these do come in our way. Still, to many these do not hurt their confidence. They manage to carry themselves through on account of self-belief. This self-belief gets thoroughly damaged when the Sun is weak or stressed. If we add weak Mercury due to 'combust', on top of a weak Sun, a lot more damage occurs. The person is sensitive to comments received from others; especially family members. This weak Mercury is quick to assume that it is not liked or it's devalued. Such a planet Mercury looks for validation elsewhere and wherever it gets it shows a dependency on them. If combust, then the Sun does that on behalf of planet Mercury to remain content. All the Sun's houses get an additional strength on account of combust planet Mercury and the houses that belong to the planet Mercury will suffer unless there is a strong and unaffected ruling planet attached to the planet Mercury's houses.

For example, let us take a chart with the sign Gemini as ascendant. The ruler of the 1st house is planet Mercury, if this planet Mercury is combust then the houses with signs Gemini and Virgo will suffer. The houses 3rd and 6th will also suffer with signs Leo and Scorpio respectively. Since the Sun has acquired power from planet Mercury, the 5th house, the sign Leo and the house where the Sun is actually transiting at the time of making this birth chart will all gain status. The good thing that happened is that the 3rd house which belongs to planet Mercury is saved because of the sign Leo. The 6th house ruler is the planet Pluto if well placed and not retrograde then even that house is saved. We must make sure of the quantity of damage if any of the planets or the Moon becomes combust.

The Moon is affected on three occasions. On a New Moon Day, Full Moon Day, and on the Quarter Moon Day, the Moon loses its power to the Sun and it channels its desires through the Sun who might not be able to oblige with all demands made. Such horoscopes with the above positions always suffer from unfulfilled desires, fear of abandonment and they constantly wait for gratification through outsiders. There is also impulsivity because the Moon is so crisis-minded that it always thinks that another opportunity might never come. If lucky, then these are fulfilled by siblings, friends, or even parents. But a time comes when these people look for outside help and we call that 'a love affair' or a 'clandestine affair' etc. When the Sun and the Moon are at sextile or trine aspect then such situations do not come. The problem that arises when the Sun and the

Moon have hard aspects between them (conjunction, square, and opposition) is that there is a difficulty in commitment and identity of the self. These people change their names, citizenship or just change their country of domicile to cover their identity so that past acts do not become public knowledge. The hard aspects have a touch of 'anaretic planets' quality to them. The anaretic planet (the last 10^0 of a house or a sign) can talk or promise many things but will never go near to fulfil it. It prefers to escape; loves 'future faking'. Always look for anaretic angle for a planet in a chart. Likewise, if a planet is in the initial degrees of a sign or a house the planet is still in the process of adapting to the qualities of the new environment. One cannot expect a sincere approach or behavior or commit as that house or the sign would. Once we deduce such qualities due to certain positions many queries get answered automatically.

Sometimes planet Venus is combust or weak or stressed then planet Venus is ready to seek validation from almost anywhere. Just remember the lost strength of these personal planets has to be restored somehow. If not in the immediate neighbourhood like parents, siblings or friends then the outsider's come. Some people have lots of friends, isn't it? Check their charts if planet Mercury or planet Venus is weak or stressed in some way. There is something lacking. That 'lack' is fulfilled first before anyone embarks on meeting other challenges in life. Do not confuse with contacts and acquaintances that people develop on account of professional needs. These are 'friends' who are ready to accompany a person anywhere and anytime. To the self-respecting person, friends are just part of life and there is no dependency. There is more of a concern than anything else. But nothing more than that. These variations are what we need to notice.

When planet Mercury is weak its compensation is not fully done with adding a few more friends. Planet Mercury is our intellect, memory, a machine that can go forward and backward in time to both guess and recall. This cannot be substituted if deranged. A small relief could be given. But not more. The solution comes from releasing the load on planet Mercury. Planet Mercury must feel relieved for a while before it enters the field of work again. Someone like a guardian, parent, spouse or anyone at the office must notice the problem faced by an individual. Then perhaps there are ways to improve. If a lot of time has passed with the planet Mercury taking that stress, then recovery will take longer. Reassurance and building confidence needs to be done constantly by someone who is close or familiar and with time improvements are sought. There will be issues like irritability, loss of focus, and unnecessary arguing. All these need to be sorted out. Moreover, planet Mercury is not conducive to taking advice immediately when weak or stressed. It prefers to try hard and make the entire issue of redemption look fatuous. It will give a number of excuses to prove the counsellor wrong. Especially from the past if there are any precedents to the contrary. A weak Mercury has an uncanny memory to remember the past just like the Moon. A strong planet Mercury on the other hand has so much to do and remember it forgets plenty of old episodes if they have occurred to disappoint the planet Mercury. Another difficulty is to keep a weak planet Mercury engaged in some activity that brings satisfaction. Their ruminating habit about past events removes their focus from anything they have started fresh. So, keeping all these in mind we all must take the initiative to advice our clients.

Then there are speeds assigned to planet Mercury and this too decides how efficient planet Mercury is in our chart. I have devoted an entire chapter to this in my previous book, "Karma is hidden". Please go through and you will understand the phenomenon of speed in the case of planet Mercury.

Planet Uranus has the habit of showing glimpses of the outcome first and excites us. The knowledge and information that this planet is supposed to provide also come in large doses in a short time. Planets like Venus, Moon and Mercury become stressed and act without their usual characteristic essence of waiting and providing good opportunities. These planets rush and cause a 'there is no tomorrow' kind of situation. That causes offense, repulsion, disappointment, and sometimes fears in others. The others feel their personal space is being exposed and their public image will be tarnished. So, one must expect that during transits of planet Uranus. In the natal chart, planet Uranus steadily provides its stock of information to the planet that it aspects and over the years the person also knows how to handle planet Uranus' energy.

Given below are the disorders that one might notice in a client and check if the symptoms tally before an advice is offered.

Mania: Mania is characterized by excessive elevations in mood and energy rather than dips-down like in depression. Mania is the hallmark state of bipolar disorder a psychiatric condition that involves both manic highs and depressive lows. Depression mania involves changes in moods. The person in a state of mania will generally describe a present emotional state as great, wonderful, and fantastic; also feel that they are on the top of this world or as if they have won a million dollars. So, what is so bad about it?

With depression, one feels sad most of the time. The problem with mania is that just like in depression, a patient's mood with mania is non-reactive. This makes them incapable of experiencing emotions other than happiness. It's a bit like a car without its brakes functioning; the car can only go at a certain speed but not stop. People with mania can go on and on with their delusive thoughts, imaginary achievements or achievements to come, and undistracted constant talking. The distraction happens only when a topic is changed without warning. There is difficulty finishing the conversation. The inner tension pulls their thoughts into many directions.

Acting without regard to consequences during pleasure-seeking activities like drug abuse, reckless driving, sex and spending are very common. In mania, it often involves displaying self-importance. These people believe that they are special and entitled. The activity taken up is usually goal directed and involves working toward some kind of reward or outcome. A direct dependency on dopamine production that involves pleasure; any act that may be repeated daily or frequently to keep anxiety down is obvious. Another common and noticeable phenomenon is an inability to get refreshing sleep. There is a decreased need. People suffering from depression suffer too of decreased or inability to sleep but they show a lack of energy afterward. In mania, no such lack of energy or lethargy is noticed. These people can go without much sleep for days or even weeks without complaining.

Courtesy: https://www.youtube.com/watch?v=y0wrW-9_cH4

Mania & Bipolar Disorder Mnemonics (Memorable Psychiatry Lecture 5)

While analyzing a chart try to notice if the Moon is combust or has been given an exaggerated desire by an aspect from planet Jupiter. The hard aspects will likely result in unfulfilled desires because the desires will be such. Planet Mercury too needs to be weak. I have noticed a combust planet Mercury causing mania; planet Mercury was in the Leo sign. It could have been a planet Jupiter's aspect too instead. Focus on self-opinion and aspirations that are unfulfillable.

Bipolar Disorder

When you become depressed, you may feel sad or hopeless and lose interest or pleasure in most activities. When your mood shifts to mania or hypomania (less extreme than mania), you may feel euphoric, full of energy or unusually irritable. These mood swings can affect sleep, energy, activity, judgment, behavior, and the ability to think clearly. https://www.mayoclinic.org/diseases-conditions/bipolar-disorder/symptoms-causes/syc-20355955

The mood swings require a weakened Moon that is at the mercy of another planet. The other planet could be from an outsider (a friend, spouse, parents) and its effects are felt stronger because in the natal chart there could be no major aspect from an outer planet or planet Jupiter. For depression to happen there needs to be failures in the attempts made. A weak or stressed planet Mercury could bring depression. I have seen hard aspects from planet Mars to planet Mercury and bringing depression. Planet Mars speeds up planet Mercury. If planet Mercury is retrograde in the chart or slow (check daily movement speed) then this speeding up will not let planet Mercury function properly on significant occasions like a test or an interview. Anxiety comes in the way.

Courtesy: https:// www.nhs.uk /mental -health/ conditions /bipolar- disorder/ symptoms/

Depression

Courtesy: https://www.mayoclinic.org/diseases-conditions/depression/symptoms-causes

During a period of depression, a person will feel sad and this feeling is also accompanied by a sense of defeat, frustration, inability to overcome a burning issue, and urgency is shown toward that issue. The difficulty in advising those affected is that they are fixated on the issue so much that they hate to think of an alternative. This is followed by a period of no contact with everyone except one or two close friends or parents. Their dependency on these confidantes is considerable and if there is any opportunity to cause a reversal it will be through these close associates.

Loss of sleep brings in a loss of energy and sleeping through the day is also seen as a relief. There is pessimism and a loss of appetite. There is hesitation that is seen as difficult to overcome, in every new resolve to adopt or take a fresh step toward improving self-confidence.

Planet Mercury is definitely involved in this phenomenon but the Moon and planet Venus cause emotional deprivation. When the Moon and planet Venus get connected through hard aspects the person has a strong attachment toward the mother. If the situation brings an estrangement, quite likely when the person has to leave home and stay away for studies or even loss of a mother, loss of a child, loss of a regular source of income, etc., become common causes. Persons who are near and dear to the subject have a better chance of giving support to the person suffering.

Borderline Personality Disorder

Courtesy: https://www.mayoclinic.org/diseases-conditions/borderline-personality-disorder/symptoms-causes

With borderline personality disorder, you have an intense fear of abandonment or instability in relationships and you may have difficulty tolerating being alone. This brings a clinging, over-caring, frequent talking to check (by phone) or keep the other engaged in an activity that serves the self, are some of the characteristics (that are fundamentally 'anxiety' driven) of people who suffer from a borderline personality disorder. The abandonment crisis is a weak 'Moon' issue. This crisis emerging out of the Moon must somehow get connected to planet Mercury (the memory manager) then this disorder can start. All disorders begin after the age of eighteen or twenty-one years of age. This is the age when children separate from their parents to go to university. Many cannot handle this. If they have inherent issues then these begin to show up.

In BPD from what I read there is a 'capture and conquer' so that abandonment may be avoided. Frequent appearances like meetings and phone calls are initially very encouraging in relationships. Telling frequently, "I miss you" for self-assurance causes the other person to believe that someone is hooked permanently. This gets exploited as the person suffering from BPD also engages in impulsive acts like sex, drug abuse, and other risks. That stages the chapter to a close because there is not much left in the relationship now and the partner believes that it is better to leave the person with BPD and seek someone else. An abandonment is self-staged in most cases. It could be similar to other members of the family and friends.

Pathologic Liars

Courtesy: https://www.healthline.com/health/pathological-liar#comparing-lies

When a person tries to portray themselves as someone who has seen it all before and nothing comes to them as something new or unheard of. Instead of appreciating the narrator, the pathological liar will now choose to tell a story very convincingly of a previous experience to be much superior to the story

Pathological lying, also known as mythomania and pseudologia fantastica, is the chronic behavior of compulsive or habitual lying. The lying emanates from a deep feeling of being inferior to others and the person struggles to stand up as an equal. It is not like lying for humour or to save a certain situation. One can catch pathological lying only with familiarity and not if you are encountering such a person occasionally or for the first time. It is practiced lying and the person lying knows how to build a story convincingly.

A pathological liar tells lies and stories that fall somewhere between conscious lying and delusion. They sometimes believe their own lies. I have an experience where my very close friend who I know for many years would love to add a false story just to show that whatever is being spoken, heard, read or seen is a 'déjà vu' experience to him. No one tried testing him but he too was sure he will get away with it with another lie. Others felt that he had issues of getting importance as his family's economic status was very poor from childhood. The lying had become a habit to somehow cover that indigence.

Pathological liars also tend to be natural performers. When asked questions, they may speak a lot without ever being specific or answering the question.

The following are to be observed:

1. Creating a false history, such as saying they've achieved or experienced something they haven't.

2. Claiming to have spent a lot of money on luxury travel, despite their friends knowing these people could never afford a taxi anywhere.

3. Boasting that their association and friends are all in high places and have access to meet them anytime.

A combust Mercury causes lying to be frequent. If planet Jupiter aspects the Sun in a hard way, then too the Sun's need to get attention becomes greater. Fundamentally there must be poverty in childhood; so, notice planet Saturn's position and aspects. Saturn aspects to the Moon and planet Venus are a must. Natal planet Saturn must be in either 2nd, 3rd, 4th, 5th, 8th or 12th houses. These houses cause a struggle to overcome poverty in childhood; bring self-hatred in the individual. To escape from that inner wound the person adopts lying and assumes that a value was earned.

Anxiety

If one has a constant fear of something that is likely to happen in the future or a fear of consequences due to what has been done or happened in the past that person is jittery always. In order to get out of that state, the person keeps certain regular habits that may be controlled. These people choose confidantes who condone their past acts and give them confidence. Such persons are much sought after by the anxiety-stricken person throughout the day. This state of worrying and seeking relief from a sympathetic source is a true sign of anxiety. Always ask the question, "From where are you seeking your relief?" and you will know if the anxiety is serious or not. Everyone has anxiety before an examination at school, college, or at university. We have experienced a fear overtaking us before an interview for a job or an oral examination. The worry or fear is about a failure in a task taken up by us. Those go away as soon as the event gets over.

In the case of anxiety, which is also a fear, the situation that is feared is not real and cannot be used to counsel someone. It must go on its own. The person suffering has to see a practical possibility of such imagined fears. For this, there needs to be a deliberation with a counsellor or someone who has experienced anxiety and has overcome that.

I shall not go too much into anxiety as there are plenty of professionals to help in case one is suffering; instead, I want to elaborate a little on planet Mercury, the Sun, and the Moon. The confidence showing houses are the 3rd, 5th, 9th, and 10th. The confidence giving planets are the Sun, the Moon, planets Venus and Mars. Mental weakness or strength is indicated by planet Mercury and the Moon.

Now let us see them as weak and occurring in confidence giving houses. Then anxiety is sure to result. Most anxiety occurs with planet Mars or planet Venus begins to push other planets, the Sun or the Moon in the natal chart. The transiting aspects are short-lived. So, observe these and come to your own conclusion.

Given below are a few more examples of how two planets get connected when a third planet comes in between to act as a mid-point. An orb of just 3^0 is to be used for accuracy.

A Walk in the Park: For Beginners -Tropical or Western Astrology ☆

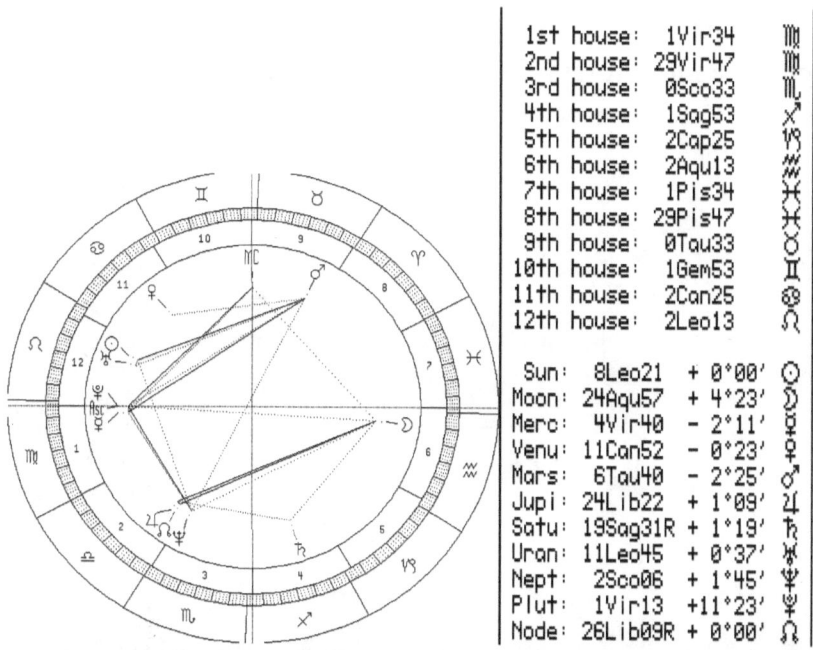

```
1st house:   1Vir34    ♍
2nd house:   29Vir47   ♍
3rd house:   0Sco33    ♏
4th house:   1Sag53    ♐
5th house:   2Cap25    ♑
6th house:   2Aqu13    ♒
7th house:   1Pis34    ♓
8th house:   29Pis47   ♓
9th house:   0Tau33    ♉
10th house:  1Gem53    ♊
11th house:  2Can25    ♋
12th house:  2Leo13    ♌

Sun:   8Leo21    + 0°00'   ☉
Moon:  24Aqu57   + 4°23'   ☽
Merc:  4Vir40    - 2°11'   ☿
Venu:  11Can52   - 0°23'   ♀
Mars:  6Tau40    - 2°25'   ♂
Jupi:  24Lib22   + 1°09'   ♃
Satu:  19Sag31R  + 1°19'   ♄
Uran:  11Leo45   + 0°37'   ♅
Nept:  2Sco06    + 1°45'   ♆
Plut:  1Vir13    +11°23'   ♇
Node:  26Lib09R  + 0°00'   ☊
```

Notice the outer planets close to planet Mercury and the Sun. planet Saturn in the 4th house. The North Node is conjunct planet Jupiter. Planet Neptune is close to planet Jupiter in 8° orb.

The ascendant is a sensitive point and has planet Pluto conjunct planet Mercury. Planet Mercury in the sign Virgo is not so power conscious. It is more servile to the world. It is happy when it finishes a job to perfection giving importance to details. Planet Pluto causes planet Mercury to go out of the way and become a power seeker. In doing so planet Mercury takes on multi personalities to get into a position where it may be noticed. The Sun is next planet Uranus and square to planet Mars in the 9th house. Planet Mars is weakened here but both planets Pluto and Mercury are trine with it and that saves the day. The North Node is close to planet Jupiter which allows the North Node to be under good care and will not indulge too much. The stress is on the Sun (12th house) and planet Mercury (1st house). Both these bodies have a job to salvage the 4th house with planet Saturn in it. That is when a person puts on different personae to impress people. Planet Venus is unaspected. This planet Venus if aspected by an outsider's planet can be swayed.

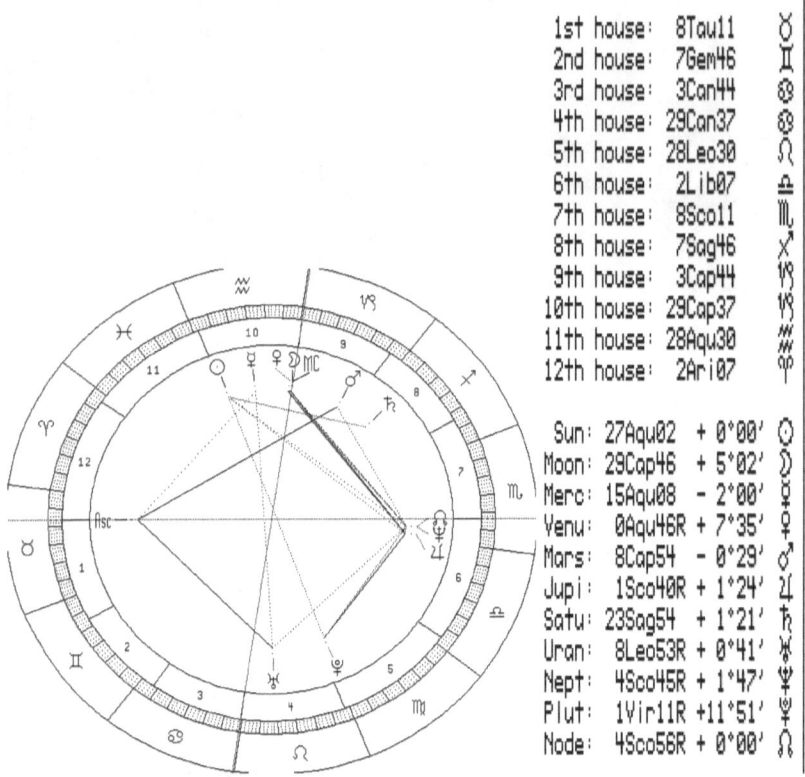

If you look at the 10th house, the Moon and the planet Venus are conjunct but appear far from the Sun. If you see the planet as a mid-point then both planets Venus and the Moon get connected to the Sun within an orb of 3⁰.

With that Venus and Moon get linked to the Sun and depend on it for manifesting their intent. The Sun is in Aquarius and is a weak sign and so also the house number ten which belongs to planet Saturn as a natural ruler. The ruler for the 10th house with the sign Aquarius is planet Uranus, who is in the 4th house. The 4th house with the planet Uranus is disturbing to the

Moon as well as the Sun because of the sign Leo on the 4th cusp. All these make the Sun desperate to work out something as an escape route and turn into a pathological liar. I know these people whose charts have been shown in (1) and (2). The idea was to show how the planets link themselves and behave as if combust. The 5th house is well supported here but not so much the 4th.

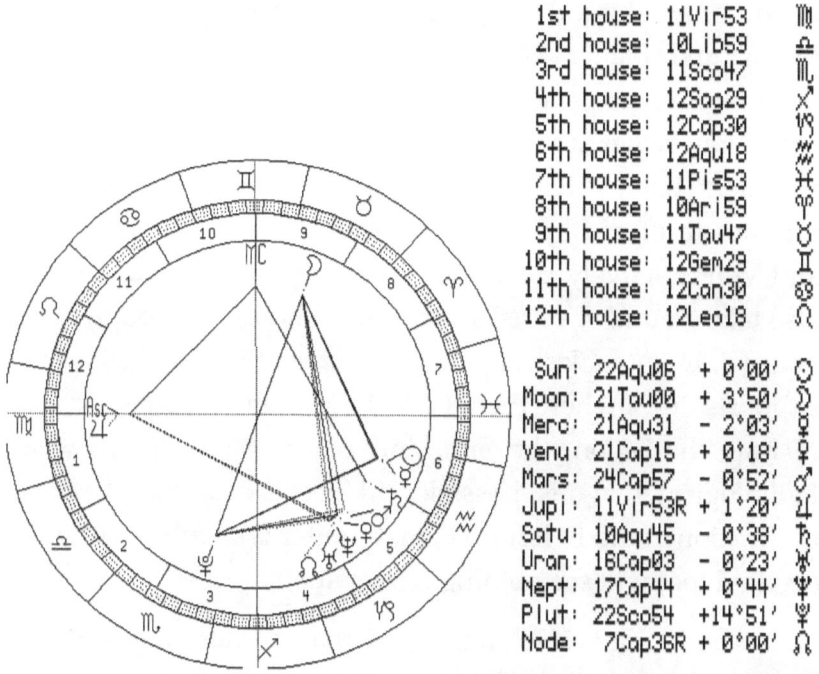

```
1st house: 11Vir53    ♍
2nd house: 10Lib59    ♎
3rd house: 11Sco47    ♏
4th house: 12Sag29    ♐
5th house: 12Cap30    ♑
6th house: 12Aqu18    ♒
7th house: 11Pis53    ♓
8th house: 10Ari59    ♈
9th house: 11Tau47    ♉
10th house: 12Gem29   ♊
11th house: 12Can30   ♋
12th house: 12Leo18   ♌

Sun:  22Aqu06  + 0°00'   ☉
Moon: 21Tau00  + 3°50'   ☽
Merc: 21Aqu31  - 2°03'   ☿
Venu: 21Cap15  + 0°18'   ♀
Mars: 24Cap57  - 0°52'   ♂
Jupi: 11Vir53R + 1°20'   ♃
Satu: 10Aqu45  - 0°38'   ♄
Uran: 16Cap03  - 0°23'   ♅
Nept: 17Cap44  + 0°44'   ♆
Plut: 22Sco54  +14°51'   ♇
Node: 7Cap36R  + 0°00'   ☊
```

The Sun and planet Mercury are squared by planet Pluto. Planet Mercury is combust. The Sun is weak in Aquarius. The ruler of the 6th house is Uranus is well placed in the 5th house.

Planet Venus is the conjunct planet Neptune and Uranus. Planet Mars is also conjunct planet Venus. Planet Mars is exalted so will definitely obey planet Saturn. Planet Jupiter increases the strength of the union from the 1st house.

Planet Saturn is also present in the 5th house. The 5th house is overloaded which leaves very little functioning power to each planet. The ruler of the 5th is Sun and is weak. The Sun and the Moon are square.

The difficulty comes from Sun square Moon which makes the planet Moon weak and it depends on the Sun. planet Mercury is also dependent on the Sun. But the Sun is weak and it cannot accommodate so much responsibility. The Sun, the Moon, and planet Mercury need supporting aspects from outside. Say, the person who wants to marry this person could have planets that can influence. Otherwise, this person will look outside. There will be a tendency to falsely represent self (optimism offered by Jupiter from the 1st house), planet Mars and Venus actively pursuing fun and entertainment, and will also take a number of risks from the 5th house. Although the 5th house does not look strong now but later on if someone's planet supports the Sun here then the 5th house can become strong. As of now the Moon, the Sun, and planet Mercury are weak. Pathological lying is possible; all because of the 5th house motivation to the 1st house. Planet Jupiter is so full of optimism (exalted too) will see nothing wrong at all.

The Moon is also stressed by planet Pluto. It is a 3rd and 9th house connection. These houses function well if we are mentally sound. There is a possibility of fears due to stress; planet Pluto forces the Moon to leave attachment for seeking or keeping power. There is a fear of abandonment (a part of BPD). Whenever planet Pluto aspects Moon or Venus this fear exists in an individual. With planet Mercury, planet Pluto causes an overload of work and suspicion about everything that is going on around. Friendships do not last long as planet Mercury always remains conscious of its superiority and its associations.

So, I think you did manage to learn something here and you will get plenty of clients with these issues. Remember people with problems and other issues related to their career and relationships will approach and not the ones who are comfortable. So be hopeful.

Chapter-XV

An Exercise

Let us consider a randomly selected planetary positional chart from the ephemeris for a day and note planetary transit positions. Later we shall apply this to any natal chart of a person and see how these affect a chart.

APRIL 3rd 2022… … … … … . (Randomly chosen day) … …free software used Astrology

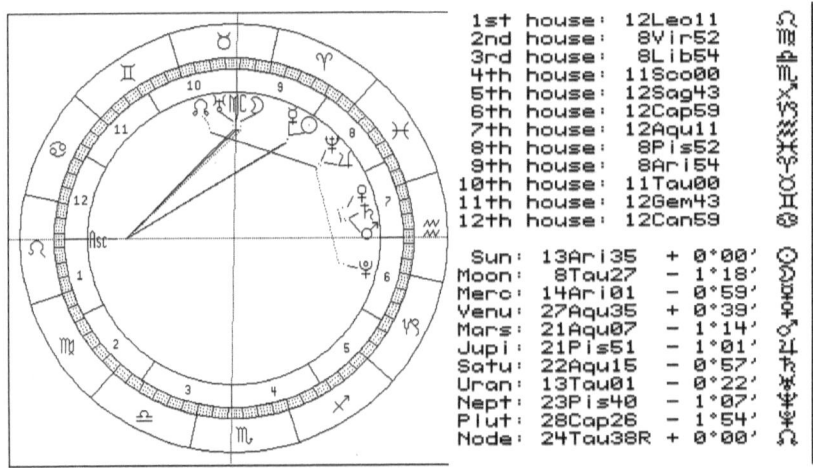

Transitory aspects: These aspects are common to all charts.

Sun conj Merc, Venus conj Mars (6⁰ orb), Venus conj Sat, Venus square North Node

Mars conj Saturn, Mars square North Node

Observations: For a week

Mercury is combust. Sun is taking Mercury's character. 5th house and Leo sign are benefited for everyone since the positions are general and hold good for all. Sun is transiting Aries. The 5th house activities and wherever the sign Leo falls in every horoscope gets benefited. Although 3rd and 6th house activities suffer, because of combust planet Mercury. The Sun may be quite enthusiastic to go out and seek entertainment, but both Mars and Venus are stuck with Saturn. So, in all charts (for everyone) 2nd, 7th, 1st, signs Aries, Taurus and Libra will show weakness. Any adventurous act will fail. Both planet Mars and Venus are well known for adventures. So, there could be mostly domestic activity. Transiting Moon can tell the mood.

With Mercury weak, our methodical ability, describing ability, the ability to talk cleverly, to use our dexterity will face hurdles and expose us to authorities. Instead, we could face trouble or irritation to the skin and erratic thoughts that bring fear and anxiety will come.

With weak Mars, trickery comes into us. The confidence, the ability to arbiter, the ability to support someone with a cause, to fight disease within the body, to co-operate and help, and to be able to work independently will suffer.

With a weak planet Venus, the wish to keep good relations, wish to confabulate with people, wish to participate in social gatherings, wish to cook, wish to invite guests, wish to be care taking toward others will all vanish. Selfishness takes over. Even when combust, slow, or retrograde these results can come.

With Venus conj Mars, in Aquarius, Mars and Venus come together to work selflessly toward the community. In the air signs, Mars is happy discussing or learning something scientific, related to literature, related to any subject that has a concern toward public welfare. Venus too is interested in dressing, decorating, be graceful in manners but experimentative in this sign. Since Mars is close to Venus, Venus is actively involved in some activity and is unable to spend time leisurely.

Saturn is conj Venus too. The conjunction is good if Venus is engaged in something that is giving satisfaction from earning some money. Saturn too will not let Venus to spend time reading, watching TV, etc. On emotional involvements if any, then this is not a comfortable period for Venus. Aquarius being a little indifferent to emotions, Venus is usually deprived of intimacy in this sign. Saturn is restricting Mars too. There will be a lot of work done but without much enthusiasm. If Mars is cooperative enough in activities of the Aquarius sign, like any activity involving research, innovation, repairs, looking for newer ways to improvise equipment, activity in performing arts, or any outdoor adventure, then it has planet Saturn's help in the form of a person cautioning Mars wherever it goes and whatever it does. It asks Mars to slow down its tempo. All legal matters are supported if planets Mars and Venus are involved in any pre-nuptial activities.

Venus, you can see is under stress and so is Mars. All horoscopes will have 1st, 2nd and the 7th houses under stress. 1st is self, 2nd is family, self-worth, and 7th are spouse, friends, and activities involving get-togethers will be affected. Since, the sign Aquarius is engaged in friction between three planets, this sign too gets weakened. So, the 11th house in all charts has limited benefits. 11th house among all is to work hard toward earning money because the 11th is 10th from the 2nd house, and the 10th house from any house is the working house.

Jupiter conj Neptune is a good combination. This materializes certain dreams if the conjunction is aspecting any planet in any chart. All charts will have their 9th house and 12th

houses activated on account of this conjunction. So future long travel may be planned, any special consultation, if required from an expert in the field of recovery from an illness (12th house) or foreign travel (9th house) is a possibility in this combination. The sign Pisces and sign Sagittarius could also tell the likelihood of an event in the future. These are common to all charts. When we apply to a specific chart, we must begin with the information gathered above...

Both Mars and Venus, with Saturn are square to North Node in Taurus. All three are strained by the conditions created by the North Node. The North Node may be trying to materialize something depending on where the sign Taurus is placed in each horoscope. But right now, all romances are on hold for sure.

Now let us apply this to a specific horoscope.

PERSON 'A' birth chart.

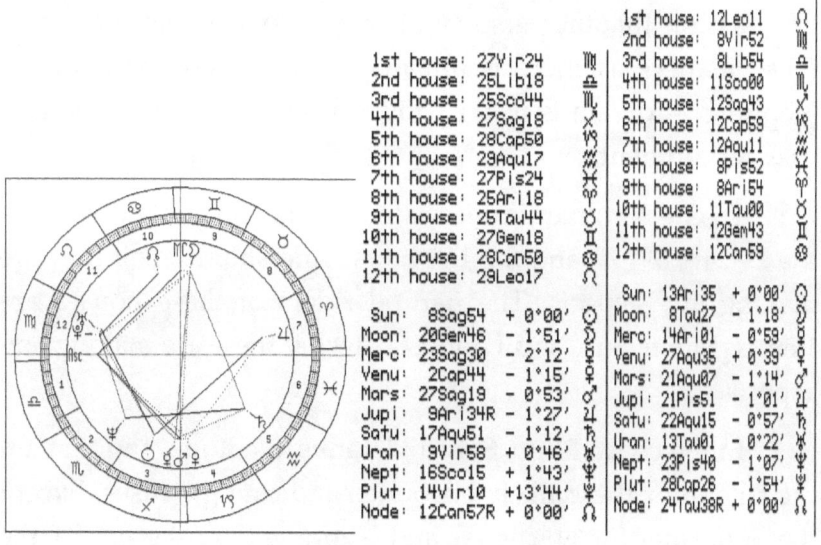

Observations: planets as on 3/04/22

The houses 12th and 9th, Signs Sagittarius and Pisces will give good results.

The 12th house has Virgo on it. The 9th house has Taurus on it. Although, Venus and Mercury are weak, these houses will give some good results in the form of relaxation, recuperation, isolation, activities related to the occult (12th) and association with friends, a little travel, some attempt at learning, some conflict with bosses are likely (9th). The sign Pisces is in the 6th house. A house for health, habits, debt repayment, friends, and earnings out of regular work. These benefits will take place on account of Jupiter conj. Neptune. Neptune has a square aspect to make with Moon, Mars, and Mercury in the chart. Even Jupiter will do the same in the horoscope because Jupiter is trine Sun and the New Moon is conj. Jupiter is in the 7th house. From the point of view of a job may be, health maybe, or taking an appointment with doctors maybe there will be dream building. It is possible that the person will happen to seek information on these matters as there is already an awareness built up by Neptune. A dream is usually toward seeking relief, a solution or entertainment.

To check romantic encounters if any, the method is to see the 2nd, 4th, 5th, 7th and the 11th house rulership lords if they are making any aspects. The natural rulers of these houses are Venus, Moon, Sun, and Uranus. Check if these are making any aspects.

In the chart, Pluto, Saturn, Uranus, Neptune, and Sun are the rulers for these likely encounter-indicating-houses. Except the Sun, ruler for 11th house and Neptune the ruler for 7th, the rest are all weak or stressed for the current week. So, the friends' network could keep the person engaged but not much of romance. The 7th house looks at legal partners more and friends with whom we share a lot are shown. Except transiting North Node no planet transiting the 7th house permits casual flirtations.

The North Node is transiting the 8th house. From the 8th house, North Node increases secret activity. So, this person could be developing certain money earning by renting property, money lending, earning on interest, consulting astrologers, trying to seek mental peace, etc. secretly. But this activity will be on for as long as North Node is in the 8th house. Later it will change to something else.

Let Us See the Last New Moon

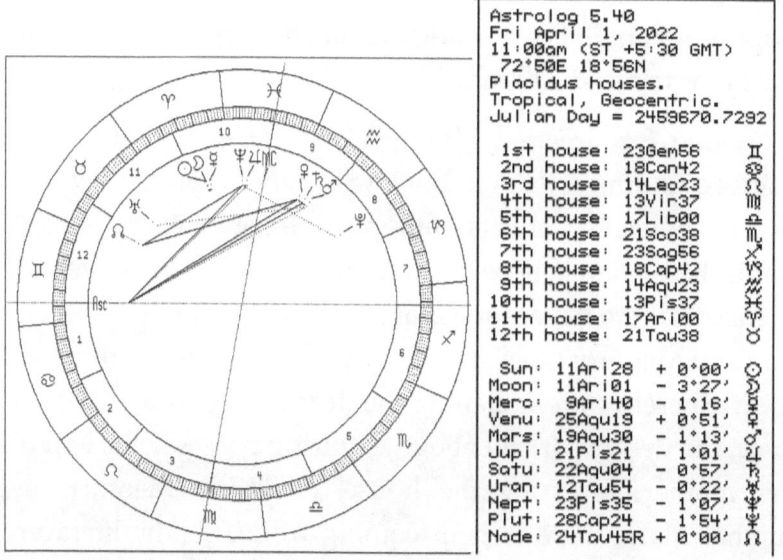

All aspects are written are happening in the natal chart above of Person A

The New Moon happened in the 7th house conjunct to Jupiter.

NM (New Moon) trined the Sun.

Mercury is combust and is in Aries....3rd, 6th, Virgo, and Gemini lose power but give it to Sun. So, 5th house and sign Leo give good results.

There is a Saturn return going on and Saturn has moved away from natal Saturn at 17^0.

This NM will help Saturn in achieving whatever it wants because it is happening in Libra. In the natal chart, Jupiter is trine the Sun. Transiting Neptune is square both Mercury and Mars on the cusp of the 4th house. It is developing a hope of receiving unconditional love. When planet Mars and planet Neptune are involved, the dreams cultivated yearn for love and affection. Unless well thought and planned there is usually a disappointment. It is expecting too much when planet Neptune only helps to build a dream.

Good for dream building. Good for setting up a new business, finding a job, relations with wife improve. Leo is in the 11th house so efforts into philanthropic work, seeking friends' help, there will be popularity gained too. This week will see success. Planet Neptune is at 23^0 approx. And the aspects to Mars and Mercury have started. In the coming years, these will repeat. Thereby, strengthening the dream. With Mars in the 4th house, the dreams are all about acquiring possessions, looking after mother, repairing the house, etc. With Mercury also conjunct Mars, there is help coming from friends, literature, associations, etc.

Final word of caution: In the current transit chart, we observed that Venus is weak, and therefore 2nd, 7th, Taurus, and Libra signs will be weak in all the charts we see. It is a universal phenomenon. The planets that are transiting in these houses are weak too. If these planets, occupying 2nd, 7th, signs Taurus and

Libra have hard aspects from other planets to them, they get weaker. If any of their houses (rulership and signs) are affected due to transiting planets making hard aspects to other, then too the planets in 2nd, 7th, and signs Taurus, Libra become weak.

Next, the North Node and the South Node are not affected by the ruling planets of any house including the outer planets. The Nodes have a complete independent agenda of their own. These will use the personal planets mercilessly. The outer planets can only co-operate if the intent is similar. For example, very soon, transiting planet Uranus and the North Node will become conjunct in Taurus. This will occur around July/Aug. Uranus is weak because it is retrograde at that time. But both North Node and Uranus are moving synchronously in the same direction. There is every chance these two will have the same motive. The North Node's motive is to be established individually. Whatever the periodicals write has little meaning. In Taurus, the North Node has the intent to give a large appetite for the senses in order that these are used to complete the execution. So, watch out and make your own notes.

So, this is the method to adopt in case you have to analyze a horoscope.

The Nodes and the Truth

Without much ado, let us look into how we might be able to use the Nodes. I write out of my experiences here, although like everyone I did start with books and the opinion of the elders who had some knowledge. So, to begin with, North Node has an effect over all of our personal planets, Jupiter, and Saturn. Even planet Saturn obliges the North Node when aspected by the North Node. North Node represents our greater greed, the suppressed pleasures and a will that needs an 'accomplice' to fulfill. The North Node creates the 'accomplice' for us as appropriate. Please understand that 'greed; is one level above 'desire' and 'ambition'. One might be able to connotate North Node's effect with a 'square' aspect. That square aspect stands for 'I must somehow and I will' and the North Node's nature is similar. It is believed that our desires of previous life remained unfulfilled and, in this life, the North Node carries us forward to fulfill them. But a 'karma' could be created that again requires that we repay. 'Karma' means a debt. What we owe others. We do return a favour with favour or with a gift but a correct equivalence of a favour received is not taken into account. Towards our children we 'pay'. We 'pay' out towards a few others too. Only sometimes do we receive. Sometimes we force ourselves to receive. They all need to be accounted for. But North Node does not care much about our Karma. It simply wants us to experience and feel sated. The South Node however, has no such interest. It tries to dissuade us from building karma and avoid taking birth again to 'pay' back. But who heeds the South Node? Virtually no one.

So how does the North Node and the South Node get their act together? I need to add a few more lines of information so that you too will be able to interpret a result when North or South Nodes are noticed in certain houses or signs in a chart. The North Node is bodyless, and has just the head. The rest of the body is South Node. Our thoughts could be good or bad, and we begin to experience, "I will, I will somehow". The South Node on the other hand, has the rest of the body but no thoughts, so no desire. It focuses on keeping its body intact, self-preservation, so to say. So, the first guideline is, wherever these two are noticed, a person will show a determination to adopt the characteristics of the sign where the North Node is in and unlike the other (South Node). It is not easy when we have to superimpose the characteristic of the house too on the information we have, so try using the basic desires to put forward to the client first. As you gain experience, you might add a few more qualities of both the sign and the house. The South Node has no compulsions like the North Node. The North Node does not concern itself with, what will happen to the body if the body too chases the desires. The South Node cannot concern itself with the activities that go on in the head of North Node. The South Node is concerned with the maintenance of sanity. For the sake of the body a few activities are required and no need for abundance, lots of food, indulgence, etc. I may be right in expecting you to be imagining already, what if South Node is placed or transiting in pleasure seeking houses? Followed by what if North Node is placed or transiting houses that increase our passions. That is what makes this section of astrology interesting because there is a difficulty too. One has to simultaneously combine two opposite natures to postulate something.

With that, I will leave you to experiment and take care of your clients.

Chapter-XVI

Epilogue

> *'The smith also sitting by the anvil, and considering the iron work, the vapour of the fire wasteth his flesh, and he fighteth with the heat of the furnace: the noise of the hammer and the anvil is ever in his ears and his eyes look still upon the pattern of the thing that he maketh; he setteth his mind to finish his work, and watcheth to polish it perfectly . . .'*
>
> Ecclesiasticus, c. 38; v. 28.

As you progress further in your pursuit of astrological knowledge there will be a number of failures. Do not be disappointed because our enthusiasm is such that we tend to over speak in the beginning. As time progresses, you will realize the small matters that you missed on your way. If you have a sparring partner while learning and later when trying out your knowledge, it is well and good. There will be plenty who will discourage and very few will encourage your good attempts; it is human nature. I call it 'cognizant dissonance'. That quality is in everyone; so that need not bother us at all. Our will and determination to complete certain tasks in hand should only matter. Each year you must look back to see what did you learn in a year that went past. There will be many years during which progress is slow.

I plan to write a small book on the outer planets because these have not been understood so well. When I started studying astrology, I was taught to consider planet Saturn to be malefic. Over the years I found that planet Saturn troubles those who are driving in the 5th gear. Anything done in moderation does not get noticed by planet Saturn.

Planet Uranus was described as sudden, shocking, and crazy sometimes. I realized that planet Uranus has the capacity to provide information that causes us to think that we wasted our time so far. It is time that we react and stop others from forcing us to do wrong or the unwanted. In your experience of planet Uranus, you too must record certain episodes and try to see where the general consensus is.

Planet Neptune was described as nebulous, foggy, uncertain, and deceptive and I was always worried whenever I interpreted this planet during consultation. In the last twelve years, I realized that planet Neptune is a dream builder. The dreams are expensive. They not only cause our resources to deplete but we begin to believe that there is a new dimension of adventure that we need to explore more. If you want to call it addiction then you are not wrong. But what to do; planet Neptune will aspect our personal planets and will cause dreams to come. It is better we see them in bright daylight.

Planet Pluto was never comprehensible for many years. Some described it as 'transformative'. Yet another new word to find its correct meaning; today Google is there to help. Fifteen years ago, I only had a dictionary and whatever it described was not convincing to me at all... I experienced planet Pluto and all words used to describe planet Pluto became clear as mountain-stream. It puts you in a situation wherein you feel you cannot blame anyone. You will realize that it was you who dug your own grave. If you want to go any further you are sure to fall into it. After that, there is no coming out. So, reading long paragraphs about the outer planets and understanding their character is very difficult. One must experience and watch others too when they suffer to understand these outer planets. None of the outer planets can bring happiness and you must remember this. They take a few years and wait until we are fully encapsulated with a particular thought of pursuit. We say 'obsessed' sometimes. Whenever an obsession or a compulsion takes over be sure you are under an influence of the outer planet.

The personal planets are enamored to be of service to us. The difficulty comes from the New Moons, Full Moons, and eclipses that have long-lasting effects. The outer planets too play a major role in arm-twisting the personal planets from doing the favours to us. That is why many times a personal planet may appear all set to do beneficence but is unable to. Check previous lunations you will have the answer sometimes.

Planet Jupiter too generously offers gifts but most of those go unnoticed because of our own unpreparedness to accept new conditions. It is important to notice each and every opportunity that planet Jupiter offers and see if that has a future in it. When planet Jupiter aspects outer planets during transits the opportunities are big and need your full attention.

You may if you want to give feedback or ask in the following e-mail and I shall try to answer whenever possible.

Email: 0akbar1@protonmail.com

www.ingramcontent.com/pod-product-compliance
Lightning Source LLC
LaVergne TN
LVHW091627070526
838199LV00044B/967